Harnessing the Power of Continuous Auditing

Harnessing the Power of Continuous Auditing

Developing and Implementing a Practical Methodology

ROBERT L. MAINARDI

WILEY

John Wiley & Sons, Inc.

For general information on our other products and services or for technical support, please contact our Customer Care Department within the United States at (800) 762-2974, outside the United States at (317) 572-3993 or fax (317) 572-4002.

Wiley also publishes its books in a variety of electronic formats. Some content that appears in print may not be available in electronic books. For more information about Wiley products, visit our web site at www.wiley.com.

Library of Congress Cataloging-in-Publication Data:

Mainardi, Robert L., 1964—
  Harnessing the power of continuous auditing : developing and implementing a practical methodology / Robert L. Mainardi.
       p. cm. — (Wiley corporate F&A series)
  Includes index.
  ISBN 978-0-470-63769-2 (hardback) ISBN 978-1-1180-0700-6 (ebk);
ISBN 978-1-1180-0701-3 (ebk); ISBN 978-1-1180-0702-0 (ebk)
  1. Auditing, Internal. I. Title.
  HF5668.25.M35 2011
  657'.458—dc22   2010037965

Printed in the United States of America

10 9 8 7 6 5 4 3 2 1

To my father, Angelo Michael Mainardi, who continues to inspire me as he watches over me, and to my mother, Lucy, who impresses me more everyday.

Contents

Preface

CONTINUOUS AUDITING HAS BEEN around for quite some time, but there has always been an active discussion regarding its true definition and how to effectively incorporate the targeted testing methodology into an existing audit department. The other challenge that internal audit departments face is to differentiate continuous monitoring from continuous auditing. Although there does not appear to be a significant difference between the two, the one thing that remains constant is that a monitoring approach will not provide any control validation.

There is always a risk that audit departments, in an effort to implement a more streamlined testing approach, will rush through critical development and implementation phases of the continuous auditing methodology. It is critically important that each department takes the necessary time to understand the objectives of the approach, adequately plan and document its own methodology, and facilitate the communication of the methodology to its own team and business partners. The development of the continuous auditing methodology is time consuming and requires adequate planning and resources. However, this up-front investment will pay off significantly as the methodology is implemented.

This book addresses many misconceptions about continuous auditing; none is more significant than the belief that in order to implement continuous auditing successfully, the internal audit department must be supported by an automated technology. This could not be further from the truth. Continuous auditing programs are being executed daily without any technology at all. The true key to a successful continuous auditing implementation is not the type of technology solution used but the detailed, documented continuous auditing methodology that you have developed to support your existing risk-based audit approach.

This book defines the continuous auditing methodology and provides a practical, step-by-step guide on how to define, develop, communicate, implement, manage, and maintain the approach. The objective of the book is to ensure that any reader—whether auditor, company executive, business unit manager, practitioner, consultant, or any other business professional interested in a target approach to evaluating the effectiveness of critical controls—can clearly understand and successfully create and implement his or her own continuous auditing methodology.

Chapter 1 provides a clear definition of continuous auditing that is used as a foundation for the rest of the book.

Chapter 2 helps you identify how continuous auditing can be integrated into your existing methodology with a need and fit questionnaire encompassing five specific questions to ensure that a benefit will be realized once the continuous auditing methodology is developed and implemented.

Chapter 3 discusses the requirements of the critical fields that are required and should be included in the formal continuous auditing methodology document and provides a suggested format.

Chapter 4 outlines the specifics of preparing to perform a continuous auditing program. This is accomplished by detailing the requirements of developing the business knowledge, understanding the specific business process rules, and identifying the technology. Each one of these topics is required to execute the corresponding work program successfully.

Chapters 5, 6, and 7 provide the individual continuous auditing methodology requirements for the three phases: (1) foundation, (2) approach, and (3) execution. Each chapter defines each phase and its purpose and specifies the particular deliverables needed to document the continuous auditing methodology properly.

Chapters 8, 9, and 10 address the continuous auditing methodology reporting requirements. They encompass the critical need for root cause analysis (Chapter 8), the suggested report format and documentation requirements (Chapter 9), and the definition of real action (Chapter 10) that must be obtained to address the opportunities for improvement identified during the execution phase of the continuous auditing methodology.

Chapter 11 focuses on the business unit management, internal audit, and technology conditions that provide guidance and assistance during the development, implementation, and management of the continuous auditing methodology.

Chapter 12 discusses the selling of the continuous auditing methodology to the business unit client and to the internal audit department staff. Although the method is not the same as a full-scope audit, it is necessary for internal audit to understand and be able to appropriately articulate the continuous auditing methodology to all parties involved.

Chapters 13 and 14 provide guidance in recognizing the challenges of implementing the custom methodology and its specific potential uses.

Chapter 15 provides a tool that can be utilized to evaluate and record the successes and opportunities for improvements in planning, testing, executing, and reporting on the continuous auditing methodology.

The Appendix provides a detailed example of a successful continuous auditing methodology as well as all the templates mentioned throughout the book.

Acknowledgments

THROUGHOUT THE BOOK DEVELOPMENT and writing process, I had tremendous support from many people. I want to say thank you to everyone who waited patiently and tolerated my unavailability from the concept phase up to and including the final revisions.

First, I owe special thanks to my son, Robert, and my daughter, Gabrielle, for all of their sacrifices during the creation of this book. Because of their understanding, I was able to focus and dedicate all of my time and effort to writing. You are both amazing, and I could not be any more proud to say that I am your father.

Thanks to Marilyn for taking care of everything while I worked on developing this book. You provided the support that made it possible for me to concentrate solely on writing during each free moment. I appreciate everything that you did and singlehandedly addressed over this long process.

Thanks to my brothers Jerry, Michael, and Stephen: Jerry for being my own personal technology help desk; Michael for being my constant supporter and motivator; and Stephen for always making me laugh when I needed it. You guys are the best brothers on the planet.

Thanks to Barumbi for the inspiration and support during this creation. I look forward to working with you long into the future. Your unique insight and skills should be shared. I look forward to seeing you often.

Thanks to my best friend, Lieutenant Colonel Henry "Pat" Campbell. You have been by my side since Penn State, and I know that I can always count on you and Laura for support or anything I could ever need. Always remember Filet, Tom Z, Kevin "Ice" Anderson, and laughing until it hurts. I want to also say thank you again for your 21 years of service in the U.S. Air Force. You are a true hero, and I want you to know how much I appreciate all you have done and that you inspire not only me but also everyone you meet.

Thanks to my two financial gurus, John "Sma Sma Smitty" Smith and Donna Whiteley. I appreciate everything that you do for me on a daily basis. Your efforts do not go unnoticed.

Thanks to two of the best people I ever hired, Stephanie Jones and Victoria Robinson. I appreciate your effort, team dedication, and willingness to follow me on new adventures at different companies. We created great work environments, produced valuable audits, and built great relationships. Your creativeness and ingenuity regarding the audit process have helped shape the initial creation of this continuous auditing methodology.

Thanks to Ken Frantzen for helping me get through all of those painful Monday morning staff meetings. Our five years together were such an adventure. I appreciate your patience and willingness to always listen. Ken, I finally made it to the "big boy" table.

Thanks to Dino and Scott Borghi at Borghi's Restaurant for always taking care of me, my clients, family, and friends. Your food, dedication to excellence, superior service, and making everyone (especially me) feel like family are just a few reasons for your success.

Thanks to my business partners over the years. Although I may have forgotten some, this list includes: Suzanne Barron, Jill Benson, Lina Borrelli, Tom Cassidy, Kristi Coombs, Arnaldo Diaz, Ken Ebbage, Cynthia Fetterman, Todd Freeman, Jorge Green, John Hall, Denise Johnson, Susan Panzer, Jimmy Parker, Vinit Rajpara, Bruce Rice, Cyndi Summers, and John Wisz.

Thanks to all my former audit team members over the years. I am sure I have forgotten a few names, but the list includes: William Baugh, Robin Benns, Bob Campbell, Lisa Chadwick, Andrew Cooper, Jayne Cravens, Jeff "Hefe" Croasmun, Lou DiGiovine, Cari DeRose, Sam "Pooh Bear" Dungee, Mike Eyre, James Huff, Denise Joyce, Alton Knight, Eric Kramer, Ola Laniya, Tomeka Lee, Cara McWilliams, Ed Merenda, Jim Mullin, Christopher Nace, Jason Pandolfo, Eric Pettis, Jack Rockenbach, Frank Satterthwaite, Deborah Sullivan, Crystal Tucker, Jennifer Valentine, and Dwayne Weldon.

Thanks to Erin and Cathy at Catarinas for always fitting me in and taking care of me; and to Maria Martin at Unique Images for taking a great picture.

Harnessing the Power of Continuous Auditing

1

Defining Continuous Auditing

 THE REAL DEFINITION

One of the significant challenges facing internal audit, control specialists, enterprise risk management teams, and business managers all over the world is being able to understand what continuous auditing is and how the approach can be used effectively. As you read through this book, keep in mind that continuous auditing has been around for decades. As I travel and speak around the world on this topic, I have found each individual team, department, or company has its own definition of what it believes the approach represents and how to maximize its value. So let us start off this educational process by establishing a clear-cut definition of continuous auditing and understanding the characteristics that make it a unique tool. The definition will be broken down into two distinct parts: (1) the formal "book" definition for personnel familiar with the audit profession and (2) the "nonaudit" definition for clients to clearly understand the objective of the approach.

Continuous auditing is one of the many tools used within the internal audit profession to provide reasonable assurance that the control structure surrounding the operational environment is:

- Suitably designed
- Established
- Operating as intended

Before discussing these three components, it is important to immediately identify a clarification regarding the definition. The assurance regarding the support structure of the operational environment is provided only for the specific controls selected during the development of the continuous audit. This is a critical distinction that must be understood by both the group using this approach and the client who is partnering in the effort. The continuous audit is not concluding on the total control environment for the process selected but only for the selected controls being reviewed. Time and time again, I have witnessed clients who receive results of a continuous audit (which was appropriately focused on a specific control) and then extrapolate the results of the control testing across the entire operation or control environment. It is not possible to use the results of a continuous audit to provide validation of an entire operation. Let's discuss the three critical components of the definition.

Suitably Designed

Auditors and control experts use the term "suitably designed" constantly when discussing control testing, but does everyone using the term truly understand what it means? When considering whether a process or control is suitably designed, you must be able to examine the supporting process documentation or clearly written policies and procedures. In the examination of the information, you should be able to identify the process flow, checkpoints, and required reviews necessary to ensure the process flows along its desired path. "Suitably designed" also implies there are documented policies and procedures detailing this process flow. These procedures should be examined to determine a sufficient level of documentation. In making this determination, a reasonableness test is applied that basically asks whether a reasonable person, without intimate knowledge of the area, would be able to follow the process and execute the tasks required. As anyone does when looking for sufficient evidence, examine the procedures and consider if there is enough detail included to perform the work. One of the difficult aspects of reviewing policies and procedures is that well over 50 percent of the time the documentation is out of date. In this situation, the reviewer will be required to perform additional steps to determine if the process is suitably designed. Those steps could include facilitating meetings with key process personnel to gain an understanding or creating detailed process maps or flowcharts. In the end, the goal is to be able to make a conclusion, based on examined information, that the process has been suitably designed.

Another component to consider when discussing design is the application and use of controls. In the review of the process documentation, there should be evidence of specific control activity. In other words, can you identify control points in the process where information is validated, reviewed, and/or approved before moving to the next critical step in the process? Control identification is critical in continuous auditing because, as you will learn in Chapters 5, 6, and 7, the "key" controls are going to be the ones selected to test using the continuous methodology. To simplify the key control concept, this type of control holds the process together tightly in an effort to ensure that the desired outcome is achieved as long as the process does not deviate from the established design. To further the explanation, consider that if this type of control fails, one of two things will happen: Either the process will come to a complete stop or the process's final result will be incorrect. Controls govern the flow of information and provide assurances to protect the outcome.

Additionally, a truly suitably designed process will include parameter requirements, established reporting, and a timely deliverable. Parameter requirements establish an upper and lower control limit. Every single control in every business process has control limits. Control limits provide the minimum (lower) and maximum (upper) range of acceptable performance. These limits communicate the range in which the business unit team must perform their assigned responsibilities. Without specific limits, there would be no way to determine whether the process was operating efficiently and effectively. As an example, when the accounts payable manager says that all expense reports submitted will be processed and submitted for payment within one to three days of being received, he is providing the control limits for expense report processing. That range of one to three days provides the control limits or standard for receiving, reviewing, and approving an expense report for payment. Each suitably designed process will have these control limits to provide accountability and guidance for the team. Without control limits, there would be no accountability for performance, which would make it almost impossible to audit with a standard for comparison.

Once the limits have been identified, examine the design of the process to determine if there are any reports generated to measure the process against the standard. In a suitably designed process, reports will be created that detail the effectiveness of the control environment to meet the standard created in the policies and procedures. These reports will also help in developing a focus for potential continuous auditing tests. The timely component mentioned earlier ties to both the reporting and the delivery of the end product. Having reporting as part of the process design is a must, but it won't help the business quickly identify potential problems or create solutions if it is not timely. If the process being considered processes items multiple times a day, every day, receiving performance reports on a monthly basis will not be very valuable. The same can be said about a daily process that just cannot meet the daily demand. If a process does not have timely reporting or cannot deliver a timely product, usually the design is flawed, not the personnel supporting the effort. You have to consider all of these factors when identifying a target area that would be suitable for a continuous audit.

Established

The next consideration after determining whether something is suitably designed is determining whether the controlled process is established. This verification may seem simple but it is mission critical in the preparation stage of developing a value-added continuous audit process. When trying to identify if a control structure is established, you need to verify that the process described in the policies and procedures or documented in the work flow *is* the actual process in place today. Too often a business unit has detailed policies and procedures that are not representative of the day-to-day operational process. The documentation of the current process is considered a low priority for the business unit due to their daily responsibilities taking precedence over the scripting of their activities. If the controlled process does not agree with the documented process requirements, identifying the control points that should be tested as part of a continuous audit is very difficult.

When presented with the scenario of the actual business process not agreeing with the policies and procedures, it will be necessary to understand and document the current process flow before attempting to develop an approach for continuous auditing. It is not that you would be unable to create a continuous audit without knowing the process was established; why would you want to test or verify a process control that is no longer critical or even applicable to the actual business process being executed on a daily basis? For the continuous audit tool to be effective and deliver the expected value, it must be based on the current control process in place and operating today. So when you are examining a department's policies and procedures, ensure that the documented process agrees with what the staff currently is executing. Once that step has been completed, it will be easier to identify and select the critical controls that govern the process to producing its results.

Another point to consider regarding an established process is the communication of the process requirements. With the speed of business and the demands of customers increasing at an almost daily rate, it is critical to understand how business units communicate changes in the process requirements and/or control limits. Very often, processes change without a formal communication plan. Without a plan to verify that all parties are aware of the change, it is not possible to ensure compliance. Communication within a business unit impacts the processing team's ability to deliver repeatable, reliable results. Ensure that you verify how process rule changes are communicated within a team before selecting it for a continuous audit. This advance knowledge will reduce the amount of potential rework as well as the number of false positives.

Operating as Intended

The last component of the definition probably seems to be the easiest one to verify. Pretty simple question: Is the process operating as intended? What this question really is asking is, is the process creating a result? It is a yes-or-no question. It is straightforward and doesn't really require any interpretation.

You must consider one simple nuance before rushing to answer what appears to be the simplest of questions. First consider this: Everyone will agree that each process, business activity, or task will produce *a* result. However, what the question is really asking is this: Is the process producing the *expected* result? After all of the activities have been completed, the question to be asked is this: Did the proper, expected deliverable occur? When a continuous audit is created according to the methodology, it will provide the data and supporting evidence to conclude on the effectiveness and efficiency of the specific controls selected for review. It will confirm or deny that the established process is producing the expected results.

It is important to have a clear understanding of the definition of continuous auditing before racing out to make your first selection. Not only is it required prior to creating your continuous auditing methodology, but it is also necessary for you and your team to have a standard definition that can be clearly explained to your clients when asked.

 ## DIFFERENTIATING CONTINUOUS AUDITING

The next step in understanding continuous auditing is differentiating continuous auditing from continuous monitoring. Many business units, internal audit teams, and risk professionals believe they are performing continuous auditing when in actuality they are not. By definition, they have implemented continuous monitoring. For example, consider a business unit that has created some form of continuous monitoring mechanism that provides activity reports detailing the business process activity that the business unit own or are trying to evaluate. The business unit begins by selecting their main process, obtaining the applicable process volumes, dollars, or man-hours. Once these figures have been compiled, they are compared to the target range or benchmark to determine whether the total number fits within an acceptable range of performance. The process of matching totals to their target or benchmark *is not* continuous auditing. Without performing any validation testing of the compiled data, it would not be possible to ensure that the key control or controls surrounding the process are working effectively to deliver the expected outcome. To conclude on control effectiveness confidently, testing must be performed.

Let's continue this example and turn the monitoring process described into a continuous audit process. Taking the same report that summarized the volumes, dollars, or man-hours would be a quick reference point in which to select the area for testing. Even if all of the data indicated the process appeared to be working effectively (because all information obtained fell within the target area of acceptable performance), testing would have to be performed to validate that the data, which appears effective or efficient, belongs within the acceptable range as the report indicates. It is not possible to conclude, from a continuous audit perspective, that a process control is operating effectively without performing detailed testing on the control environment for a period of time. That is the only way the process can be proven to produce repeatable, reliable results.

Table 1.1 further illustrates the differences between continuous auditing and continuous monitoring.

Table 1.1 first identifies the process owner. It is important for all parties involved to understand and agree that management owns monitoring. Management has a responsibility to provide oversight of the process it owns. This oversight should be able to provide a status of the key process deliverables on demand. What that means is that management has the ability to produce status updates of its process at any time during the day, week, or month in which it is requested. If the information is not readily available, how does management run the operation and adjust to changes in demand, availability, or client needs when appropriate? It would seem difficult, if

TABLE 1.1 Continuous Auditing versus Continuous Monitoring

	Continuous Auditing	Continuous Monitoring
Responsibility	Internal audit	Business unit management
Definition	Methodology used by auditors to perform control validation on a recurring basis	Management process that assists in meeting its fiduciary responsibilities
Focus	Process that tests selected transactions or key control points based on a predetermined criteria Part of the assurance process of internal audit responsibilities	Process that verifies acceptable performance based on department or industry standards Part of the ownership responsibilities of management

not impossible, to effectively manage an operation without a formal reporting process in place to support the business. If a person encounters an area without management reporting, consider whether this area is ready and willing to commit to a continuous audit. The reason for the skepticism is that without standard monitoring reports, the business owner may struggle when trying to discuss the critical controls and convey the established control limits supporting the process potentially under review. Be cautious in this situation, and be sure to communicate client expectations and the objective of the continuous audit.

Just by name alone, it would appear that internal audit owns continuous auditing. Although that is true initially, many times established continuous auditing tests are developed and executed by internal audit and then handed over to the business unit to use as part of its self-assessment process. Although it may be common for continuous auditing tests to be given over to the business unit for its use, it is very rare for the business to give internal audit one of its monitoring procedures. Any business unit can execute the continuous audit work as a proactive measure to identifying potential opportunities for improvement and trends in the workload.

Next, review the definition of continuous auditing and monitoring in Table 1.1. Monitoring is management's primary tool to meet its fiduciary responsibility for oversight of the operation. As the owner, management must maintain the quality of the process and institute checks and balances to ensure that the process is as efficient and effective as possible while meeting business, regulatory, and client demands. Management will not be successful in this endeavor without a monitoring process. One word of caution regarding business unit monitoring: For the monitoring to be effective, it must be formal. Business owners who say things like "I trust my people" or "That will never happen to me" are managing by feel and experience. That approach is dangerous and has been proven to work only for so long before something negative impacts the business. The best way to manage and monitor any process is by obtaining data and analyzing it to verify that it is complying with the process standards.

We have discussed the continuous auditing definition, but here is another summation definition more from a nonaudit perspective. This type of definition is one that could be provided to a potential client to explain the concept more easily:

Continuous auditing is another method to verify that the critical controls in a business unit process are working effectively.

SEGREGATING CONTINUOUS AUDITING AND CONTROL TESTING

Now that we have established the definition of continuous auditing, let's further clarify the methodology by comparing it to a full-scope audit or control testing. A full-scope audit is a very foundational approach. It begins with an understanding of the area to be reviewed. From that information, a detailed process map is created. From the process map, a risk control matrix is developed to identify the process objectives, inherent and residual risks, and their corresponding likelihood and significance ratings. Control identification and effectiveness are also scored on the matrix. Once the matrix has been completed and validated with the client, internal audit will build the detailed audit program to test the control environment effectiveness. In its most basic form, the detailed steps from information gathering to execution of testing are the major components to executing a full-scope control testing review. This type of audit or review evaluates the implemented process from start to finish.

Although continuous auditing requires business knowledge, just as a full-scope audit does, it does not require any other of the listed major document deliverables. This alternate approach does not focus on all of the controls to execute the process from start to finish but strategically identifies the critical controls that anchor the process. Once the key controls have been identified, they will be selected and tested to ensure that they are operating as designed. This is a streamlined approach to validate the performance of the critical controls.

The key difference between these two types of audits is that continuous auditing is a results-focused methodology that has been created to determine proper performance of a selected control. The methodology is not concerned with the ancillary controls in the process from start to finish but only the controls identified as critical during the planning. Continuous auditing is a drastically different mind-set from traditional auditing focused on the delivery and execution of an individual control. The same selected control will be tested on a recurring basis to ensure that it produces repeatable, reliable results. The

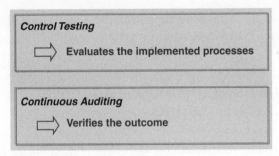

FIGURE 1.1 Definition: Continuous Auditing versus Control Testing

frequency of control testing is discussed in Chapter 5 as part of the foundation phase of the continuous auditing methodology.

Remember, a full-scope audit evaluates all of the control points from start to finish in a process; a continuous audit evaluates the selected controls on a recurring basis for a specified period of time. Figure 1.1 provides an illustration of this point.

CONTINUOUS AUDITING OBJECTIVES

One of the most difficult tasks is to clearly articulate the objective of a process, tool, or approach. However, if you want to be successful in your efforts to develop, implement, and manage this continuous auditing methodology, you must be able to identify the objectives. Before discussing the specific objectives of this approach, let's clarify what an objective represents. An objective must depict the purpose or reason for doing whatever it is you are planning to accomplish. The reason that the continuous auditing objective is so important is simple: If the objective is not known, no one will be able to grasp the concept of why the work is being performed. The lack of a fully developed continuous auditing objective can and will cause confusion for the individuals performing the work and any clients involved. Now that we have clarified the definition, let's discuss the objectives.

First and foremost, the objective of continuous auditing is to conclude on the efficiency and effectiveness of selected controls through targeted testing performed on a recurring basis for a specified time period. In simpler terms, continuous auditing is a strategic testing approach to verify that selected controls are working. From an audit perspective, it provides additional objectives. For one, the application of continuous auditing allows audit departments to expand coverage and depth of critical areas that would not have been covered under the traditional audit approach. Additionally, when developed and used correctly, continuous auditing saves time by streamlining control verification testing.

Another objective is that continuous auditing verifies the implementation and operation of newly created action items. Because audit teams are concerned with the timing and quality of significant management actions in response to audit reports, audit departments have implemented continuous auditing to authentic action plan completion. It is difficult for audit departments to perform detailed follow-up or field visits to areas with significant action plans due to the time, cost, and resource commitment such an effort would require. As an alternative solution, continuous auditing can be used to verify that the action has been addressed and is operating as intended. To ensure reliable results, this type of continuous audit should be executed after the business unit action has been in place for at least 90 days.

An additional objective for continuous auditing is to expand audit universe coverage. In this day and age, audit departments are being asked to take on additional work, participate on company-wide projects, partner with external auditors, and own Sarbanes-Oxley work, just to name a few areas. It is difficult, if not impossible, for some audit departments to take on these new requests on top of the existing workload and commitments to the audit committee and senior management. Continuous auditing can provide the flexibility to increase audit coverage without sacrificing quality, dedicating new resources, or demanding overtime.

Imagine being able to complete your existing audit plan, verify newly implemented action items surrounding critical risks, increase audit coverage, and drill down deeper in higher-risk areas without adding staff or altering required work hours. All this is attainable when you plan properly and incorporate continuous auditing into your department.

 ## DISPELLING THE CONTINUOUS AUDITING MYTHS

Even though continuous auditing has been around for a long time, there are still misconceptions about what it is and how it should be used effectively. Here are a few of the myths along with the corresponding truths.

Myth: Continuous auditing has to be automated.

Truth: Continuous auditing can be either automated or manual.

Automation is definitely not a requirement. Continuous auditing is about performing testing on a recurring basis to ensure viability of control effectiveness. Whether the testing is automated or not, the testing still can be completed. Remember, manual testing is not being completed for a full-scope audit but only for selected controls. There is a misconception that if it is not automated, it cannot be done. That is simply not true.

Myth: Continuous auditing requires internal audit to be in the business unit too often, and it will cause a disruption.

Truth: Continuous auditing, when implemented correctly, will be less intrusive than a regular audit.

A regular audit requires a significant investment in time for both the audit team and the client. In addition, one to four consecutive weeks are spent in the client's business unit meeting with key personnel, performing detailed testing, and soliciting feedback and explanation for all testing throughout the fieldwork. With a continuous audit, clients commit minimal time up front to understand the methodology and then have to meet with internal audit only if a discrepancy is noted with the recurring testing performed. In actuality, clients will see internal audit much less during a continuous audit than during a regular audit.

Myth: Continuous auditing is too time consuming and difficult to implement.

Truth: Continuous auditing is not difficult to implement if the objectives of how the methodology is to be used are clear and communicated to the audit team.

Continuous auditing is incorporated into an audit department's existing methodology to complement its current risk-based approach. The most challenging part of creating the continuous audit methodology is getting the audit team to understand that this is a totally different method to test and conclude on the efficiency and effectiveness of an internal control environment. Because the continuous auditing methodology has like phases when compared to risk-based auditing, the transition between the two is not a huge hurdle. From the continuous audit perspective, the testing and reporting are very similar to a regular audit; the biggest difference is the targeted scope and control selection. The

development of a continuous auditing methodology can be drafted, for-
matted, and implemented in three months. Although there are teams
that have implemented a continuous auditing methodology in 30 days,
usually the documentation of the methodology and approach along with
a marketing and communication plan are not completed in advance of
the rollout.

 ## SUMMARY

Clearly understanding the definition of "continuous auditing" is a critical first
step in the adoption and implementation of the methodology into your audit
department or business unit. First and foremost, establish the objective for your
team and communicate that same objective to the team throughout the
development process. In order to successfully integrate continuous auditing
into your current operation, you must understand the approach, document the
process, and recognize the opportunities to use the methodology effectively. In
Chapter 2, you will learn to recognize those opportunities and review your
current methodology to determine how to expand the services you offer at
this time.

2

Where to Begin

RECOGNIZE THE NEED

It does not matter if you are in an audit department, an enterprise risk management group, a compliance department, or a business unit. It does not matter if you are a team of one or work with a team of over 50 individuals. There never seems to be a sufficient amount of time or resources to accomplish all of the department goals that were set at the beginning of the year. Why that happens should not be a mystery to anyone who has worked in a business unit for more than a year. Each year begins with optimism and excitement and the belief that, as a team, we can accomplish more than the previous year because of experience.

The reality is that it is very difficult, if not impossible, to take on more than the previous year, even with an experienced team. Why? Because a high-functioning, successful team, especially an audit department, will be looked to as a resource in subsequent years. As resources, departments that have met or exceeded their goals will be asked to partner on company-wide projects, expand their breath of coverage, or guide and direct other business units on how to be successful. So with all of these potential additional activities, how will an audit team handle its new popularity? Keep in mind that while accepting the invitations to partner is an excellent marketing opportunity for internal audit and a significant morale boost for the audit team, it does not alleviate the existing commitments to the audit committee and senior management. Internal audit will still be required to complete the audit plan, partner with external auditors, and work closely with regulatory agencies. Please remember the goals and objectives of your department before accepting every invitation to partner on projects and initiatives of other departments.

Regardless of whether your team is being asked to participate on large projects or assist other departments with specific initiatives, continuous auditing still may be able to provide assistance with the execution of work and generation of control effectiveness conclusions. The question becomes: Is there a way to become more efficient and effective as a team without sacrificing quality or increasing the size of your staff? I do not believe there is an audit department or business unit out there today that does not want to be able to operate with a more efficient and effective team, especially without increasing department size. In the current environment, business units and companies are trying to find ways to reduce expenses. So asking for more staff for any department would be a futile effort.

However, it would be worthwhile to consider a methodology that could provide a reasonable assurance over critical or key controls without increasing the size of the team instead of begging for additional headcount or passing up on an opportunity to become more efficient. Before deciding whether a continuous auditing methodology would be the right fit for your department, consider the next questions to assist in identifying your opportunity for maximizing the benefits from this approach.

 ## POTENTIAL NEED/FIT CONSIDERATIONS

Believe it or not, fit is critical when considering incorporating continuous auditing into an existing operation. The methodology has a drastically different approach from traditional auditing and requires discipline in its development, execution, and maintenance. As defined in Chapter 1, continuous auditing is focused on validating the performance of a critical control and not with the examination of the process from start to finish. This key distinction sounds simple in explanation but is difficult for auditors to maintain in real-life performance. The reason why is because internal audit traditionally has reviewed business processes from start to finish, verifying that all controls are in place and operating as intended. Also, the traditional audit will occur once every 12 to 18 months for a higher-risk area.

Continuous auditing is going to require an auditor to examine a process, consider all controls in place from start to finish, select the critical control(s), and test the specific performance of the selected control on a recurring basis. Supporting or ancillary controls involved in the process are ignored. This is the most difficult concept for auditors to accept since they are accustomed to testing all controls in a process as part of a regular, or full-scope, audit. To determine whether continuous auditing is a methodology that could help your team, review the next five questions. Each question includes a brief explanation to ensure a clear understanding prior to answering.

1. Do you have a comprehensive annual risk assessment in place?

   This question is trying to determine if your audit methodology contains a formal risk assessment process of all auditable entities in your audit universe. A formal risk assessment would include a risk profile (documented background of the area's processes, systems used, staff size, production volume numbers and dollars, etc.) of the auditable entity, area objectives, inherent and residual risk, existing controls, and quantifiable questions detailing the overall risk level assigned. The risk level assigned should be based on the likelihood and significance of the inherent and residual risks with consideration given to the controls currently in place.

2. Do you have adequate coverage of all higher-rated risk areas?

   This question is focused directly on your annual audit plan to determine how comfortable you are with the audit activity of the high-risk areas of your audit universe. Sufficient coverage would mean every high-risk area is reviewed in a 12- to 18-month period. Most audit groups are unable to perform work in every one of these areas and rely heavily on their risk assessment process to triage or risk-rank the highest areas of the company. In the ranking process, ensure that there is consistency of application of the risk scores given and that subjectivity is kept to a minimum. These coverage decisions should be based on quantifiable data, previous audit activity, external reports, and outstanding action items.

3. Do you complete your annual audit plan every year?

This question requires more thought than may be apparent on the surface. In determining whether the audit plan gets done, think about the effort and dedication needed to complete every assignment as well as how many audits got postponed or reassessed to a subsequent year. Look for indications that the department was too optimistic about what could get completed during the audit cycle. In addition, determine how much time was diverted from the plan to address special requests from clients, senior management, and committees.

4. How much of your audit plan includes activity in areas in which the audit team has an intimate business knowledge and previous audit experience?

The more business knowledge an audit team has of its target areas, the more effective members will be at identifying the critical controls that support the process. Couple the business knowledge with previous audit experience of the area and the audit team is not only versed with an understanding of the operation but also has an established working relationship with the business unit team. There is no skill more valuable to an internal auditor than business knowledge. The efficiency at which the continuous auditing approach can be applied and used effectively is impacted by the audit team's ability to identify the true key controls in the business process.

5. Do you have the right team makeup to adapt to a methodology enhancement?

This question requires each team leader to examine the background, experience, and flexibility of members of the audit team. Before incorporating continuous auditing into your audit group, consider the background of the staff. Do staff members have sufficient business knowledge of the industry and company to understand the business process from start to finish? As discussed in question 4, intimate business knowledge is a prerequisite to implementing continuous auditing successfully. When considering experience, the team needs to have, at a minimum, two individuals with significant audit experience. For almost every audit department, it will be no problem to have two members with this level of experience. However, there is always a qualifying statement. Experienced auditors must be willing to share their knowledge and have the necessary communication skill set to instruct other auditors on how to identify and verify key controls in a process. Team leadership and direction by example are core competencies for all auditors in charge and managers but have to be assessed honestly when considering a methodology diversification from the standard risk-based approach. The leadership team has to have solid communication skills, lead by example, and be able to listen, clarify, and address questions throughout the development process. Flexibility is the final consideration regarding the audit team profile. For this purpose, the term "flexibility" has a dual meaning. From an audit team perspective, it represents the ability to adjust to new situations, environments, and client styles while at the same time being able to differentiate and execute two distinct audit approaches. Auditors are continually placed in challenging scenarios; nowhere is this more evident than when an auditor is trying to launch a different audit methodology with an existing client. After navigating the challenging launch, auditors must apply their audit and business knowledge to the revised approach and maintain the discipline to execute the methodology without reverting back to a full-scope, risk-based audit.

As previously discussed, the success of any audit activity relies on the client partnering and working with the audit team to provide business process details, activity data, and explanations regarding deviations from the business processing standard. To understand the current state of the audit/client relationship more effectively, the next section discusses how to identify the audit department's client relationship score and provides suggestions on how to strengthen existing relationships and foster new ones.

 CLIENT RELATIONSHIP SCORE

Every auditor knows the value of a strong relationship with business partners. Even though it is impossible to measure specifically the importance of the auditor/client relationship to the success of an audit, the client relationship still remains the number-one priority of all audit teams. Why? Because all audit activity requires the client to provide:

- Information about the process to be reviewed
- Documentation and data evidencing the current business process
- Time and resources to work with the audit team
- Agreement and acceptance of issues noted
- Action plans to address the opportunities for improvement.

An auditor, even one with no experience, knows the client is not going to just open up and share business information without feeling confident about the auditor and having a clear understanding of how the information is going to be used in the examination of the business process.

To assist in quantifying the audit/client relationship, complete the Client Relationship Scorecard in Table 2.1. To determine the client relationship score, read the statement and then place a checkmark under the corresponding

TABLE 2.1 Client Relationship Score

Relationship Statement	1	2	3	4	5
1. IAD has a specific marketing plan.					
2. IAD creates a relationship on every assignment.					
3. IAD is knowledgeable of the company operations.					
4. IAD is technically proficient.					
5. IAD communicates constantly throughout the audit.					
6. IAD validates all issues before the exit meeting or draft report.					
7. IAD consistently applies ratings.					
8. IAD issues reports in a timely manner.					
9. IAD uses client surveys after each project.					
10. IAD completes audits with minimal client disruption.					
11. IAD clients understand internal audit's objectives.					
12. IAD obtains complete action plans from the client.					
13. IAD is asked for input from the client on projects.					
14. IAD provides a value recognized by the client.					

number that best describes your current work environment. After reading and scoring all 14 statements in Table 2.1, calculate the total number of points accumulated for each answer and average the total by dividing by 14. An average score of above 3.5 indicates that your audit department recognizes the importance of establishing relationships with your clients and is on the way to fostering positive partnerships on every audit. If your average score is between 3.0 and 3.5, you have begun to develop relationships but still need to focus on the core competencies (communication throughout the process, validation of issues, and timely delivery of the audit product) that are critical to a partnership's success. Any average scores below 3.0 require the audit department to analyze each statement and determine which ones represent the biggest opportunity for improvement. The analysis should include a ranking of the relationship statements from most to least critical. When performing this ranking, consider the objective of the audit department and the steps needed to meet them on a consistent basis. Once the ranking is completed, develop specific action plans with the business process owner to address each opportunity for improvement.

Each statement in Table 2.1 is explained in detail in the numbered list. In scoring, 1 indicates Strongly Disagree; 2 means Disagree; 3 is Neutral; 4 means Agree; and 5 means Strongly Agree. The acronym IAD represents Internal Audit Department.

Relationship Statement Explanations

1. **IAD has a specific marketing plan.** Every internal audit department should have a marketing plan that details the services performed by the group and provides an overview of the audit process itself. Also, the marketing plan should include an organizational chart to provide clients with an understanding of how the group is structured and the reporting hierarchy. Other marketing plan examples may include:
   - A projected timeline of a risk-based audit
   - The deliverables for each audit phase
   - The report opinion ratings along with their corresponding definitions

   Having a marketing plan for the audit department better prepares the audit team for the introductory meeting with the client and demystifies the audit process (especially for a first-time client).

2. **IAD creates a relationship on every assignment.** Traditionally, internal auditors always looked at audits as an assignment. The assignment was given to an audit leader and supporting staff to execute, and that team was to perform the work as efficiently as possible and move on to the next area to be reviewed. Audits should never be looked at as an assignment. Auditors need to adjust their thinking and consider every opportunity with a client as another chance to create, build, and maintain a relationship. Always remember that a strong relationship takes time to establish and is based on trust. Obviously, it is much simpler to perform an audit as an assignment because building a relationship requires dedication. However, in order to complete an audit, the audit team is going to rely on the client to work closely with the auditors and provide the detailed information to be tested. If the audit is executed as just an assignment, there will be challenges throughout the audit that will prolong the delivery of the final audit product. Building a strong relationship is about partnering on every project. Keep in mind that a partnership requires two parties to work together to achieve the same goal.

3. **IAD is knowledgeable of the company operations.** Every auditor should be able to agree that there is no greater asset to an auditor than knowledge of the company. More and more audit departments are recruiting individuals who possess business line experience. The "company experienced" individuals are being brought into internal audit to provide the detailed business process knowledge perspective. No matter how experienced auditors are, they will never have the understanding of the business process nuances that business line employees have acquired over their tenure of working in the day-to-day operations. To try to compensate for the lack of actual operational experience, auditors must constantly build on their business process knowledge. Auditors can accomplish this through independent research and learning about company policies and procedures, industry standards, and audit experience.

4. **IAD is technically proficient.** Like any other profession, auditors must work diligently to become technically proficient. Drilling down into that concept, auditors first must clearly understand the audit methodology that has been developed and implemented within their team. The methodology should detail the guidelines and explain the steps necessary in the three main phases of an audit: planning, fieldwork, and reporting/wrap-up.

The audit team is responsible not only for understanding the phase requirements but also for the expected performance and deliverables of each phase of the audit. Technical proficiency is acquired over time by reviewing the established methodology, asking questions in times of uncertainty (the most underused skill), completing all required/assigned steps, and learning from the audit team leaders.

5. **IAD communicates constantly throughout the audit.** Constant communication throughout the audit means that the audit team communicates consistently:
   - Beginning with the kickoff meeting
   - Through the planning regarding the approach and scope of the audit
   - During fieldwork by keeping the client up to date on the testing and validating all potential issues prior to concluding on the adequacy of the control environment
   - In the reporting phase by delivering a clear, concise message in a timely manner

   A high-functioning audit team communicates consistently through the entire audit process. At no point during an audit should a client be wondering how the audit is going. Communication should be the cornerstone of the audit department and a core competency for every auditor on the team.

6. **IAD validates all issues before the exit meeting or draft report.** One of the most common mistakes auditors make is to rush to a conclusion without examining all of the information. That is not to say that auditors will conclude on testing without finishing the sample. What it means is that a conclusion will be made without first validating the testing results with the process owner or subject matter expert. Statement 3 said that auditors, no matter how experienced, will know the process in as much detail as the operational processing personnel. So why would any auditor finalize an opinion without validating the testing results first? Take a simple three-step approach to conclude on testing confidently:

   1. Double check the results
   2. Validate the results with the process expert
   3. Develop the testing conclusion based on the data

   If an auditor follows this simple three-step approach to validation, there will be much less debate about the testing results and much less confusion regarding the overall audit opinion.

7. **IAD consistently applies ratings.** Truly one of the biggest challenges facing audit departments today is applying ratings (individual testing and overall audit) consistently from one audit to another. No matter what the assigned area, testing technique, or type of audit, the ratings must be applied consistently based on risk. Risk is clarified by the likelihood of the risk being realized and its impact once it has occurred. Regardless of the area being reviewed, if the same risk exists for department A and department B, they must both be given the same rating. Who works in the department, the tenure of the team, friendliness of the managers, or physical location should have absolutely no impact on the assigned rating. Remember, ratings are based on the risk identified in testing the data. Always base the audit conclusions on the process and supporting data.

8. **IAD issues reports in a timely manner.** An audit report issued within 30 days of the completion of the fieldwork would be considered timely. The benchmark for reporting is 15 days from the completion of fieldwork to the issuance of the final report (not the draft). Believe it or not, communication throughout the audit (as discussed in statement 5) significantly reduces the time it takes to draft, review, and issue a final audit report. No surprises and up-front communication and discussion of the pertinent issues throughout the audit assist in the delivery of the final audit product.

9. **IAD uses client surveys after each project.** Client surveys are the most effective way to solicit independent feedback regarding audit execution. Surveys should be sent to the key client contacts that were relied on during the audit, not just the head of the business operation under review. Many audit departments use client surveys, but the surveys are sent only to the manager or head of the client department. Many times this person was not involved in the daily operations of the audit and completed the survey without understanding all of the effort required to finish the job. It is important to identify the client survey recipients throughout the audit and independently solicit their feedback. One note of caution: The survey will improve the effectiveness and efficiency of audit operations only if client feedback is reviewed and validated where necessary, and if action is taken to address the opportunity for improvement.

10. **IAD completes audits with minimal client disruption.** Many audit clients assess the success or failure of an internal audit based on how much disruption the audit team imposes on daily business operations. Business

units in any company are focused on providing customer service, whether the client is internal or external. The last thing an operational unit wants is to have the assigned audit team bothering them or asking questions when its employees are trying to do their job. Effective audit teams allow business units to perform their daily responsibilities throughout an audit, even during the fieldwork phase. The key to minimal disruption during an audit is planning. If the audit is planned effectively and client expectations are agreed to in advance, there will be no need to interrupt the client during the audit. To complement the planning, be sure to establish specific times for the validation of testing results and the discussion of potential issues.

11. **IAD clients understand internal audit's objectives.** A simple concept taken for granted by audit departments is that business units understand what audit does and why auditors are performing the work. The truth is that most people outside of audit honestly don't know the objectives of an internal audit function. Some believe it is a necessary evil while others think internal audit is part of the external audit function. Communicating the objectives of internal audit is critical to building the foundation of the audit/client relationship. Demystify the unknown for clients and ensure that they understand that one of the primary objectives of the audit department is to partner with the business units to strengthen and validate the control environment.

12. **IAD obtains complete action plans from the client.** Clients who provide complete action plans to address items in an audit report recognize the value of a strong relationship with their audit partners. For clarification, a complete action plan has three characteristics.

    1. The documented action addresses root cause.
    2. The action has a true owner (meaning the person has the ability and authority to make the action happen).
    3. The action has a realistic target date.

    Obtaining this type of action should not be a battle of wills between internal audit and the client. Strong relationships foster a partnership where both sides discuss root cause and work together to develop a solution to address it.

13. **IAD is asked for input from the client on projects.** Fully developed relationships will foster an environment of solicitation of input and feedback from internal audit on business unit projects or initiatives. When a

business owner asks for internal audit's assistance, no matter how big the project may be, the audit team should realize it is working with a client who truly recognizes and respects the value of internal audit. These situations are great opportunities to build on existing relationships, but the audit team must be careful not to take on too many projects because it is afraid to say no to a client.

14. **IAD provides a value recognized by the client.** Quality is one of the most difficult concepts to quantify because it is subjective and based on an individual or a group's opinion. Unfortunately, internal audit's clients are the ones who get to judge whether a service provided any value. When trying to determine the level of quality the audit department delivers, don't just look for quality with clients who are given a satisfactory rating. Every client has an opinion. As discussed in statement 9, the survey is the primary tool to solicit feedback directly from the client. However, contrary to popular belief, more value is recognized from a client who receives a less-than-satisfactory rating. Why? Because critical opportunities for improvement were identified during the audit, and the client has recognized a positive gain from a negative rated report. When audit teams hear positive praise from a client who received a less-than-satisfactory report, they know their efforts are being recognized for delivering a value and a benefit to the business unit.

 ## SUMMARY

Internal audit has the unique ability to review and conclude on operations throughout the company. It is increasingly relied on year after year to provide confirmation and validation of the strength of the control environment as well as opportunities for improvement. To achieve its objectives, internal audit must use all the tools at its disposal while leveraging the relationships with the business units to continually provide support and information to execute the work. Additionally, internal audit must clearly understand its existing process methodology before developing an alternate approach, such as continuous auditing, to address the opportunities to expand audit coverage and depth in certain areas in the business. Once the decision has been made to expand the audit product offerings to include continuous auditing, a new methodology will have to be developed to explain the alternate approach.

3

Continuous Auditing Methodology Development

 CONTINUOUS AUDITING METHODOLOGY

In an effort to expedite the documentation of the continuous auditing methodology and reduce the amount of development duplication, the audit team can use the existing audit methodology as a guide/outline. The continuous auditing methodology will contain the same components as the risk-based audit approach except that it will be a more streamlined version. Your current methodology should contain the approach objectives and detailed directions on how to plan an audit, document process flows and controls, develop a test plan, and effectively communicate the test results.

When presented with any new technique, approach, or methodology, there is always the temptation to jump right in and start using it without developing the proper standards. Speaking from firsthand experience, I can tell you that that is not the smartest or best course of action. One of the biggest mistakes an audit department can make is assuming that the audit team fully understands the methodology and how, when, and where using it would be the most beneficial. Remember, this methodology, while similar to a full-scope risk-based audit in some respects requires a totally different mentality and specificity, starting with the selection of a target area, through the planning, to the testing selection, all the way through to the execution.

Consider the level of planning and effort that went into the development of your current audit methodology to create a complete profile and step-by-step guideline for executing an audit from inception to final report. Your audit methodology—or any methodology, for that matter—should contain the necessary details to communicate explicitly process objectives and the executable tasks to reach the desired end result or deliverable. This development process takes time, a clear understanding of the approach, and dedicated resources to document the entire work flow.

Let's examine the methodology requirements for the continuous auditing approach.

METHODOLOGY REQUIREMENTS

A complete audit methodology is designed to provide the department with the road map or outline to execute the process effectively in order to achieve the desired result. Keep in mind that while any process will generate a result, only the process with a detailed methodology supporting it will produce a valued result. Often, more time is wasted correcting the problems and filling in the gaps of a process that was not thought out from the beginning. Even though it may seem expeditious to select the next audit and begin testing the area on a recurring basis, it is much more efficient to take the necessary time to determine how your department can benefit from a continuous auditing methodology and document your process. It will be time well spent. In the next sections, we discuss the document requirements to be included in your formal continuous auditing methodology.

Continuous Auditing Purpose

Every methodology begins with a purpose statement. This statement provides an overview of the document and explains why it has been created. It does not need to be a couple of paragraphs; more often than not, it is a few sentences describing why the methodology has been developed and officially declaring this process as the methodology to which the company will adhere for the implementation and maintenance of its specific continuous auditing program. The aim of the purpose statement is not to convince the reader that this tool is needed but to explain the formal documentation requirements of the approach. Do not confuse or combine the purpose statement with the detailed objective of the continuous auditing methodology. The continuous auditing methodology objective is described separately and in greater detail.

Transitioning from the purpose listed to the objective is like moving from the title of an article to the opening statement of the first paragraph. The objective is the reason why the methodology has been developed and how it is to be used within the department.

Typical continuous auditing program objectives include wording such as "provide an ongoing validation of the effectiveness of the selected controls" or "determining that key controls over a critical process are in place, established, and operating as intended." From my experience and perspective, internal audit departments that I have worked in or partnered with had two reasons for creating an internal audit continuous auditing methodology:

1. To expand the coverage over their audit universe
2. To drill down into critical controls to ensure they produce repeatable, reliable results

Due to their subjective nature, objectives will be developed based on the individual needs of the each department. Every audit team that considers creating and implementing a continuous auditing methodology must examine its current methodology and evaluate the potential need and fit (as discussed in Chapter 2) before incorporating an additional work product into their service offerings. I have told all of my business partners, colleagues, and clients not to expend time and resources to develop the continuous auditing program unless it will benefit your team, department, and company over time.

After you have performed the analysis of need and fit and decided that a fully developed continuous auditing methodology would benefit your department, consider documenting the goals of the program. When creating goals, ensure that they are realistic. Some departments set such a high bar in measuring the benefits of a continuous auditing program that the dedicated effort to meet those expectations becomes counterproductive. When setting your team's goals, detail the benefits that the program will produce. Consider the

TABLE 3.1 Continuous Auditing Benefits

Business Unit	Goal/Benefit
Internal Audit	Increase auditor business unit knowledge and exposure
	Proactive identification of trends and root cause focus
	Establish and foster business management relationships
	Enhance audit product offerings
	Manage audit workload more effectively and efficiently
Audit Committee	Expansion of risk and audit coverage
	Standardization of audit results
Management	Validate compliance with existing policies and procedures
	Provide potential methodology for self-assessment
External Partners	Potential reduction in external work performed
	Advanced reliance on internal audit work

items listed in Table 3.1 as potential goals of the continuous auditing program once it has been established and is up and running. The table provides some goal definition suggestions and the targeted area that will recognize the benefits.

In developing your continuous auditing objectives and goals, it is critically important to recognize in this section what continuous auditing is designed to accomplish. Moreover, ensure that there is a clear understanding that continuous auditing in no way, shape, or form is created to replace the coverage that a full-scope audit would provide. The overall objective of the methodology is to enhance the current product offerings of internal audit departments while providing an expansion of coverage over identified areas of risk in the business operations.

As added detailed support for the continuous auditing methodology, it is recommended that the documented continuous auditing methodology include a brief explanation of the difference between continuous auditing and continuous monitoring. As discussed in Chapter 1, this difference is the cornerstone component of what determines the effectiveness and recognized benefit of a successfully implemented continuous auditing program. Remember to document the recurring testing aspect of the approach as the differentiating factor separating a monitoring process from a true auditing process. The power of the methodology is always going to be in the detailed results it generates on a recurring basis.

Continuous Auditing Phases

The phases of a continuous auditing methodology are no different from the phases of a full-scope audit. The continuous approach has planning, fieldwork, and reporting phases. Existing audit methodology requirements can be used as an outline in the development of the continuous auditing methodology.

The continuous auditing planning phase requires the same discipline and dedication to obtaining a detailed understanding of the business operation being examined. Without the proper business knowledge, it is very difficult to perform any audit services, let alone try to develop a focused approach to evaluate specific critical controls in a continuous auditing program. Chapters 4 to 6 explain the planning phase objectives and major deliverables.

As with any audit work, in continuous auditing, the planning phase requires the biggest commitment of time to complete; nothing works well if it is not planned correctly. Insufficient planning is one of the biggest mistakes audit departments make. It does not matter if an audit team has been assigned a full-scope audit, a limited-scope review, or a continuous audit; there is always a temptation to begin testing as quickly as possible to start generating results. The planning phase usually does not get the right amount of attention for a multitude of reasons. As an example, some teams believe they already know enough about the business and how it operates on a daily basis; others believe the planning can be accomplished concurrently with data testing. The problem is that it is not efficient or effective just to test data based on previous experience or another individual's recommendation. Proper testing is achieved only when the audit team not only has a clear understanding of the existing policy and procedure requirements but also has obtained a validation of the current process being performed by the operation under review. This need to plan properly becomes even more critical during continuous auditing testing because the auditor has specifically selected an individual control(s) to examine. If the selected control is not one of the critical controls in the operational process, the value of the continuous auditing program will be significantly diminished.

The fieldwork phase is basically self-explanatory. This is the phase where all of the time spent planning is put into action. The fieldwork phase requires a detailed program to guide the auditor through the intricacies of testing and the process standard requirements. And just as in any audit service performed, during fieldwork auditors will be compiling results, identifying potential exceptions, and summarizing results. In a continuous audit with a couple of enhancements, this phase will most closely mirror the fieldwork phase of a full-scope review. The continuous auditing program methodology requirements for the fieldwork phase are discussed and detailed in Chapter 7. This phase creates the basis and support for all of the conclusions you will draw as a result of the focused testing performed. The strength of the audit and the recognized value of the work completed will be evidenced in the documentation of the fieldwork. Be certain to document your testing approach and results properly in your work papers. Doing this will ensure that the data will be relied on to support the conclusions and not just the auditor's opinion. Remember always to let the data drive the results. More often than not, it is the process that has opportunities for improvement, not the personnel.

The reporting phase of the methodology details how the results of a continuous audit are going to be communicated. This phase should indicate the type of report to be issued along with the potential corresponding ratings that an area could receive based on the risk of the observations noted. The report phase also provides a standard report format in which all continuous auditing activities will follow regardless of the client, location, or operation type being reviewed. Consistency of report format, rating, and delivery are what drives the success failure of the final audit report. The continuous auditing methodology requirements for the reporting phase are discussed and detailed in Chapter 9.

How Much Detail Is Needed?

Everyone inevitably asks how much really needs to be included in the documentation of the continuous auditing methodology. One thing I have learned over my 20-plus years in internal audit is that there are absolutely no shortcuts, especially when it comes to the documentation of work. The methodology, when it is developed, represents the blueprint that guides the audit team through the process from start to finish. No matter how much experience you have or your audit team has and no matter how well you believe you understand the nuances to the continuous auditing methodology, it has to be documented in a clear, concise manner and format that does not require any special skill, education, or experience to execute.

The level of detail has to document the steps in each one of the phases and should also contain a checklist of deliverables required in each phase. The checklist will serve as a self-monitoring mechanism instructing each person involved in the process to ensure that all necessary steps have been completed prior to moving from one phase of the methodology to the next. Although this step will not guarantee that all steps have been completed, it can be used as a quality control measure when determining the effectiveness and efficiency of a completed continuous audit. Consider the documentation detail as a recipe for the successful completion of a continuous audit. Just like cooking something for the first time, if the prescribed recipe is not followed, whatever you were trying to cook will not turn out right. The same can be said about the continuous auditing methodology. If the steps are not detailed in the methodology and followed as designed, the expected results will not be achieved. Take the necessary time to detail the methodology phase requirements adequately to keep your auditors on track and focused on the assigned task.

Methodology Outline

Table 3.2 details a suggested format for a continuous auditing methodology. The information contained in the table is not required for every methodology developed nor is it meant to be an all-inclusive list.

TABLE 3.2   Continuous Auditing Methodology Section Suggestions

Section	Details
Purpose and Scope	What does this document contain and represent?
	Expectations being set forth for the approach
Objectives and Goals	What is the reason for using this methodology?
	What are the expected benefits of implementation?
Planning	Business knowledge development and education
	Target area selection and objective development
	Testing frequency and scope
Fieldwork	Work performance
	Exception identification and validation
Reporting	Report format
	Rating definitions
	Distribution requirements

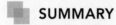 **SUMMARY**

The audit department is scrutinized and judged whenever results are presented to a client or business partner. To avoid unnecessary discussions and challenges, take the time to fully develop and document the continuous auditing methodology. Internal audit teams face enough existing barriers when executing assigned audits; the introduction of a "new" approach will be met with immediate skepticism by clients. To prepare your clients, team, and partners, document the continuous auditing methodology. Ensure the methodology clearly states the objectives of the approach and potential recognizable benefits and provides sufficient details of the executable phases for your audit team to follow. The time invested in the proper development of the continuous auditing methodology will save numerous hours of potential rework and benefit the development and ongoing maintenance of the audit/client relationship.

CHAPTER FOUR

4

Preparing for a Continuous Audit

 BUILDING THE BUSINESS KNOWLEDGE

As discussed in Chapter 3, planning is the most critical component of any audit activity. To reinforce its importance and focus on developing a sound approach, Chapters 4 and 5 are dedicated to creating a strong structure for the successful development and planning of a continuous auditing program. Many times, planning for audit activity is done on the job during the fieldwork or even as an afterthought once the preliminary results are being compiled.

No matter how strong an auditor you are or how experienced your audit team may be, there is absolutely no reason to stop trying to learn about the current business operations, challenges, and risks facing the operational business team every day. Nothing is a more powerful tool for an auditor than business knowledge. If auditors focus on developing and maintaining their business knowledge, they will become much more efficient and effective at objectively analyzing the process and identifying the corresponding risks. Once auditors develop a solid working knowledge of the business area, they will be able to strategically dissect the process and create targeted programs to validate the control environment. Remember that no auditor is expected to understand the process at the same level of detail as the operational personnel working in the area. The goal is to build on the business knowledge each time you have an opportunity to interact and discuss the process with the business owners and technical experts in the area.

The primary purpose of this chapter is to identify and explain the information needed to create a successful continuous auditing program and to introduce the three main phases of preparation. Additionally, the chapter also focuses on how to develop important business knowledge as you create your continuous auditing programs. Let us begin by identifying the three phases of preparation:

1. Developing business knowledge
2. Understanding the rules
3. Identifying technology

 ## DEVELOPING BUSINESS KNOWLEDGE

One concept that everyone can agree on is that over the past decade, internal audit has been held to a higher standard than before. This is not just the result of the most popular and publicized scandals; rather, individual companies have had control breakdowns in their core business areas that have caused them to lose money and recognize a serious drop in expected deliverables and/or production quality. "With this higher level of expectation on internal audit," business unit management is looking for internal audit to ensure that the business process control environment is in place and operating as intended. Remember, any process will generate a result; the question that must be answered remains: Is the process producing the *expected* result?

To ensure that internal audit provides the value it is relied on to deliver, the audit team must develop a strong working knowledge of the business operation under review. The most difficult scenario for internal auditors, regardless of their audit tenure, is to be assigned an area to audit that they have never examined before. When faced with this type of scenario, it is incumbent on the assigned auditor to gain an understanding or working knowledge of the business process. Most business units are not overly excited and welcoming when internal auditors come into their area for a review; assignment to an area where there is no baseline information to start planning increases the pressure on auditors.

With no existing information available on which to develop their plan and audit approach, auditors need to discover the necessary background on the new area in the most efficient and effective manner. There are seven different ways to gain business knowledge background on the area:

1. Independent research
2. Previous audit activity and results
3. External examinations and results
4. Action items
5. Walk-throughs
6. Process map
7. SIPOC

Independent Research

Where does someone go to find out information about anything? It used to be the library, where you would spend hours upon hours looking through card catalogs to identify a topic close to the one you were searching for, only to be directed to a particular section in the building. Upon arriving in the specified section, you remained hopeful that the particular book, magazine, or periodical you needed was on the shelf. Even if you were lucky enough to have found the materials, you could spend a significant amount of time paging through the information just to find the background or fact you were looking to learn.

Those days have long since passed with the invention of the Internet. Now searching for information, or even a specific word, has become a much more manageable endeavor. When given an area about which you have no baseline information, start with the Internet to gain background on the topic. Use the power of the Internet to narrow your search and focus on the general business process. Do not waste time trying to find the process details for your exact business. The goal in developing business knowledge is to find background information that you can use to begin the learning process for an area for which you have no previous knowledge. Many audit teams try to identify, examine, and read every topic identified during their search and end up wasting valuable time. Remember that the objective of using an online search engine is to quickly identify business process topics to build the foundation of learning. Technology alone will not provide any audit shop with a complete background on a process area.

Also, even though the Internet is the most powerful search engine available, examine current periodicals maintained by your company or department. Most companies subscribe to the latest industry journals and newspapers. These types of documents can provide you with a profile of the business industry that may be beneficial as you learn about a currently unknown process. Through their independent research, audit teams will be better equipped to develop the specific testing objectives required by the continuous auditing methodology. The more business and industry knowledge the audit team can obtain, the more effective its continuous auditing testing will become.

Previous Audit Activity and Results

Auditors planning a continuous audit of a new business process should review any and all documentation maintained in their own department. To begin this research of internally held information, auditors must first identify all the work that was done in the business unit under review. One word of caution with this approach: Be careful to select the previous audit activity that pertains to the specific business process being targeted. The common mistake of many auditors during planning (especially in the continuous auditing methodology of a new area) is that they pull and read every piece of audit activity for a division, department, or functional area. Although this is a valuable exercise to fill downtime, it will not benefit an auditor who is always looking to be more effective and efficient especially when it comes to saving time during part of an audit. To streamline and shorten the learning curve, the auditor needs to be strategic and identify and examine only the completed audit work that has a direct link to the area or process selected for the continuous audit.

Once the applicable audit documents have been identified, the auditor should review the work papers to gain an understanding of the key testing elements. These key elements include:

- Business, audit, and testing objectives
- Scope of the work
- Risks

- Current controls
- Test plan
- Results
- Overall rating

Let us briefly examine each element to clarify the review and learning approach.

One of the most overlooked elements is the objective. Whether it is the business, audit, or testing objective, it must be identified and clearly understood. Every objective answers the question as to why the process, audit, or test is being performed. It is the rationale behind the business unit being established, the reason the audit is being performed, and the purpose of the specific audit testing. The critical answers to the objective questions establish the foundation of learning for any area. Once the objectives are clearly identified and comprehended, the auditor can begin to understand all of the activity that takes place to support the function.

Scope, which on the surface appears the easiest to establish, is the element that usually does not get documented properly. Scope in the work papers you are reviewing should detail the specific items to be covered during the testing and identify any exclusions made during the planning of the work. A properly documented scope statement will assist the researching auditor in determining whether or not the subsequent testing documentation should be reviewed in an effort to build the business knowledge. If the documented scope does not pertain to the continuous auditing target area, do not waste the time reviewing the audit work. The building of business knowledge is benefited by the auditor staying disciplined and not trying to learn every aspect of the business based on all audits completed in the functional area. Understanding the scope will direct the auditor to the most valuable work performed previously.

Other valuable information in the knowledge-building phase is understanding the specific risks and controls currently identified. The continuous auditing methodology is designed to take the numerous risks and controls in a business area and narrow the list down to the most critical ones. Critical risks are the ones that have the largest likelihood of occurring and significance or impact if and when the risk is realized. Conversely, the established controls (the ones currently functioning in the operation, not the desired controls) will be targeted and tested to determine that they are established, in place, and operating as intended. The work papers and supporting testing will tell the researching auditor how well or poorly the established controls performed and mitigated the biggest risks.

After gaining an understanding of the business process and the corresponding risks and controls, the auditor should review the test plan. The test plan details the specific steps utilized during the audit to conclude on the effectiveness of the control environment. There can be instances where the actual steps used in a full-scope audit are transferred and used in the continuous audit plan. The testing and results will provide the researching auditor with a road map on how to test controls effectively. Each one of the test plans reviewed should link directly back to the documented risks and controls. There are times when more testing is performed than is required to validate a specific control. The continuous auditing methodology requires that the targeted test be linked directly to the process risks identified during the planning. That is why it is critically important to gain a detailed understanding of how the process was tested. This understanding is easily attainable by examining the test plan.

The final elements to be considered when developing your business knowledge through previous audit work are the test results and overall rating of the work performed. The test results and overall rating provide a picture of the efficiency and effectiveness of the control environment of the target area that is being examined. When trying to gain an understanding of an area for a continuous audit, many auditors focus only on the poorly performing controls identified in the audit work. This method will provide a perspective on the business operations, but it is important to examine all controls tested, regardless of how they performed during the audit. When the business unit places more emphasis on the failing controls, the continuous audit may want to focus on other controls to ensure they are still working as designed even though they are not getting the same level of attention.

The bottom line for expanding your business knowledge through previous audit activity is to spend a sufficient amount of time understanding the objectives before diving into the detailed testing. This will level set the researching auditor as to why the audit was being performed in an effort to validate the control environment of the particular business objective being tested. Also, take time to understand the testing and if possible ask questions of the auditors who worked on the completed project previously.

External Examinations and Results

As discussed in the previous section, valuable information about a business unit can be learned by examining completed audit work, and external examinations are no exception. Although the external exam may have a different objective and may have been completed by someone other than internal audit, it still will provide a perspective on the business function reviewed.

Copies of all external examinations usually are provided to internal audit. If not, the results of the examination can be obtained upon request. Although researching auditors will not be able to examine the actual work papers used in developing the external report, the results can be used to establish a better understanding of the status of the control environment of the area tested. Even though the actual work papers are not available, the report will detail the target area, scope of the review, testing results, and overall opinion. This report coupled with the internal audit work performed will help researching auditors develop a more well-rounded business knowledge and potentially higher level of confidence of the business unit being targeted.

Action Items

Another way to build your business knowledge is to examine action items linked directly to the business area being researched. As discussed in the previous audit activity and results section, the action items selected for review will be valuable in building your business knowledge only if they are tied to the area being researched. There are so many action items being tracked in an audit department that it is critically important to be selective in the items read. Auditors sometimes can get lost in all the details and lose focus on why the research began in the first place.

To start this review, select any action items (matching the business unit area under review) that are currently open or have been closed in the past six months. To build on the foundational understanding, it is important to identify what the business unit currently is focusing on as well as what it has completed recently. During the action item review, determine if any of the action items, closed or open, are linked. If so, take some extra time to understand the relationship between the action and the time it is taking to address the issue or time it took to put the action into place. Also, if the business unit being researched is already working on a significant number of open actions, it may not be the best time to introduce a continuous audit on top of the current list of responsibilities. Even if your research does not identify any outstanding action items, you may want to consider a different target area if the business unit has recently (within the previous three months) made significant changes to its control environment. If you launch a continuous auditing program into a process that has just completed recent control enhancements, there may not be sufficient time for the business unit team to adapt to the new process. This short time frame between the new control enhancements and the continuous audit program could result in false positives or even a lack of sufficient sample sizes available to conclude on the effectiveness of the control environment.

The action item database or tracking system can provide an in-depth profile of the business unit's control environment status, but it may also provide an indication that the business unit is not ready for a continuous auditing program. If the action item data is telling you that significant changes have just been made or that the business unit management is in the process of addressing known control issues, do not waste the time and resources to build a complete continuous auditing program until the business unit has developed some stability in its process. This constructive approach will benefit the auditor, the audit department, and the business unit relationship.

Walk-Throughs

One of the most effective ways to develop business knowledge is to perform a walk-through of the existing process. Nothing can replace an in-person explanation of the process while watching the business unit personnel performing the functional requirements. This type of knowledge transfer requires a commitment from the business unit management to dedicate the time and a process expert to explain the operational steps. The auditor performing the walk-through must have experience in performing walk-throughs and clearly understand the business unit objectives. Without experience and objective understanding, the auditor will not know what questions to ask to clarify the process steps or when to ask them. It is very easy for a researching auditor performing a walk-through to get overwhelmed by the complexity of the topic or lost in the details being explained. Asking qualifying questions or even requesting the process expert to clarify a particular step is critical in the development of a detailed understanding of the business.

The final step in completing a detailed walk-through is to document the understanding in a narrative. Once the narrative has been completed, it must be validated with the technical expert who provided the operational information. This validation step ensures that the knowledge transfer was provided and received without any critical information being excluded or missing during translation.

Process Map

The other option to documenting the walk-through exercise is to create a detailed process map in lieu of a narrative. Although narratives written by experienced writers can document the process details adequately, a process map forces the creator to have a true understanding of the functional area at a granular level. It is possible to perform a walk-through and document a high-level overview of the process providing any reader with a basic explanation of the functional process in a narrative. A process map, however, breaks down the functional process to a detailed step-by-step level.

Process maps may require a little bit more time to create, but they are well worth the extra investment. The additional effort required also helps researching auditors develop their communication skills and helps facilitate the detail questioning process. In addition, it is a document that can be updated easily from year to year to ensure that the business unit process is accurately depicted in the process map for future audits, continuous audits, and knowledge transfers. Automation plays a key role; process map generation has become much easier using computer software.

During process map development, be sure to highlight the existing risks and corresponding controls directly on the map. Doing so will provide readers with a more detailed profile of business unit operations. It also gives researching auditors the guidance to focus on the key controls as they develop their business knowledge during the process of creating a continuous auditing program.

SIPOC

A SIPOC is a Six Sigma tool designed to document a process. The SIPOC acronym stands for Suppliers, Inputs, Process, Outputs, and Customers. Everyone in internal audit—and business, for that matter—is familiar with the concept of input, process, and output. What a SIPOC does is require the thought process to be expanded to include the suppliers and customers who are involved in a business process. Even though the SIPOC is heavily used and was originally designed to be used to document manufacturing processes, it is a very valuable tool in internal audit and process excellence departments.

The SIPOC process directs the user to consider supplemental information that surrounds the business process. For example, instead of just documenting how the process information flows, the SIPOC asks: Who provides the required information used in the process? The additional details utilized to complete the SIPOC increase the depth of knowledge of any business unit function being researched. The SIPOC also provides a profile of the interdependencies of all business units involved in the generation of a particular product, transaction, or process. Internal audit is constantly challenged to find the root cause of a control breakdown; it can use a SIPOC in this effort to provide direction as to the ownership of a particular piece of information that can be causing the failure of the control being tested.

Over the past 20-plus years of my audit career, I have found the SIPOC to be the most effective way to develop business knowledge of an area for which I did not have a solid process-level understanding. Without the business knowledge of the process, it is very difficult, if not impossible, to perform any audit activity effectively, especially a continuous audit. Next is a more detailed explanation of the SIPOC and some helpful hints for completing one.

First, we start by defining each of the components of the SIPOC and explain how to complete each one.

Suppliers

Suppliers represent any group, team, department, or individual that provides information to support the process being examined. Consider suppliers as the group that supplies information to make the process run from start to finish. Suppliers are also known as providers because they provide the elements necessary to ensure success of the operational process. The elements the supplier provides could be materials, information, forms, or even individuals. The most effective way to identify suppliers is to ask who provides the information that is listed under the Inputs column of the SIPOC. Consider suppliers who are internal as well as external. The supplier element of the SIPOC commonly includes third-party providers contracted by the business unit.

Inputs

Inputs represent any information used in the process. Inputs usually contain raw materials, reports, figures, process detailed information, or staff used to complete the process tasks. The question to ask when completing the Input element of the SIPOC is: What information is required to perform the process successfully? Asking qualifying questions during the information-gathering phase will assist the auditor in identifying all the necessary inputs that feed the process. The feeders or inputs to the process should be able to be tied directly to a process step listed under the Process element of the SIPOC. Remember that the inputs listed should represent only those inputs used in the current process, not inputs that would be used in the redesign of a stronger control environment.

Process

Process is the section of the SIPOC where the high-level functional process map is documented. This element can be documented by referencing a formal process flow chart or listing the process flow under the column heading. The key to completing the process element is to document the process from start to finish. Use whatever method you are most comfortable with to complete the process requirement of the SIPOC. In practice, the process element is the one that is completed first when developing the SIPOC because all of the other SIPOC elements flow from the process details.

Outputs

Outputs represent any deliverable that is generated from the process detailed in the SIPOC. Many times the outputs represent a single event or a key deliverable of the process. Consider the audit process, for example. The main deliverable of an audit is the audit report. When audit departments create a SIPOC of their operations, the audit report is listed as one of the outputs in the SIPOC. When detailing the outputs of the business process SIPOC, what output is generated by the process and provided to the internal and external customers? An output can be a report, an approval, a completed assembly, or a delivery of information to another department.

Customers

Customers represent any client or partner who receives the outputs listed in the SIPOC. Customers can be internal or external to the process. In order to be considered formal customers documented in the SIPOC, they must receive the output directly from the business unit process documented in the process element of the SIPOC. Another key clarification of customers is that they do not have to be users of the process output. They could just be an area or partner who receives the output for informational purposes.

SIPOC Helpful Hints

Here are a couple of tips for documenting the elements in order to make the SIPOC process less cumbersome:

- **Consider the order in which the SIPOC is completed. The recommended approach is to begin with (1) process, then (2) outputs, (3) clients, (4) inputs, and (5) suppliers.** Logic would suggest that the SIPOC be completed in the order in which it is listed, beginning with suppliers flowing through to the customers. However, in practice rather than theory, it is more efficient to start with the process element of the SIPOC. Doing so allows auditors to document the business process flow and also provides the basis for them to complete the other elements of the SIPOC. Once the process element has been completed, the next step is to fill in the output. With the business process detailed, it is easier to list the particular outputs generated by the process. To keep the SIPOC exercise moving, follow the business process flow by completing the customer element by asking who directly receives the output generated by the process. After completing the right side of the process element, move to the input element, and list any information utilized to ensure that the process runs from start to finish. Once you have listed the required inputs to the process, document which partners provide the specific inputs under the supplier element of the SIPOC.
- **Ensure that every input listed has a specific supplier.** Any information detailed under the input element must come from somewhere or someone, and that group or individual has to be listed specifically under the supplier element. There does not have to be a one-for-one correlation between the supplier and input elements because some suppliers can provide more than one input that is used in the business process.
- **Validate the details with the business process owner just as you would for a drafted process map.** Validation with the process owner is a critical step to ensure the integrity of the data included in the SIPOC.

Remember that the SIPOC is going to be used to select the controls to be tested in your continuous auditing program.

Now that we have completed discussing the first phase of preparation, let's move on to the second phase, which is understanding the rules.

 ## UNDERSTANDING THE RULES

To build on and complement auditor knowledge of a business process area, it is necessary to obtain a clear understanding of the rules that govern the business process that is going to be tested using the continuous auditing methodology. Think of the process rules as the standards by which the process should be operating. These rules not only guide the process from start to finish but also identify the parameters of acceptable performance. A key factor that must be considered when trying to understand the business rules and requirements is that these rules can come from only two places: internal and external to the business. Internal rules are created and enforced by department management or company standards. External rules are created and enforced by governmental agencies. These are the only two sources for rules that maintain the business unit procedural requirements. Next we discuss different rules that must be considered as you continue to build your business knowledge.

Policies and Procedures

The primary source of rules guiding the business process is the policies and procedures created by the business unit to direct the operational team in the execution of the function. The biggest challenge when it comes to policies and procedures is obtaining the most current version of the documentation. A majority of the time, business unit policies and procedures are not up to date; often they do not reflect the most current process. Policies and procedures seem to be the last item on the task list for business unit management. The reason these documents are not kept up to date is because it is more important for the business to address customer needs; maintaining updated internal documentation almost always takes a backseat to satisfying the customer needs. Although that may work in achieving business objectives, it makes life very difficult for auditors attempting to document the process and build business unit knowledge. It becomes the auditors' responsibility to ensure that the policies and procedures are up to date and represent the current process being followed by business unit personnel.

If the policies and procedures are not updated, auditors must perform additional steps to validate the current process and document the differences between the policies and procedures and the actual operational steps being performed. Again, validation becomes a critical step in the effort to build current business unit knowledge. If auditors fail to complete the validation step, they likely will create a continuous auditing program based on antiquated data; when executed, the program will provide non-value-added results.

Fully developed policies and procedures should include the transaction requirements for all activities being performed in the business unit. When discussing transactions, the definition of a transaction is not restricted to a financial transaction with a debit and a credit. For the purpose of building the business knowledge in our effort to create a targeted continuous auditing program, transaction can be compliance, financial, or operational in nature. For example, an operational transaction could be as simple as a handoff between departments or the delivery of a report from one processor to another. Compliance transaction requirements are excellent sources for continuous auditing programs, as compliance transaction requirements are very specific.

Another factor to be considered when examining policies and procedures are whether there are any process workarounds. A "workaround" is defined as any variation to the established process requirements that would allow an exception to the current rules. A true workaround is documented in the policies and procedures and represents an exception to the rule, which means it should happen very infrequently. If the workaround is happening on a daily basis, it could mean the current process needs to be revised to represent the day-to-day business that requires the business unit to handle the process in a new way.

Although it is acceptable to have approved process workarounds, it is not acceptable to establish or use a workaround to bypass a critical control. Keep in mind that fully developed processes have been built with proper controls implemented at key process stage gates. If a workaround is built to avoid the established critical control, the control environment is weakened and the probability for errors and mistakes increases incrementally. Many times workarounds go unnoticed because errors do not surface immediately as a result of the process change until a process exception has been noted as a result of the completed testing. The business process will continue to generate results even though a new workaround may have been implemented. To continue to build detailed business knowledge, consider workarounds as you develop your SIPOC and plan for your continuous auditing program.

Manual Processing

Manual processing poses different risks depending on the business process. In and of itself, manual processing increases risk because human error is injected into the business process. There are discussions everyday on whether manual processes pose more risk than automated ones. Each audit department has its own interpretation, but before concluding which method has a higher level of risk, consider this.

If a business operation contains a manual part of the process, there is the possibility that the person responsible for that process piece could make a mistake. Everyone will agree with the previous statement describing the potential risk of manual processing. The debate begins when estimating the frequency of the number of manual processing errors. The truth is, it is impossible to determine the rate at which an individual will make a particular mistake. There are probabilities or percentages but not a real factual way to conclude on the number.

Conversely, consider automating the same control that currently is done manually. If the same control is automated and it is not set up correctly, the control will fail every time the process requires that particular step. In this example, the automated control would have a higher frequency of failure and a larger error rate than the manual control.

When developing your business knowledge in an effort to build a complete continuous auditing program, be sure that you consider any manual processes included in the business unit operations. Both manual and automated processes must be documented in the business unit SIPOC to accurately document the process and build the strong foundation of operational business knowledge.

Supervisory Overrides

Supervisory overrides are another important rule to understand while building your business knowledge. It is perfectly acceptable to have a supervisory override built into the process, but it must be documented clearly in the policies and procedures. A supervisory override also can be described as a supervisory approval. No matter how the exception process is described, it represents the need for a supervisor to grant permission to process a transaction that does not follow current policies and procedures specifically. Additionally, there should be very specific, established, documented parameters of the scenario and business process requirements for which a supervisory override will be needed, requested, and approved.

There is one caution to be considered when discussing supervisory overrides. When gathering the business process data, determine if the supervisory override or approval has created an environment in which the business unit personnel have developed an optional process flow in an effort to avoid having to go through the supervisory override process requirements. Consider this instance in which a business unit team was bypassing the supervisory override process in order to expedite wire authorizations. The wire operations business unit had strict requirements detailing the approved amounts that each wire authorization clerk could approve without a secondary approval. In this example, the clerks were allowed to individually authorize up to $10,000. If a wire request was more than anyone's approved amount, the clerk would have to present the wire to a supervisor for subsequent approval prior to the release of funds. Although on the surface the control looks effective, the clerks figured out that they could process over their approved limit, without getting a supervisor approval, by splitting the wire request into two separate wires. So if a wire request was submitted for $12,000, instead of getting a supervisory approval, clerks would just send two wires to the same account for $6,000 each. From a policy standpoint, there was no violation of the clerks' approval amount. However, the critical control of validating a wire request over $10,000 was bypassed. Remember, the controls are built into the process to protect the company's assets and strengthen the control environment.

As you document the process and develop your business knowledge, be aware that there are always techniques to bypass controls, especially if you are dealing with the same transactions day after day in the business operations processing unit. Most of the time the operational personnel are not creating this revised procedure to avoid the supervisory approval in order to deceive or commit a crime but more from a convenience standpoint. The processor believes the wire is authentic and tries to save time and effort by processing two separate wires for the correct amount instead of requesting the supervisory signature, as required by the policies and procedures. The dollar limits were established for a reason and are not optional. As you become more familiar with the business unit requirements, you will build a stronger knowledge of the business. This increase in knowledge will ensure a stronger, more efficient identification of the critical controls that should be tested as part of your continuous auditing program. The goal of building this understanding of the business process and the corresponding rules is to create value-added audit services.

External Regulatory Requirements

One of the most efficient ways to develop your business knowledge is to obtain the regulatory requirements that govern the particular business process you are considering for your continuous auditing program. The Internet is a good starting place to identify the applicable federal, state, and local regulatory laws that the business unit must maintain in order to be in compliance.

Knowledge of the regulatory rules pertaining to the business will complement the policy and procedure knowledge you have developed from your initial review. The goal is to create as complete a picture as possible. This additional detail regarding applicable laws should also be included in your SIPOC. The other aspect of regulatory rules to identify and learn is how the business unit handles the receipt, communication, and subsequent compliance with new laws and regulations as they are implemented and introduced to the industry. The business unit should have a comprehensive program to handle the identification and interpretation of need to implement the new rule. Without a process to evaluate whether a new law impacts its process, a business unit could be in noncompliance and not even realize it.

As you complete the process of understanding the rules that impact the business operations, you will be better equipped to develop a comprehensive continuous audit program strategically focused on the critical controls currently in place in the operational unit.

To complete the three phases of preparation for a continuous auditing program, we examine the third phase: identifying technology. As noted in the myths in Chapter 1, continuous auditing does not have to be an automated process. Continuous auditing can be developed for a manual process as long as the audit department has a clear understanding of the business unit process. However, to continue to learn as much as possible during the preparation phase, technology must be considered.

IDENTIFYING TECHNOLOGY

To continue preparing for the development of a continuous auditing program, we now discuss how technology can impact or influence your continuous auditing program development, execution, and maintenance. In the development of your custom program, you should include these four areas:

1. Technology requirements
2. Origin of the data
3. Import and export process
4. Third-party agreements

Technology Requirements

When identifying your technology requirements, consider the level of technology in the business unit operational area needed to maintain the function. Once you identify that requirement, you must determine whether the internal audit department has the expertise to handle the specific technology requirements of the business process. The biggest mistake an audit team can make is trying to work with a technology that it does not understand. The pace at which technology moves today makes it more difficult for audit teams to effectively understand technology requirements. Business units obtain advanced software and new versions frequently; internal audit departments must update their documentation as well as their knowledge of the systems being used in the business areas to process data.

Besides determining level of expertise needed to perform the testing is going to be the identification of where the data is maintained and processed (data storage and source system requirements). Be sure to consider whether the same operating systems are used to receive, store, process, and distribute the data before, during, and after they are processed. Compatibility of the data process, storage, and distribution systems could impact data integrity of the subsequent product generation.

Origin of the Data

When discussing a highly technical process, it is critical to obtain a clear understanding of where the data originated in the system. In other words, you must learn where the SIPOC Input elements originate. Is data being keyed into the processing system directly from the business unit personnel? Is data coming in from another internal system in the company? Or is data coming from an outside party? Determining the origin of the data is a critical preparation step in the development of a continuous auditing program because the data source specifically impacts the program steps and potential dependencies on the accuracy of the data being tested.

Validation of the data origin sometimes must be obtained from system personnel outside of the business unit because internal business processing personnel may not be familiar with how the data end up in their work queue. All they know is that the data is in their system and how they push that data through the process. To design a comprehensive continuous auditing program properly, auditors must identify the origin of the data before they can begin testing the process.

Import and Export Process

It is critically important to identify the specific details of how data is imported and exported between different systems. Even importing and exporting in the same business unit can become a control problem or a version issue based on the process being used to store and share the data. Many times auditors are told that system data is being directly fed from the source system to the processing system and that there is no chance of there being a data integrity issue. Although that seems like a reasonable conclusion to draw based on the source system transmitting the data directly into the processing system, differences in the data may be revealed during testing. The reason that happens is that even though the data is transmitted from one system to the other, it is not a direct system feed. Often systems are not compatible and cannot recognize data formats from one system to another. Therefore, in order to make the transfer work, the data is downloaded from the source system to another program, manipulated to meet the requirements of the processing system, and then sent from the secondary system (not the source) into the processing system. During that manipulation, the data could be corrupted.

When developing a continuous auditing program, auditors must understand how data is moved into and out of the business processing system. If you do not understand the movement of data between systems, you will waste time researching false positives or reviewing program code for potential errors. Take the time up front in the preparation phase to better understand the data movement before you begin the testing and always remember to validate the technology process described by the business unit personnel.

Third-Party Agreements

All third-party agreements, especially the ones dealing with systems, must be obtained and reviewed to ensure that there is a clear and documented understanding of what is expected from external business partners. All third-party agreements should contain a service-level agreement that details the specifics of the agreement made between business unit management and the outside firm. The service-level agreement also contains the details of how the data is to be compiled, processed, and delivered to the business unit and in what form and time of the day or month they are to be delivered. Many continuous auditing programs are developed specifically to test the details of service-level agreements.

 SUMMARY

An auditor's most powerful tool is the development of his or her business knowledge. The only way to build an adequate audit approach and program to validate the control environment of a business process is first to gain a detailed understanding and working knowledge of the business. As a member of the audit team, you will face increased expectations of performance and sometimes may be expected to have all of the answers. In addition, some audit departments will challenge themselves to try to be as knowledgeable in the business process as the personnel who are working in the processing unit on a daily basis. Both of these statements are unrealistic expectations for any audit department. The auditor's goal is to develop a working knowledge of the business process, not to master it, prior to developing the continuous auditing program.

Use the suggestions and techniques mentioned in this chapter for developing your business knowledge, understanding the rules, and identifying the technology requirements of the process under review. But do not try to understand all the specific details of the process to the same level as the person who has been working in the business area for the past year. Instead, leverage the knowledge and expertise of experienced business personnel to guide you in the ongoing and continuous development of your own business knowledge.

5

Continuous Auditing: Foundation Phase

 TARGET AREA

Understanding the concept and basics of how continuous auditing works is a good start when implementing a continuous auditing program but one of the more difficult questions to address is where to begin using this new and different approach. Selection of a target area to validate using a continuous auditing methodology becomes an important decision that impacts the level of success recognized in the testing approach and results. Let us start with where to begin.

Where to Begin

When considering all of the auditable entities in a risk-based audit universe, deciding which area would be more suited to be tested using the continuous approach can be confusing. Before selecting the pilot area, take a step back and examine all of the potential areas for review in the current year as well as any and all commitments you have made to your business partners, external partners, committees, and boards. List all of the required work for the audit year, and ensure that each item on the list is a true audit assignment. Keep in mind that a true audit assignment represents confirmed work, such as Sarbanes-Oxley testing, cyclical audit areas, external partner commitments, and any regulatory requirements. Do not include potential areas that you believe may come up or audits on your wish list. The selection process has to be made from a "pure" sample, including only that work that must be completed in the current audit year.

Once you have finalized the audit work list, it is time to evaluate the work to be done and consider the different methods available to conclude on the effectiveness and efficiency of the control environment of each unit under review. When making these decisions, you must examine these points:

- Risk level of the area
- Transaction type processed
- Technological dependencies
- Audit activity
- Audit team input
- Business unit observations

To ensure that you make a fully informed selection, we discuss each of these topics in more detail.

Risk Level of the Area

When examining the risk level of a business function or process, it is important to have a clear understanding of the business objective. Specifically, documenting and understanding the business objective is the foundation on which the risk level can be determined. To make an accurate determination, discuss and document all of the potential barriers or obstacles (risks) that could prevent the business unit from achieving its stated objective. Once the risks have been noted, determine the likelihood and significance of each individual risk identified. Then use the potential exposure of all the risk information noted to determine the risk level.

Risk will always be a primary factor when examining an upcoming audit. Here continuous auditing is no different from any other audit activity. However, continuous auditing is used to validate the control environment that have a higher-risk level than those areas with medium- or lower-risk due to the recurring nature in which the continuous auditing testing is performed. Given the heightened awareness of higher-risk areas and the critical dependencies placed on the control environment, the recurring nature of a continuous auditing methodology makes it a more suitable approach for validating control effectiveness. A different testing approach might validate control effectiveness, but in continuous auditing, the results determine that the controls being tested are producing repeatable and reliable results.

Transaction Type Processed

The type of transaction processed by a business unit is another factor considered for a potential continuous auditing review. The term "transaction type" does not refer specifically to a debit or a credit. When most auditors hear the term, they automatically assume that a financial transaction took place representing a movement of money. For the purposes of the continuous auditing methodology, the term "transaction type" indicates *any* financial, operational, or compliance transaction that occurs in the normal course of business to achieve the stated objective.

Review the type of transactions that take place within the business unit to keep the operational processes moving. Continuous auditing methodologies work best in areas where a high level of transactions are processed on a daily basis. Remember, the transaction volume you are looking for could be a hand-off between business units, an approval, or a completion of required documentation. It does not have to be the receipt or payment of monies. Often, audit teams implementing continuous auditing methodologies do not consider higher-risk areas because the auditors do not see the potential risk in the operational process. Most audit teams tend to focus on high-dollar items, which are important but do not always represent the highest level of risk in the business process cycle. That is why it is necessary to understand the business process objectives and corresponding risk levels when reviewing transaction types. Without knowledge of the business objective and process, it is difficult to make an informed, educated decision about the type of transaction to be tested using the continuous audit approach.

Technological Dependencies

No matter what type of audit is to be provided, the current skill set and business unit knowledge of the audit team must be considered to ensure that the agreed-upon audit objective can be accomplished and the corresponding value of the audit service can be delivered. This is especially true when it comes to technology. The frequency at which business units expand and use technology everyday to build more efficient and effective processes places additional pressure on the internal audit departments to understand the technology being used. The speed of technology change is a factor to be considered when planning to execute any audit. The question that must be asked is: Do we have the technical knowledge to perform this work? If you are considering performing a continuous auditing review of an area that executes most of its processes using technology, you must be intimately familiar with the technologies being used to build an effective test plan.

Although technology can be an excellent tool to increase production in a business unit, additions, upgrades, or changes in technology often present a challenge to internal audit departments. This is a significant consideration that has to be examined before deciding to build a continuous auditing program to determine control effectiveness.

Audit Activity

Existing and previous audit activity in the business unit being considered for a continuous auditing review has to be incorporated into the evaluation process. It is important to determine how much and what type of audit activity has taken place in the targeted area. The audit history of a business unit can provide a profile of the level of attention that a particular area has received from the internal audit department. If a business process has been examined within the last six months or is included each year in your external auditor partner's areas of coverage, it may not be appropriate to consider instituting a continuous auditing review. This is especially true if it is a business process that has to be tested and validated by the external audit partner. In those instances, the internal audit department must review the continuous auditing methodology with the external partner and obtain their approval prior to initiating the testing plan under a false assumption that it will be accepted by the external partner. Doing so will ensure that there is no duplication of effort if the external partner does not believe the continuous auditing methodology provided sufficient coverage and requires the process to be retested.

Even business functions that require significant audit activity each year can be a target area for a continuous audit. The continuous auditing testing approach provides auditors with another method to validate a specific control or controls and over a period of time as opposed to testing it once from a historical perspective.

Audit Team Input

A critical but often overlooked consideration is communicating with your audit team about a potential area being targeted for a continuous auditing review. Talk to audit team members about any area being considered for any type of audit services: continuous audit, full-scope audit, or even a special project. Each time an audit service is to be executed, there should be a discussion about the business unit's objectives, personnel, and existing relationship with the internal audit department. This discussion will provide a guide to the type of audit partner the business unit is as well as information about whether the area is having any turnover issues or challenges in the day-to-day operations.

An additional step to take when soliciting team input is to ask the managers and supervisors if they have any additional information they could provide regarding the potential target area. Managers and supervisors are exposed to different audiences and business unit personnel just based on their job titles. Most companies have manager and new leader training that all company managers must attend. This training provides another forum for the internal audit managers to listen and solicit information from their business unit counterparts in an informal setting. Valuable information is exchanged among company leaders during these informal encounters, and this information can provide insight that would not normally be shared in an audit discussion. Remember always to keep communication as a cornerstone for your department and share business unit information with your team when appropriate.

Business Unit Observations

One final consideration when linking the type of audit activity to a particular business unit is the current audit observations for the business unit under review. If business unit management is currently working on a significant amount of outstanding observations, it may not be the best time to try to introduce an audit activity, especially a new one such as the continuous auditing methodology. Internal audit activity already provides a certain level of stress to business management; attempting to implement a new technique only compounds the issue. Also, if there are existing observations or even recently closed ones, it is not the right time to use a continuous auditing methodology because the process is either in a state of transition or adjusting to a recent process change. Either instance will create inconsistent results in a continuous auditing review and not provide any value to the client because the testing is being performed on a moving target.

There is one exception to this rule when it comes to using the continuous auditing methodology for newly implemented processes. Continuous auditing has seen a significant increase in use from internal audit departments to validate the proper implementation of a new control that was identified during the most recent full-scope audit. Here is how it works. An internal audit department performs a full-scope audit and identifies a critical control weakness. Management agrees that it is an exposure and creates a new control to address the issue. To ensure that management has addressed the issue adequately, as agreed in the audit report, internal audit creates a continuous auditing test plan specifically targeting the newly implemented control. The key to successful validation is to ensure that internal audit provides the business unit sufficient time—usually 60 days—to implement the change fully. This amount of time also ensures that there is a proper population of transactions to select from for the testing.

Making the Decision

After evaluating the auditable units and the corresponding factors previously discussed such as audit activity, audit team input, and technology, it is time to determine which business units appear to be the most appropriate for the continuous auditing methodology. The best fit for continuous audits are the business operations that have these characteristics:

- **The area has transactions (operational, compliance, or financial) that occur multiple times every single day.** This ensures a solid population for sampling that is going to take place on a regular basis for the length of the continuous audit.

- **The area has documented policies and procedures.** This will assist the audit team in the proper development of the continuous auditing test plan.
- **The process has been established and operating under the current procedures for at least three months.** This reduces the number of false positives which may occur if the process is in a transition period.

This list is not all inclusive but should provide you with a guide to launch a successful pilot program.

These tips will help guide your selection of an area that will most benefit from a continuous audit.

Next we turn to some business process characteristics in which caution should be applied before selecting them for a continuous auditing review. Let us look at each one individually.

Judgment

Although the continuous auditing methodology can provide validation of a business process producing repeatable, reliable results, it can also be a challenging tool requiring extra work to eliminate and/or validate false positives. Nowhere is this truer than in the case of a business process that requires the business unit team to use judgment. If the operational procedures allow for variations to the standard process, it becomes increasingly difficult to test the control effectiveness on a continuous basis. This is the result of the testing standard potentially being different for the sample items selected. This is because each sample will have a different standard to be tested against, which makes it nearly impossible to compare the data results from one period to the next as required by the continuous auditing methodology.

As an example, consider term life insurance. Although the process of reviewing and approving a term life insurance policy is strictly governed and has existing guidelines for approval, it is possible for a life insurance underwriter to decide to take additional risk on a customer based on any number of factors. There is nothing wrong or illegal with the decision to extend or expand the approval guidelines; it is just based on the underwriter's judgment. The judgment factor allows the underwriter to expand the boundaries of acceptable risk based on his or her evaluation of the situation. This type of processing environment is not really conducive to a continuous auditing methodology because judgment makes it difficult to specify the processing standard. Also, with the recurrence and ongoing nature of a continuous auditing test plan that requires testing on a monthly or quarterly basis for a set period of time, it becomes difficult to keep up with the stringent time frames of a continuous audit while trying to clarify and explain the underwriting decisions and understand the thought process for the decisions.

In general, it is recommended that a full-scope audit be performed on an area that incorporates a significant amount of judgment in the operational procedures. Even though you could use a continuous auditing approach, you would spend too much time researching potential exceptions to recognize the full value.

Complexity

Like judgment, complexity poses another caution when considering using a continuous auditing methodology to test a process environment. The unique feature of a continuous auditing methodology is that it focuses testing on a specific control that has been identified as a critical or key control in the business process. These critical controls are strategically tested on a recurring basis to ensure they are producing the desired results. However, when looking at a business process as a potential candidate for using the continuous auditing methodology, examine the process from start to finish to identify how many critical controls are involved and if this type of audit methodology is the best way to evaluate their effectiveness. In a complex business processing environment, it sometimes is difficult to identify the one or two critical controls that regulate the process results.

For example, consider an investment company that uses financial hedge transactions to address interest rate risk. You do not have to understand all of the details surrounding an interest rate swap transaction; you just must know that it has many moving parts that need a strong control environment to ensure its success. Because this is a complex transaction requiring not only strong financial controls but also strong operational controls, it is not that easy to select a single control to be tested using the continuous auditing methodology. The more complex the business process, the more difficult it is to identify the critical control to be singled out for testing.

Again, it is recommended that a full-scope audit be performed to validate the strength of the controls over this complex financial transaction processing area. If you tried using the continuous auditing methodology, the testing would cover so many different critical controls that it would feel like a full-scope audit to the client. Plus, with many controls being selected, it would be impossible to keep up with the workload of testing the selected controls on a recurring basis.

Suggested Starting Areas

Any time the internal audit department tries to introduce a new concept, approach, or methodology to its clients, clients always feel uncertain. They are not sure what may be coming out of internal audit or what internal audit is looking for or attempting to identify. To ease the tension, consider selecting an area where there is a crystal clear objective and no need for interpretation. Table 5.1 contains some examples to consider when you begin implementing your continuous auditing methodology.

The proposed areas listed in Table 5.1 include a baseline or beginning objective that could be used to start your continuous auditing program. If there is another objective you would like to use, that is fine. But remember to verify that the testing objective directly links to the business objective and has the corresponding risk associated with it to make the testing worthwhile for the time invested. Do not test just to test. Create a value-added objective to ensure that the testing will prove the control environment is producing repeatable, reliable results.

TABLE 5.1 Continuous Auditing Suggested Topics

Area	Objective
Payroll	Determine valid Social Security numbers for all current employees
Accounts Payable	Determine valid addresses (no PO boxes) for all vendors
Vendors	Determine each vendor has a current contract
Procurement Cards	Determine appropriateness of usage
Benefits	Determine correct charges for selected benefits
System Access	Determine system access matches job description
Reconciliations	Determine timeliness of completion

TESTING OBJECTIVES

Table 5.1 introduced testing objectives for the first time as part of our discussion of the development of a continuous auditing methodology. The detail presented in this section defines and explains the creation of a continuous auditing objective. The first thing we need to do is explain what an objective is and what it is meant to represent.

By definition, a testing objective is the bottom-line or baseline reason the corresponding testing is being performed. The testing objective specifically answers the direct question of why this testing is being performed. It is meant to represent the purpose of the test. Sometimes audit testing is created and completed without anyone on the internal audit team that performs the work being told the objective of the testing.

For example, we have all worked on a project and been asked to move off of the current assignment to assist on another audit that has been identified as either a higher priority or having fallen behind schedule. In these instances, when we arrive on the scene of the new assignment, we are put to work immediately during the hectic fieldwork phase and really never told the overall objective of the testing. If the established testing objective is not clearly communicated, it is difficult to execute the work without knowing the overall purpose of the testing being performed. The testing may be straightforward and simple to execute, but without knowledge of the objective, it is difficult to know what the expected results should be and how it impacts the overall audit.

Developing a Testing Objective

In the continuous auditing methodology, the creation of the testing objective is crucial to the success of the development of the foundation phase of the continuous audit. To begin, the testing objective must be created from the business objective. While that sounds like a simple request, sometimes it is challenging to get business unit management to clearly articulate its own business objective. Usually, when asked to state the business objective, the business unit provides auditors with task-level activities. It is up to the assigned auditor to accurately solicit and identify what the true business objective is prior to creating the continuous auditing testing objective. Auditors should help management explain why the group was created and what it has been assigned to do. The business objective is the reason or purpose the business unit was created. Once auditors are able to identify the business objective, they can formulate the testing objective.

Testing objectives begin with "to determine" or "to ensure," followed by the business objective. As an example, consider a business objective for an accounting department responsible for bank reconciliations. The reconciliations team of the accounting department would have a business objective to perform all bank reconciliations timely, accurately, and completely with the supporting documentation attached evidencing the corresponding balances. The testing objective would be to "to ensure" all bank reconciliations were performed timely, accurately, and completely with the supporting documentation attached evidencing the corresponding balances. It is as simple as it appears; the difficult part for auditors is validating the correct business objective. If the business objective is not accurate, all work developed to support the testing objective will not be valid and will provide no value to the customer.

Now that we have explained the development of a testing objective, we need to refine the development of a testing objective for a continuous auditing methodology. In the continuous auditing approach, the testing objective will follow the same format but will not be an all-encompassing objective, as it is in a full-scope audit. The continuous auditing methodology is focused on one or two critical controls that must be validated to ensure they are producing repeatable, reliable results. Since the focus has changed from testing all controls supporting the business objective to selecting specific or key controls supporting the business objective, the continuous auditing objective must be refined to specifically indicate inclusions and exclusions.

Inclusions and Exclusions

The testing objective is designed to communicate to audit customers exactly what is going to be covered during the audit activity to be performed in their area. Although documenting the continuous auditing testing objective may seem like a simple and relatively straightforward concept, often it is not documented sufficiently. Any audit customer would tell you that it is important to clearly understand what and how the audit work is going to be performed and specifically what the work is going to include. At no point in an audit should customers be uncertain or in the dark about what is happening in their own area.

The testing objective is an excellent opportunity to build on the audit/ client relationship by ensuring that the auditing objective for your continuous auditing program is detailed and explicit. The proper development and documentation of the testing objective will provide the foundation for your audit/client relationship. In no other audit activity is the clarity of the audit objective more important than in a continuous audit. Remember, one of the key distinctions between continuous auditing and other audit activities is that in a continuous audit, the coverage is going to be very specific and focused on a key control or two. Correspondingly, the audit objective supporting this targeted approach must match and clearly communicate the focus.

To ensure that the continuous auditing objective is complete, it must communicate not only the specific controls to be tested but also the detail that is going to be included as part of the validation testing. If the testing objective does not provide the exact inclusions and exclusions, the audit client and possibly the auditor may have a false sense of stability of the control environment of the process being tested. For example, if a continuous auditing program is going to be developed for the account reconciliation process and the focus is going to be on the handling of adjusting entries, the audit objective should state that exact purpose. In addition, the audit objective should have a clarifying statement detailing the account reconciliation controls that are not going to be tested (timeliness, approval, aged items, etc.). Without a fully developed testing objective, an independent reader could extrapolate the positive continuous audit results for adjusting entries across all account reconciliation process requirements. This could lead to a potentially incorrect conclusion that the account reconciliation process is operating effectively. However, the reality of the independent continuous auditing activity verified only that the processing of adjusting entries was operating effectively. No other testing was performed to validate the other controls supporting the account reconciliation process.

Fully developed testing objectives for all audit activity should detail both what is to be included and not included for the continuous auditing testing to be performed. This will ensure that the audit team as well as the audit customer clearly understand why the audit activity is taking place.

Review and Validation

As the continuous auditing methodology becomes part of the audit services your department provides, the discipline for reviewing, verifying, and validating the testing objective will also become a constant. Because of its approach, the continuous auditing program requires working knowledge of the business area to ensure that the time and effort will provide value to the audit customer. As previously discussed, business knowledge must be developed and used as you select the target area and develop the corresponding continuous auditing objective.

The continuous auditing objective should be created using the internal auditor's existing business knowledge to evaluate the targeted operational process and select the control(s) to be tested. Once the targeted control(s) has been identified, the audit objective must be developed and documented. After the objective has been drafted, it should be reviewed to ensure that it is complete and properly details the inclusions and exclusions and focused on the true critical control(s) governing the process. At this point of development, a review is required to determine if the objective contains the critical documentation requirement and is clear in its message and also targets the appropriate control(s).

The final step in the continuous auditing testing objective development process is to verify with the audit customer that the true key controls have been identified and will be covered as described in the objective. The business process personnel are contacted by the responsible auditor planning the continuous auditing testing to communicate and verify the continuous auditing objective for two reasons:

1. Ask the business owners to validate the objective for appropriateness (as it pertains to the risk communicated by the audit team).
2. Obtain the audit customer's agreement as to what is going to be covered during this specific continuous audit.

Without validating the appropriateness of the continuous auditing objective with the customer, the audit team could waste time developing a custom audit program that will not provide any value or benefit to the audit customer upon completion. If the continuous auditing objective is developed properly, it will explain why the audit activity is being performed, what is going to be concluded on at the end of the work, and, most important, directly linked to the business objective.

Validation of the continuous auditing objective will entail verifying that you have:

- Identified the most critical controls supporting the business objectives.
- Clearly understood the corresponding risks that may impact the achievement of the business objective.
- Discussed the objective and the testing focus with the audit customer to verify your understanding and interpretation of the business process and risks.
- Believe your audit team has the business knowledge, technical audit knowledge, and tools to complete the testing as described by the business operational personnel.

After completing these validation steps, you can be confident that the continuous auditing objective you have created is not only complete but also will provide valuable feedback to the audit client in an effort to make the business process more efficient and effective.

Objective Development Mistakes

Because there are so many rules and requirements involved in the successful development of a continuous auditing objective, it is important to discuss some potential mistakes that can be made during the process. These mistakes include lack of communication, insufficient detail, the missing link, and infeasibility. Next we define and explain each mistake, and provide proposed solutions.

Lack of Communication

Communication is the foundation of any audit department. Auditors must be skilled communicators. That means everyone on the audit team must be able to write, speak, and listen to peers and customers. This rule has never been more important than in the communication of the continuous auditing objective. The objective has to be clearly conveyed from the responsible auditor who planned the continuous auditing program to the audit team as well as the audit client so that there is no misunderstanding of the reason for the testing and what the target area is going to include. Audit clients need to be certain as to what is going to be examined in their area, especially when the audit department is introducing a new product, such as continuous auditing. Without proper communication of the specific objective, audit clients will feel insecure as they partner with the audit team on the first continuous audit.

If the continuous auditing objective is properly developed, well written, and clearly communicated to the audit client, the foundation will be built to support the subsequent testing and possible process improvements based on test results. Never underestimate the power of strong communication with audit clients, no matter what audit services you will be performing.

Insufficient Detail

What is insufficient detail? What would seem like a very good question does not have a simple answer. The challenge with answering a question like this is that the answer will always be a judgment call. However, here is a tip to help ensure that there is sufficient detail in your continuous auditing objective: The objective must be clear enough not only for the business owner to understand why the work is going to be performed; any individual, with no prior knowledge of the area or the testing, should be able to read, understand, and follow the reasoning for the testing objective. If neither reader can recognize the meaning of the objective or if interpretation is required, the continuous auditing objective is not clear and must be rewritten.

When crafting a continuous auditing objective, it must be based on the current operational processes, not on risk and control assumptions. It would not be possible to test what *should be* happening in the business process. The objective should detail the specific controls to be tested and have sufficient depth and support so that the reader does not have to interpret why a continuous auditing approach is to be used to validate the control environment.

Missing Link

Another common mistake in the development of a continuous auditing objective, especially the first one, is that the audit objective itself is not linked to the business objective. Every operational department, no matter what the industry is or what the company does, has a business objective. The operational business objective clearly defines why the business unit was created and details the purpose of the operation. Be careful not to mistake the mission statement or individual tasks for the business objective. A mission statement is a very broad overview of the department; usually it does not define the department's objective and purpose. Also, the task-level activities support the effort exhausted by department personnel trying to achieve the business objective. These individual processing tasks, while critical to the operational success of the business unit, do not represent the business objective. The business objective falls somewhere between the broadly based mission statement and the task-level detail. Be certain to focus on the true objective; ask qualifying questions to determine and understand the purpose of the department and the function it represents in achieving corporate objectives.

Developing an Infeasible Continuous Auditing Objective

Almost everyone I have worked with to implement and integrate a continuous auditing program into an audit department wants their program to be the best and to have a huge impact on the company and the audit department operations. That is an attainable goal if the continuous auditing objective is created in accordance with the outline. However, due to the unique nature of the continuous auditing approach, sometimes it is difficult to keep the approach focused and direct. Internal audit departments believe that if the continuous auditing objective is bigger and more inclusive, it will produce better results and have a larger impact on the business unit. This could not be further from the truth. The fact of the matter is, the more direct and focused the continuous auditing objective is, the more useful the results.

Also, if the continuous auditing objective is too big and covers multiple controls throughout the operational process, it will be very difficult to manage, maintain, and report and will appear to the business owner to be exactly like a regular audit. A continuous audit focuses on a key control or two; the corresponding objective should specifically detail why the audit activity is being performed and clearly identify the controls to be validated. Bigger is not necessarily better. A clear continuous auditing objective should be attainable and directly linked to the business objective to ensure that the client and the audit team are not frustrated at any time during the execution.

FREQUENCY

Anytime internal audit departments begin to discuss the implementation of a continuous auditing methodology, the topic of frequency tends to spark the greatest debate. To a normal person, the term "continuous" would immediately connote a definition that must include the terms: constantly, every, or all. However, for an internal auditor, continuous in an audit approach would be defined as a predetermined interval in which testing was going to be performed. Determining just how frequent continuous should be will have to be established based on the process being reviewed. When it comes to the development of your specific continuous auditing methodology, frequency is another piece of the puzzle that must be clearly defined and consistently applied each time the continuous approach is used.

Process Delivery Frequency and Volumes

When setting the frequency at which to perform the continuous auditing testing, you must first clearly understand the business process under review. In identifying the most appropriate operational process for a continuous review, it is mission critical to understand the process timing for generation of a result. Examine the process to determine not only how the process operates from start to finish but also how many items are processed every day, week, and month. Without this knowledge of process volumes, it becomes increasingly difficult to create the corresponding testing frequency for your continuous auditing program.

For example, if the account reconciliation process is being considered for a continuous auditing review, it is important to learn the frequency at which reconciliations are completed. Although the account reconciliation process appears to be a straightforward process creating reconciliations on a monthly basis, some reconciliations are performed weekly and some are performed quarterly. So, if you decide to execute the continuous audit on a monthly basis, there could be weekly reconciliations that may be missed or quarterly reconciliations that will appear as potential exceptions during the monthly testing. A detailed understanding of the output timing and delivery of the targeted process is mandatory when creating the frequency for your continuous auditing methodology.

One other aspect to consider in the frequency development is volume. In gathering the process information details, ensure that you obtain as much supporting information as possible pertaining to the volumes produced. The reason volumes become a consideration factor is that you have to ensure that there will be a sufficient number of events to select from to realize the full potential of the continuous auditing methodology. Remember, hundreds of critical controls and processes in every company support the control environment of the operations, but not every one of the processes has the amount of activity or volume that would benefit from a continuous audit. Every business has high-risk processes, but there may not be a sufficient population to select from each month or quarter to benefit from developing, executing, and maintaining a continuous auditing approach. Obtain all the necessary details before selecting the targeted area and creating the corresponding frequency to perform the testing.

"6-9-12" Methodology

A majority of the continuous auditing techniques being executed today are done on a monthly basis. There are three key reasons why monthly is selected most often.

1. Monthly appears to be the most appropriate frequency for testing because it provides sufficient time for the audit team to select and test a representative sample.
2. For business operations that process multiple transactions per day, every day, monthly is the recommended frequency, given the daily and weekly volumes available for testing.
3. Any frequency interval shorter than monthly puts unfair stress and pressure on not only the audit team for execution but also on the business management for participation and partnership. Shortening the frequency is dangerous and does not provide any additional validation of the control environment as compared to monthly. Also, with a shorter frequency, the continuous auditing testing will appear to business owners never to end; owners will feel that they are being watched constantly. For value-added results and strong audit relationships, select monthly as the frequency for your continuous auditing methodology for any business process that produces multiple transactions every single day.

To further enhance the monthly testing frequency for your continuous auditing program, the "6-9-12" methodology is the recommended frequency.

The "6-9-12" methodology is a monthly testing frequency specifically designed for continuous auditing programs where the process is generating results multiple times every day. This frequency was developed to be used as a predictive cycle as well as an effective testing cycle for high-volume-producing areas. Here is how the frequency methodology works.

This monthly testing approach requires the first six consecutive months be sampled, selected, tested, and reported. The sample size in each one of the months remains consistent, as does the tested approach. Assuming no reportable exceptions were noted, after the first six months of testing, months 7 and 8 are skipped and a sample is selected and tested at month 9. This sample taken in month 9 will encompass activity from months 7, 8, and 9 inclusive but will be testing them all at once. Again, assuming no reportable exceptions were noted, months 10 and 11 are skipped, and a sample is selected and tested at month 12. This sample includes the previous three months of activity as indicated in the testing performed in month 9.

To illustrate the "6-9-12" testing frequency methodology, consider a process that is going to be continuously tested with a corresponding recurring sample size of 15. According to this frequency approach, 15 items will be selected and tested for the first six consecutive months; then in month 9, 15 items will be selected and tested with a representative sample of 5 from month 7, 8, and 9; in month 12, 15 items will be selected and tested with a representative sample of 5 from months 10, 11, and 12. In total, 120 items were selected and tested over the 12-month period representing 90 items from the first six months and 30 over the second six months. This is the recommended testing frequency as long as there were no reportable issues identified during any of the testing. This frequency methodology is a proactive approach on a recurring basis designed to provide a validation that the control(s) tested produce the desired repeatable, reliable results. It was created to be used proactively. When executed properly, it can be used in some instances as a predictive tool as well as a validation of the existing control environment. Remember, every process produces a result, but not necessarily the desired one. Always validate the results of all audit testing.

The "6-9-12" frequency can be followed without adjusting the samples selected as long as no reportable exceptions are noted during the first six months of testing. However, if a reportable exception is identified during the first six months, the approach for the second half of the year will have to be adjusted as needed. As an example, say that during month 2 of the continuous auditing testing, a reportable exception is identified and has to be addressed by the business owner for remedy. The first question that will be asked is: Should the testing proceed as identified in the methodology, or should the testing be postponed until the control weakness has been addressed by business unit management? The answer is simple; the testing is executed as designed, whether opportunities for improvement have been identified or not. Continuing the testing validates that the full issue has been identified and tracks the progress of the implemented improvement suggestions. The continuation of the testing also validates that the correct remediation has been put into place. This validation will be evidence in the subsequent month's testing. If an exception has been identified and validated along with a corresponding corrective action, the results should begin to improve within the following two months after the control has been addressed. If the subsequent months' testing does not improve, the wrong action plan to address the root cause was implemented. This self-validation helps to ensure the appropriateness of business actions taken as well as the root cause analysis performed by the internal audit team.

The other part of the continuous auditing testing frequency that will be impacted by a reportable exception is the increase in the samples taken. In our example where the reportable exception was noted in month 2 of testing, the number of samples would have to increase to ensure that the control environment has been strengthened through management action and is producing repeatable, reliable results. With this exception in month 2, the following four months would be tested as originally planned, but the third-quarter testing would be done as three separate samples testing 15 in month 7, 8, and 9. As long as no other reportable exceptions were identified after the original one, the fourth-quarter testing would require only a sample of 15 be tested in month 12, representing five from each month. Table 5.2 illustrates the recommended "6-9-12" frequency for a continuous auditing program.

Frequency can be set at any interval deemed appropriate based on the business process. If the business process does not produce results on a daily basis, then monthly testing could be too frequent. In that case, consider setting the continuous auditing testing frequency at quarterly. In a quarterly approach, each quarter is selected throughout the year with no quarter being excluded. The key to establishing the continuous auditing testing frequency

TABLE 5.2 "6-9-12" Continuous Auditing Frequency Chart

Month	Satisfactory Results	Remediated Results
1	Pass	Pass
2	Pass	Reportable exception noted
3	Pass	Same exception identified
4	Pass	Pass
5	Pass	Pass
6	Pass	Pass
7	No Testing	Pass
8	No Testing	Pass
9	Pass	Pass
10	No Testing	No testing
11	No Testing	No testing
12	Pass	Pass
Following Year	Internal Audit Discretion	Included

is to match and validate the testing interval to the production of the business process. The one caution to be aware of is that once you commit to a frequency, you cannot alter or adjust it during the testing. This means that you cannot start off a continuous auditing program with the "6-9-12" testing frequency and then decide, in month 3, to switch to quarterly since you did not identify any reportable exceptions and you believe the process is working as designed. There is not enough testing evidence through the first 3 months to conclude on the results as part of your continuous auditing methodology unless you complete the full cycle of testing. Do not be fooled early on by positive results. Complete the testing and truly identify the strength of the existing control environment.

TESTING TECHNIQUE

The final step in completing the continuous auditing methodology foundation is the determination of the testing technique to be used to perform the actual validation of the selected sample. In this section, we discuss different techniques that could be used. Ultimately, the technique chosen will depend on the type of business process control being reviewed. Choosing a testing technique for a continuous auditing program is exactly the same as choosing one for a full-scope audit. The business process is reviewed, controls are identified to be tested, and the corresponding testing technique is executed for control validation.

In this section, we identify and discuss four different testing techniques that can be used in the continuous auditing program: inquiry, inspection, exception, and transaction. Table 5.3 summarizes the advantages and disadvantages of each testing technique. Although any of these techniques can be used in a continuous auditing program, it will be up to the internal audit team to determine which technique would be the most appropriate, given each individual situation. With any audit testing technique, a decision

TABLE 5.3 Testing Techniques Advantages and Disadvantages

Technique	Advantages	Disadvantages
Inquiry	Easy to administer	Requires skill to develop
	Yes/no format	Yes/no format does not allow for follow up
	Standardized	Reader knows what answer should be
	Quick to implement	No opportunity for clarifying questions
Inspection	Easy to administer	Time consuming
	Observation of the operational procedure	Requires experience to identify critical process points
	Provides opportunity to ask qualifying questions	Operational person being shadowed is on their best behavior
	Blank sheet of paper approach	Requires business knowledge to identify deviations from process requirements
Exception	Easy to administer	Only validating outliers
	Quick to implement	Time consuming
	Specifically identifies potential process exceptions	Requires knowledge of the process and requirements
Transaction	Reperformance of the process	Time consuming
	Validates full sample	Diligence to complete all testing
	Most useful technique for continuous auditing programs	Requires knowledge of the process and requirements

also will have to be made as to whether the testing will be manual or automated. Since every testing scenario is different, it is impossible to develop and discuss an all-encompassing list. The judgment of the internal audit team and its experience will lead the way in the selection of the technique. No matter which testing approach you choose, document how and why the decision was made. Your audit documentation, especially when it comes to a continuous auditing program, is closely scrutinized and must be able to stand on its own.

Inquiry

By definition, inquiry is the process by which client data and supporting information are tested using a question format or standard questionnaire. This testing technique is used most often by companies that have multiple locations that are created, operated, and managed under the same policies and procedures. In a business operational environment like this, the questionnaire testing technique allows auditors to gather and evaluate standard critical controls across multiple locations, states, or even countries. This technique is used most often when an internal audit department is challenged with the task of reviewing multiple locations with limited resources. In this scenario, the best approach to take is to develop a standard questionnaire based on the established corporate guidelines and solicit independent feedback from each selected location. The questionnaire is developed directly from corporate policies and procedures and focuses on the critical controls. The format of the questionnaire is confirmation based (yes/no) and requires the developer to have detailed process-level knowledge of the operation under review. Even though the questions themselves are in a yes/no format, they must be clear, concise, and not require interpretation from the reader. Complicated or confusing questions will lead to interpretation on the reader's part and ultimately to a variety of answers that will not be able to be compiled for an effective evaluation. Although a questionnaire will not take the place of a site visit, it will allow the internal audit team to compile critical process-level information from the site management team. An example of this type of company could be a bank, restaurant chain, or storefront. In each of these companies, the location of the business should not make any difference as corporate policies and procedures should be applied regardless of location.

Inspection

Inspection by definition is a testing technique performed by visual verification. For this reason, the responsible internal audit team member performing this type of testing will have to be in person to view the operational control being executed. This type of testing is performed when all of the other testing techniques would not be effective in verifying the strength of the control environment. Although this type of testing does not require the business-process-level understanding of the inquiry technique, auditors will need to know the basic process requirements in order to ensure that what they are observing and documenting is being performed according to established policies and procedures.

The inspection technique is commonly compared to performing a walk-through of a process. A walk-through usually is completed during the planning phase of an audit and requires the internal auditor to observe, follow, and document the control process from start to finish. It is time consuming and requires commitment from the process owner to assign a subject matter expert to guide auditors through the process. This is an excellent method to gain an understanding of the process control requirements, but it may not be one of the most effective testing techniques. The challenge with using inspection as a testing technique for a continuous auditing program or even a full-scope audit is that the processor being followed or watched is usually on his or her best behavior and very attentive to the process requirement details while under review. However, this review environment may not reflect the normal day-to-day business and thus may not reveal some challenges or stresses in the control environment. The objective of the inspection testing technique is to verify that the existing control structure has been suitably designed, established, and operating as intended. This technique focuses on "operating as intended" as auditors trace the steps from start to finish in the process to identify control effectiveness and potential opportunities for improvement. From an effectiveness standpoint, this testing technique works but would not be the first choice selected unless the situation and control environment required it. The most common situation in which the direct inspection technique is used is in the gaming industry. Due to the high-risk nature of the gaming industry, direct inspection is the most effective control and testing technique available to ensure compliance with gaming regulations as well as established company policies and procedures.

Exception

By definition, the exception testing technique (also known as the outlier technique) is performed by identifying, selecting, and researching any population or sample items that fall outside of the acceptable parameters as established in company policies and procedures. Every operational business process has established parameters that provide the control limits for satisfactory performance. These control limits create boundaries in which all transaction activity should take place, if the controls are operating effectively as designed. When using the exception technique, internal audit performs testing only when the transaction activity result is outside of acceptable control limits. This technique requires additional time to execute due to the fact all items outside of the acceptable parameters must be identified and explained. Although it is an acceptable type of testing technique, there is no validation that the activity currently within the acceptable control limits belongs there. Control validation should contain a sample that includes the outliers as well as the apparent satisfactory results.

Simply running the reports to see if any items fall outside the control limits without any additional testing is monitoring, not auditing. One of the biggest mistakes that internal audit departments and others make is that they consider the ongoing review of key performance indicators or metrics a form of continuous auditing. In reality, this type of technique without testing is continuous monitoring, not continuous auditing. Testing must be performed to satisfy the requirements of continuous auditing.

Transaction

By definition, the transaction testing technique requires the reperformance of work as it should have been executed by the operational business personnel. This is the exact same testing approach that is used when performing full-scope testing on a selected sample. The transaction approach requires the same discipline and commitment to understanding the business process and then tracing the information through the designed control environment.

This technique is used most frequently for testing in the continuous auditing methodology because it provides the most accurate depiction of the work being executed. It also gives the internal audit personnel the opportunity to better understand the key process controls by analyzing the data and evaluating the effectiveness and efficiency of the control environment.

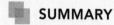 **SUMMARY**

In every strong audit product, there is a foundation supporting the objective and the corresponding testing. In the continuous auditing methodology, the foundation represents the selection of the target area and the establishment of the frequency that defines continuous auditing. It is critical to determine the foundation components for your continuous auditing methodology to ensure that the approach will provide the validation of the control environment in the production of repeatable, reliable results. Take the time to fully develop your target area selection process as well as to determine how often and how it will be tested. The extra time that you dedicate to these components will prove invaluable in the implementation of your continuous auditing program.

CHAPTER SIX

Continuous Auditing: Approach Phase

 APPROACH PHASE

In this chapter, we identify and discuss the second phase of the continuous auditing model as well as the keys to creating strategic test procedures that will be specifically used in your testing. In addition, we explain the five key component development factors that comprise the approach phase to validate that the information identified in the foundation phase is accurately translated to the continuous auditing testing approach. The five components to be discussed are:

- Scope
- Volumes
- Sampling
- Criteria and attributes
- Technology

SCOPE

From an internal audit perspective, the scope is developed based on the planning information compiled. It details what will be included in the continuous auditing testing. The scope should be linked directly to the continuous auditing objective and include the proper amount of detail to accurately conclude on the specific continuous auditing testing objective. The scope also provides your business partner with the parameters in which the testing is going to be executed. In the ideal situation, the scope that has been established by the internal audit team should not change once the testing has begun. Let us discuss some of the specific components that make a scope statement more effective and efficient and reduce the number of times it is changed or altered once the testing has begun.

Time Frame

One of the main components related to scope is time frame. Time frame in this instance represents the start and end date to the information that would be tested as part of a particular audit service. For example, a typical scope, from a full-scope audit, would be all audit activity from January to December or all audit activity since the last audit. Most full-scope audits have a historical time frame; they try to capture all business activity during the scope period. Internal audits in general are historical in nature and provide a testing approach that is most often described as detective. In an effort to change the audit approach, the continuous auditing methodology creates an environment where the audit activity to be performed is as close to real time as possible. To accomplish this, the time frame in a continuous auditing methodology focuses on the business process activity for the last completed month. This drastic change in scope time frame is the result of the continuous audit approach being performed on a recurring basis, such as the "6-9-12" testing frequency discussed in Chapter 5. This testing frequency provides the support necessary to facilitate the ongoing testing of the key control selected in an effort to validate the delivery of repeatable, reliable results. This shift in time frame changes the audit approach from detective to directive. The scope adjustment is one of the main selling points of the continuous audit methodology.

Inclusions and Exclusions

When documenting scope, whether it is for a full-scope audit or a continuous audit, it is critically important to ensure that the scope statement is fully developed and contains the necessary details to convey the complete message to the reader. The scope detail must communicate to audit customers exactly what is going to be covered during the continuous audit. Although this may seem like a simple and straightforward concept, often scope statements are documented without the proper level of detail.

Throughout all audit activity, clear, concise communications provide the foundation for delivering value-added services to audit customers. For a continuous auditing methodology, the scope must be documented clearly, concisely, and completely. Audit clients should have no question or doubt as to what the continuous audit activity scope includes.

The properly developed and documented scope statement provides the audit client and the audit team with the specifics of what is going to be tested in the continuous audit program. The specificity of the scope statement of a continuous auditing program is another key distinction separating this approach from the traditional full-scope auditing methodology. To achieve this distinction, the scope statement must be adequately detailed and link directly to the continuous auditing testing objective.

To ensure that the continuous auditing scope statement is complete, it must not only detail what is going to be tested but also tell what is *not* going to be included. If the scope statement does not provide a clear distinction of inclusions and exclusions, audit clients and independent readers of the report might receive the wrong message. To assist in the development of the continuous auditing scope statement, it is beneficial to review the continuous auditing test objective to ensure the specific scope statement links directly to the stated objective. Fully developed scope statements not only link directly to the specific testing objective but also document the particular aspects of the process that will not be covered or tested as part of the continuous auditing program.

Scope Statement Development Keys

There are many different thoughts and suggestions for creating complete scope statements. The one overriding recommendation for developing your continuous auditing scope statement is that the scope must be specific and provide adequate details to explain the reasoning behind the parameters set for testing. These parameters must articulate the exact attributes that are going to be tested along with the corresponding time frame to be used in execution of the continuous auditing program.

The biggest benefit of a fully developed scope statement is that it reduces the possibility of the scope having to be adjusted once the testing has commenced. The scope statement represents the boundaries of testing that can be performed; adjusting the scope after the completion of planning is frustrating for both the audit client and audit team. To ensure that the scope statement does not have to be adjusted during the fieldwork phase, it is important to dedicate the necessary time and resources to identify the specific information that must be tested to support the continuous auditing objective.

Lack of sufficient planning is one of the primary reasons why scope statements have to be changed after fieldwork has begun. This lack of planning corresponds to an inadequate level of understanding of the business process that is to be tested using the continuous auditing methodology. Without a solid baseline understanding of the business process, it is very difficult to develop a complete scope statement detailing the inclusions and exclusions of the continuous auditing program to validate the effectiveness and efficiency of the selected controls.

VOLUMES

Volume plays a critical role in the determination of the final scope. Since the scope sets the specific parameters of what is going to be tested as part of a continuous auditing program, it is important to ensure that there is sufficient volume to be tested on a recurring basis. Without a sufficient amount of data or transactions, it will be difficult to conclude on the validity of the selected controls that are to be tested. Next we describe number and dollar details to explain the details surrounding the interpretation of pure volumes.

Number

The first component of volume to be discussed is number. In regard to scope volume, the term "number" represents the number of transactions that occur during the corresponding scope period. Transactions, as used here, represent any compliance, operational, or financial activity. An example of an operational transaction would be the review and approval of an application. Another example of a transaction for a compliance process would be the timely submission of a regulated government form. This definition recognizes that any hand-off, sign-off, review, approval, or posting of an amount could represent a transaction as defined in the continuous auditing methodology testing requirements. In auditing, when the word "transaction" is used, most people immediately think of a pure debit and credit financial transaction representing the movement of money.

It is important to identify how business processes with smaller volumes of transaction of activity directly impacts the continuous auditing program scope. The question becomes: What is an appropriate number to ensure a valid sample can be selected during the scope period to support the successful execution of a continuous auditing program? In the ideal situation, auditors developing the continuous auditing program should identify the business process that generates multiple transactions every single day. With this type of volume, auditors are guaranteed a more than sufficient population to sample in support of the continuous auditing program requirements.

If a sufficient number of transactions are not executed in the target area during the scope period, it may be necessary to reconsider the original continuous auditing target area. As a reference point, the minimum number of transactions during scope period for a continuous auditing program should be approximately 50. This baseline number should provide an appropriate population from which to select a representative sample for a continuous auditing program on a recurring basis. Of course, the larger the number of transactions that are processed during the scope period, the broader selection and sampling can be to support the continuous auditing scope statement and to link to the continuous auditing objective.

Although it is possible to select and develop the scope statement for an area that does not have at least 50 transactions processed during the scope period, auditors must be certain that the continuous auditing program is the most effective testing technique for a processing area with lower-than-normal transaction volume. If the corresponding risk for this business processing area is significant, it is appropriate to plan and execute a continuous auditing program focused on validating the key controls in the area. Accordingly, the pure number of transactions processed could be lower than normal and result in the testing of *all* transactions processed during the scope period. Just like the continuous auditing testing performed in a high-volume business process, this continuous auditing program will be executed to ensure that the control environment is producing repeatable, reliable results. The only caution to recognize when selecting a business process with small volumes of transactions being executed during scope period is that these transactions are usually closely monitored in the smaller business processing functions. This is the result of having the necessary staff to examine and approve all transactions. Continuous auditing programs, in general, usually are focused on high-volume business processing units to validate that the control environment, for the selected key controls, can withstand the rigors of increased volumes without sacrificing output quality.

Dollar

The second component to be discussed regarding volume is dollar. The pure financial factor of the transactions executed during the scope period represents the perfect complement to volume when developing the final scope for your continuous auditing program. Although dollars provide a good indicator for the potential risks related to the transactions being processed, they can be misleading when it comes to determining the most effective scope for the continuous auditing program. In many instances, auditors instantly gravitate to areas processing the highest dollar transactions and believe that these transactions represent the biggest risk. That might seem like a logical conclusion, but auditors who are developing the continuous audit program often are led to make incorrect assumptions.

Consider this example. We will use the wire operations area as our target area for our continuous auditing program. In developing our scope, we noted that there is transaction activity, but it does not occur every single day. In accordance with the scope guidelines for volume, this business process could fit into the continuous auditing program requirements even though it does not meet the suggested minimum transaction volume for proper sampling. However, as we continuously perform our research into the scope requirements for volume, we discover that the average dollar for wires executed represents the largest dollar amounts during the scope period. Any time large dollar transactions are being executed by a business processing function, the corresponding risk of executing these types of transactions is inherently high. However, when developing a continuous auditing program, auditors should be looking for high-volume transaction processing business units; they should not just focus on low-volume, high-dollar transactions. The reason for not developing and establishing a continuous auditing program surrounding a business unit that processes high-dollar transactions on an infrequent basis is that, more often than not, these types of transactions receive an increased level of review and scrutiny prior to execution. This example does not state that all business processing units executing infrequent high-dollar transactions are all doing so, without exception, and in an always well-controlled environment. There is no way to draw that conclusion without specifically testing the process execution. However, it is a fact that processes which execute these types of transactions have multiple controls in place over the execution. In the development of the continuous auditing program, the scope statement must be well researched and appropriately linked to the targeted continuous auditing objective. Additionally, continuous auditing programs usually focus on high-volume transaction environments regardless of the corresponding dollar amounts of the transactions processed.

In general, dollar amounts are a critical consideration when developing the continuous auditing approach and detailed scope. It is important to note and be aware that higher-than-normal dollar transactions receive an increased level of review prior to execution and may not be the most effective indicators of the overall strength of the processing environment, if no representative sample of different dollar amounts across the scope period is taken.

SAMPLING

The next component to discuss regarding the approach phase of the continuous auditing methodology is sampling. Because of the recurring nature of the continuous auditing program requirements, it is critical to determine how each recurring sample is to be selected. Although there are many different types of sampling techniques, we are going to focus and discuss the three most widely used: random, judgmental, and statistical. Each technique has advantages and disadvantages, but one sampling approach, judgmental, is used primarily in the development of the continuous auditing program requirements. The sampling technique selected plays a critical role in the development of the continuous auditing approach phase, which is focused on creating the most comprehensive testing plan to support the continuous auditing objective. Due to the specific and focused nature of the continuous auditing objective, the sampling technique has to be developed strategically to ensure the targeted transactions are properly included in the testing. Also, as you develop your continuous auditing methodology, keep in mind that whichever sampling technique you select should be used consistently throughout the execution phase. For example, if you choose a random sampling technique during month 1 of the continuous auditing program, you must use random sampling in each subsequent month until the completion of all auditing testing.

Random Sampling

Random sampling, by definition, is the unbiased selection of items within a population based strictly by chance with no discernible pattern to describe the method of individual item selection. The critical or unique component of selecting a test sample using random sampling is that every single item in the population has an equal chance of being chosen regardless of size, amount, date, location, or value. The moment any parameter or restriction is placed on the selection criteria, the sample selection is no longer random. Random sampling is also known as haphazard, meaning there is no specific primary reason as to how the items chosen to be tested are selected.

In building the approach phase of your continuous auditing program, random sampling could be the preferred selection method if no special or particular factors need to be included in the testing sample. This could be the case, for example, if the continuous auditing program was being performed to validate the use of a standard application in a business processing unit. In this example, the assumption is made that every item process by the business unit uses the same exact standard application being tested. In any business process being tested using the continuous auditing model, random sampling would be an appropriate method for selecting recurring sample items.

Most internal audit departments use random sampling not just for continuous auditing programs but also for full-scope audit reviews, because this method of sampling provides the most unbiased selection technique. However, when using random sampling, it is possible to unintentionally exclude potentially critical transactions. The internal audit departments that use random sampling are willing to take and accept a certain level of risk. This risk is related to the possibility that an incorrect transaction was processed and unintentionally left out of the sample tested due to the random nature of the selection. Random sampling provides no guarantees that the specific type of transaction identified during the continuous audit planning phase will be included in the random sample selected.

The most compelling argument against using a random sampling technique in internal audit is not the risk of missing a potential exception in the sample selected. That is a real risk and poses a challenge in the sample selected, but it is not the main barrier to using the technique consistently. The real challenge with random sampling is that it is extremely difficult to execute a truly random sample without applying a single bias during the individual item selection. For example, when selecting random samples, many auditors subconsciously pick items to be tested based on file size, folder color, name, date, or some other obscure factor that has a particular meaning for the person making the selection. To further illustrate this concept, it would be like an auditor opening a file drawer and subconsciously choosing a sample of the folders that were his or her favorite color. This bias is not intentional but does happen in random samples where auditors are asked to choose any item at all for testing.

Judgmental Sampling

Judgmental sampling, by definition, is the process by which auditors select items to be tested that meet specific predetermined criteria. The unique characteristic of judgmental sampling is that the selected items can be matched specifically to meet the testing parameters being verified as part of the continuous auditing program. The selection parameters used provide a strategic advantage in an effort to maximize the continuous auditing program results by selecting only those sample items that match exactly the control requirements being verified.

In developing the approach phase of your continuous auditing program, judgmental sampling is the preferred method of selecting the sample items to be tested. Judgmental sampling is the most widely used technique when executing a continuous auditing program because the method mirrors the targeted approach that supports the continuous auditing methodology. Remember that the continuous auditing methodology requires auditors to examine the business process and strategically select the key control or controls that anchor the business process in order to ensure that the control environment is effective and efficient. Correspondingly, the sampling method that most closely resembles the methodology approach is judgmental sampling. By definition, the continuous auditing methodology judgmentally identifies and selects the key control or controls to be validated. To guarantee that the sample items chosen are going to be processed through the controls identified in the foundation phase of the continuous auditing methodology, the judgmental sampling technique is the only way to link the testing transactions to the identified controls. This sampling technique ensures that the sample items selected are directly linked to the testing objective because the selection was made based on the parameters set forth in the continuous auditing objective.

For example, if the foundation phase of the continuous auditing methodology identified the reconciliation process as the target area and aged items over 60 days old as the key control to be tested, judgmental sampling would be the most effective sampling method that could be used. The judgmental sampling technique would ensure that all the items selected for testing would be at least 61 days old. Using any other sampling technique, such as random or statistical, would not guarantee that the items selected for testing would specifically match the requirement of being over 60 days old.

The judgmental sampling technique allows auditors to focus their entire testing sample on the specific control parameters being tested as part of the continuous auditing program. This type of focus selection provides sufficient data on a monthly basis to determine the effectiveness and efficiency of the control being tested.

Statistical Sampling

Statistical sampling, by definition, is a mathematical method that auditors use to determine the specific size of the sample to be selected. We are not going to discuss the specific details of how to execute a statistical sample here; this mathematical method requires an exact knowledge of the population to be sampled and the development of specific components to be factored into the calculation of the sample size. Without a working knowledge of the calculation factors and the exact number of items in the population, it is not possible to use statistical sampling as your selection method. Many statistical samples are developed without knowledge of the specific population size; the population, incorrectly, is usually estimated.

However, there are advantages to using a statistical sample. These advantages include a mathematically calculated sample size that has been quantitatively developed to accurately represent a valid sample to be tested on the population. Another advantage is that statistical sampling is recognized as the most objective and defensible selection technique. This is because the number of items selected was mathematically calculated while the random and judgmental collection techniques are based on the decision of the auditor performing the test. The mathematical selection eliminates the possibility of bias on the auditor's part and sets the sample to be tested based on true volume. However, in a continuous auditing program, it is more efficient and effective to not use statistical sampling because there is no guarantee that the type of transaction being validated will be included in the testing sample. Even though auditors are selecting samples based on risk and experience, the samples cannot be explained through a mathematical calculation.

The main reason audit departments use this technique is due to what can be done with the results. The primary advantage of a statistical sample is that the error rate identified at the completion of the testing can be statistically extrapolated across the entire population without question. This statistical conclusion cannot be made when using a random or judgmental sampling technique.

Being able to statistically conclude on the error rate across an entire population is very powerful and provides auditors with a concrete conclusion based on the sample testing performed. Considering the advantages discussed as well as the extrapolation of results, it would seem logical to use statistical sampling in the approach phase of a continuous auditing program. However, the biggest problem with statistical sampling is that the mathematical calculations usually result in a sample size greater than 85 when the population exceeds 1,000. The recurring nature of the continuous auditing program and the short time required to execute the testing on a monthly basis makes statistical sampling not the most effective technique for selecting items to be tested in support of your continuous auditing methodology.

TESTING CRITERIA AND ATTRIBUTES

The next component to be discussed regarding the development of the approach phase of the continuous auditing methodology is the criteria and attributes of the testing to be performed. The formalization of the criteria and attributes will follow the same development process that auditors use in the creation of the testing attributes for any audit testing to be performed. The focus and source of the criteria and attributes should be matched directly to the business process policies and procedures. In order to build the criteria and attributes to be tested, the operational policies and procedures must be up to date and represent the current process being executed by the operations team.

Testing Keys

Once you obtain and validate the most recent policies and procedures, it is critical to identify the selected control process standard. The process standard to be tested can originate from only one of two places: internal and external. An internal process standard is developed from a management decision or a policy and procedure requirement. These internal standards are usually the result of the processing environment and are based on the experience and expertise of the management team in an effort to process transactions through their department process requirements. An external process standard is developed as a result of a federal, state, or local law or regulation. These external requirements spell out the specific standards to which the business unit must comply to process transactions through the department.

The operational standard establishes the acceptable range of performance for all transactions processed according to it. The acceptable range of performance is identified with an upper and lower control limit. These control limits provide the minimum and maximum standard for a transaction to be considered acceptable when performing the continuous auditing testing.

Once you have identified the specific process standard for the control(s) to be tested in your continuous auditing program, the next step is to create the individual test steps to be performed to validate control efficiency and effectiveness. It is critically important to ensure that the test steps are clear, complete, and inclusive of all of the operational steps to re-perform sample items selected. This level of detail will ensure that regardless of which auditor is asked to execute the continuous auditing program, it can be performed without a significant amount of explanation. This process of developing specific test steps should be no different from the development of an audit program for a full-scope review. Whether you are creating the test steps for a continuous auditing program or developing an audit program for a full-scope review, each step should provide clear direction and explanation as to how the work is to be performed. Without the proper level of detail, the testing may not be useful and relevant to conclude on the specific testing objective. The most effective technique for validating the existence of a sufficient level of detail for the program steps is to perform a test transaction through the documented program details. If the desired result is achieved, the test program contains a sufficient level of detail for auditors to follow and execute.

Information Retrieval Plan

Once you have established and validated the testing approach for your continuous auditing program, the next step is to identify and develop a plan to receive the information necessary to execute the testing successfully. Because this information and/or documentation is going to be required each and every month that the continuous auditing testing is performed, a process retrieval standard must be developed. Doing so will ensure that the required information is received on a timely basis so that the continuous auditing testing can be performed as scheduled. This retrieval plan provides both client and auditor with the specific process steps to be followed in order to obtain the transaction details to be verified.

Keep in mind that this information retrieval plan must contain the same level of detail as the individual steps. Auditors developing and documenting the retrieval plan must create the most effective and efficient means of obtaining transaction details to be tested with minimal disruption to the business process operations. Once auditors draft the retrieval plan, they must present it to the business unit management, not only to verify the process but also to obtain the manager's approval. Additional items that may need to be discussed during the verification process with business unit management include the method of retrieval (automated or manual), specific selection criteria or constraints, the timing of selection and/or delivery, or where the work is going to be executed.

The development, documentation, and verification of the information retrieval plan make up one of the most critical components of the approach phase of the continuous auditing methodology. The complete and full development of this plan determines the success or failure of a continuous auditing program. If the retrieval plan contains the necessary steps to gain access and retrieve the transaction details, the continuous auditing testing can be performed in a timely fashion. Conversely, if the retrieval plan is not clear or has not been approved by business unit management, executing the continuous auditing test plan will be difficult if not impossible. If there are any challenges or difficulties in obtaining the source documentation, the scheduled continuous testing will not be able to be completed. One of the significant challenges to the successful execution of the continuous auditing approach phase is that if the responsible auditor falls behind while performing the recurring testing, it will be impossible to catch up in subsequent months without altering the original testing requirements.

Challenging Control Limits

One more topic to be discussed is the concept of challenging the internally generated control limits of the business process standard that were communicated by the business unit. Although externally required process control limits cannot be challenged due to the originating body, it is important and also required to examine the internally generated control limits to ensure their reasonableness in regard to the operational process requirements. The continuous auditing methodology does not require the audit department to question the business knowledge or experience of the process owners but to consider the established upper and lower control limits that govern the process to be tested using the continuous auditing methodology.

The most common approach to evaluating the apparent validity of the business process control limits is to apply a reasonableness test to the established control limits. The controls limits are the guidelines or range established by the business unit that indicate the parameters in which each transaction should be processed to be considered accurate and acceptable. Many audit departments create audit program steps that ask auditors to review a particular process and determine whether it is reasonable. However, most individuals do not realize that a specific methodology must be applied to determine reasonableness. A process or action is determined to be reasonable if and only if a reasonable person with limited or no knowledge of the topic would agree with the process or action being taken. In other words, would an average person agree that the action or process being described is reasonable? If that is the case, the process or action is considered to be reasonable.

Most of the time, when auditors are assigned to execute the continuous auditing program, examining the internally generated control limits is important to determine that the limits represent reasonable guidelines for satisfactory performance. This consideration of control limits is critical to the success of the continuous auditing program, because all of the testing executed will be based on the control limits established in the approach phase. To ensure the validity, applicability, and usefulness of the continuous auditing testing results, the criteria and attribute development must be not only well thought out and discussed with internal audit and business unit management but also appropriately documented. The documented details of the criteria and attributes provide internal auditors with the specific steps to execute a successful continuous auditing program.

 TECHNOLOGY

The final component to be discussed regarding the approach phase of the continuous auditing methodology is technology. Although technology is not a requirement, it is important to recognize that technology may complement the continuous auditing program. Usually, technology tools are designed to perform various tasks, such as data evaluation, sample selection, and, in some cases, continuous auditing testing. Technology is not a requirement in order to plan, build, execute, and report on the continuous auditing program. Many internal audit departments implement continuous auditing methodologies without purchasing a specific technology tool designed to select and analyze large series of data. Technology, as discussed here for the approach phase, focuses on the technological aspect of testing in the continuous auditing environment.

Identification of Technology Needs

The most critical step in the consideration of incorporating technology into the approach phase of the continuous auditing methodology is to determine how technology is going to be used. One of the most common mistakes that internal audit departments make is to go out and purchase a technology solution to perform their continuous auditing programs. This is not necessary in order to incorporate continuous auditing into your audit department to complement existing audit services offered. Technology can enhance and expand the potential uses of continuous auditing but is definitely not a requirement. Many internal audit departments successfully perform continuous auditing without any assistance from technology or an automated tool. Also, keep in mind that your existing technology (such as Microsoft Excel and Access) can be leveraged to perform such tasks as sample selection, analysis, and testing. Examine your current audit methodology and how you use technology; then, after you develop your continuous auditing methodology, determine how to leverage the same technology in your new approach. Continuous auditing methodologies can be successful with or without the use of technology; likewise, they can be further enhanced using technologies already in use. Next we discuss how to use your audit team's technology experience and knowledge to expand and expedite the development of the approach phase of the continuous auditing methodology.

Authority and Use

In this day and age, when technology has been integrated into almost every aspect of the business process, it is only natural that technology plays a role in the specialized approach of developing test procedures. Requesting the authorization and approval to gain direct access to business unit data is the first step in incorporating automation into continuous auditing testing. It is crucial for the responsible auditor to request system access (for the system in which the target data are stored) independently from the business process owner in order to develop and maintain a strong relationship with your business management partners. Although your information technology team may be able to get access to the data independently or possibly could already have access for another project, it is beneficial and ethical to inform the client of the requirement to obtain the data to complete the corresponding continuous auditing work. This system access request provides management with the confidence that internal audit always will notify clients that business-level data is going to be accessed to execute the audit services described.

Once the authorization has been granted, internal audit should review the system field value tables to understand how the data is stored and identify the fields that directly correspond to the previously developed continuous auditing scope and objectives. One of the keys to using technology for the retrieval of the sample data is that the technology selection program must be focused and accurately written. This focus ensures that the technology program is strategically designed to obtain only the field values that need to be tested and verified to complete the testing. A common mistake made when incorporating technology is to have the selection program retrieve all corresponding fields for the sample items to be tested. When this occurs, internal auditors responsible for executing the continuous auditing program will have to dedicate time and resources to review, interpret, and identify the fields selected for testing. This additional investment of time can cause unnecessary delays in the completion of the approach phase of the continuous auditing methodology and reduce the amount of time available to execute, evaluate, and report on the testing results. Keep in mind that the continuous auditing methodology requires a detailed, dedicated execution and any wasted time is almost impossible to recover. To that end, stay focused on how the technology is being used in your continuous auditing program and select only the required fields.

Besides using a technology tool to obtain sample data, technology can be used to develop customized selection programs. The most obvious selection is a statistical sampling model discussed earlier in the chapter. Remember, this technology model mathematically selects sample items based on a formula. However, other selection tools may be automated in an effort to expedite the approach development process. For example, technology can be used to randomly select items in a population (which is stored online) by creating a random number generator or selecting every nth item from a population list. Or a technology program can be built to select a judgmental sample of transactions over a certain dollar amount, from a specific region or salesperson, or a specific type. Technology provides limitless opportunities to automate the selection of the continuous auditing sample and increases the efficiency and effectiveness of the approach phase from month to month during the execution.

The other primary use of technology in the approach phase is to develop the specific continuous auditing testing that will be launched and run every month to perform the testing without any manual processing. This is the most advanced use of technology in the continuous auditing methodology and requires experience, discipline, and source (where the sample data is stored) system knowledge. If you have an auditor with the corresponding skill set, it is possible to create an automated continuous auditing test program. Technology experience will be necessary to develop the system program code to go out to the source system, retrieve the data, and execute the corresponding steps. The auditor developing this system code will have to ensure that the automation steps directly match the testing objective developed in the foundation phase of the continuous auditing methodology discussed in Chapter 5. Additionally, the auditor must be disciplined and dedicated to validate that the automated testing developed does not incorporate any other test procedures or source data in the execution of the testing. The only way to verify the clarity of the technology test developed is to run a couple of sample items through the automated test to ensure that the correct information is retrieved and tested and produces the expected result. If possible, perform a manual test of the test results produced by the technology to double-check for validity of the results. Also, without source system knowledge, the auditor will need assistance in identifying the correct field values that directly correspond to the continuous auditing testing objectives.

Expanding Samples

Technology usually is included in an audit process for the purpose of expediting the process or increasing the number of samples or sample transactions to be tested. Anytime the audit process can be performed more effectively and efficiently (expedition of the process requirements), technology is a welcome addition to any internal audit department. However, technology solutions that are incorporated into a continuous auditing methodology in an effort to increase productivity sometimes have the opposite effect. The reason technology sometimes can hamper the continuous auditing process is that there is a temptation to expand the number of samples or individual sample items selected for each of the continuous auditing months being tested. Although doing so may seem like a good idea, it tends to bog down the process because more time is spent evaluating and explaining the potential exceptions than is spent determining the control effectiveness based on the well-developed foundation and approach phases of the continuous auditing methodology. Also, consider how difficult it would be to perform testing on multiple samples or significantly larger samples every single month. From an execution perspective, it is not feasible to expand and increase samples. These actions usually result in frustration from the both client management and internal audit.

If the continuous auditing methodology is followed properly, the specific sample to be chosen and the corresponding sample size are strategically developed and directly linked to the continuous auditing objective. Be confident in the research and planning that was performed in the foundation phase as well as in the custom development of the scope, sampling technique, and testing criteria that were developed during the approach phase. These well-thought-out and effectively planned techniques will ensure that your continuous auditing program will provide the validation of the control environment for the particular controls to be tested. Consider using technology as an enhancement to the completed foundation and approach continuous auditing methodology requirements and not as a replacement for all of the dedicated work that was committed to creating the details already completed. Technology should be incorporated into the continuous auditing process to enhance the execution of the phases and not used as an additional step. With this disciplined attitude, your continuous auditing program will generate positive results and confirm whether the controls being tested are producing repeatable, reliable results.

 ## SUMMARY

As the continuous auditing methodology begins to evolve and take shape, the approach provides the final components that will detail the specific scope, sampling technique, and testing attributes to complement the foundation components described in Chapter 5. It is important to remember that the scope must be detailed and specific not only to the items that are going to be included in the testing but also to any items that will not be included. This is one of the critical differentiating factors between continuous auditing and full-scope auditing because only a single control or possibly two controls will be tested as opposed to all of the controls in a process from start to finish.

Take the time to consider and select the most effective sampling technique and the particular test steps that will be necessary to evaluate the selected control(s) effectiveness. And remember, technology can be a powerful partner to internal audit, but it can cause problems if it is not used in the specific techniques described. The extra time dedicated to the approach components will prove to be invaluable as you move into the execution phase of your continuous auditing program.

CHAPTER SEVEN

Continuous Auditing: Execution Phase

EXECUTION PHASE

In this chapter, we identify and discuss the final phase of the continuous auditing model as well as the keys to performing the testing in accordance with the methodology to obtain maximum value of the testing results. In addition, we explain the three key component development factors that comprise the execution phase to validate that the information compiled during the foundation and approach phases is accurately translated to the continuous auditing testing approach. The three components to be discussed include performance, exception identification, and summarizing results.

PERFORMANCE

When the continuous auditing methodology was being developed, it contained only two phases: the foundation and the approach. However, upon implementing the methodology, it became clear that there were nuances in the performance of the customized audit methodology that would require strict adherence to ensure that the continuous auditing programs would deliver the value-added benefits for which it had been designed. Although performance may seem like a commonsense concept, it is here where deviation from the established guidelines and approach will impact the efficiency and effectiveness of the continuous auditing methodology. The specific requirements of the foundation and approach phases set the stage for the detailed execution phase to be performed in accordance with the developed guidelines and frequency. Both the guidelines and frequency have been custom created to link directly to the business objective for the process being tested and the timing in which the selected process delivers the intended result. To clearly communicate the importance of the execution phase requirements, we begin with the basics of completing the continuous auditing program requirements.

Completing Program Requirements

It does not matter if internal audit is completing a full-scope audit or performing a continuous auditing program, all testing should be executed as specified in the corresponding audit program. This concept seems to be common sense and a very basic beginning auditor technique, but there are many times in which the audit program, developed throughout the planning process, gets changed or altered by the team executing the work. The question becomes: Why would a member of the audit team change or alter the approved program? Is it because the program was created incorrectly or does not contain the appropriate steps to match the business process? Or perhaps the audit objective gets altered on the fly. Whatever the reason, the approved program should be changed only as an exception in the event that the planning phase failed to uncover the true business operations process and the program had to be altered to match the actual work being performed.

In the continuous auditing methodology, the program steps that have been designed and validated with the business owner should not be changed during the execution phase. For internal audit departments to recognize the full value of a successfully implemented continuous auditing methodology, it is paramount that responsible auditors perform the continuous auditing work program exactly as it was designed. This will ensure that the results maintain focus on the effectiveness of the selected control and validate that it is delivering repeatable, reliable results. Responsible auditors must trust in the information and work compiled during the foundation and approach phases of the methodology that have been used to craft the specific program steps being executed.

Although completing the testing as originally designed is often overlooked or considered as an afterthought, the completion of any audit program requirements, especially in the continuous auditing methodology, is the only way to provide documented evidence to conclude on the stated audit objective. The concept of staying focused on executing the approved program steps cannot be reinforced enough times. Many times auditors make adjustments or interpretations to the continuous auditing program with the best intentions only to have the program produce inaccurate or non-value-added results. Trust in the foundation and approach development process and execute the work. The main goal in completing the program requirements in the continuous auditing methodology is to execute without removing or altering any of the program steps. Remember, the scope and corresponding testing parameters have been set. Altering the program in any way could result in a scope change that will impact your ability to conclude on the audit objective that was discussed and approved with the audit client. Changing the approved scope or testing objective could impact the established business relationship that internal audit has been developing throughout the implementation and introduction of the continuous auditing methodology. If you focus on accuracy of execution, the work program will provide a true validation of the selected controls. This concept is truly easier said than done because auditors, by nature, constantly look to increase the support for the work being performed, and that usually means an increase in testing or the attributes that are being tested. Stay focused and believe in the work already completed as part of the continuous auditing methodology. Above all, resist the temptation to alter the established scope and program requirements.

Resisting Temptation

Temptation by definition is the act of tempting or the condition of being tempted; something tempting or enticing. These are words that you do not often hear when discussing internal audit departments. No one has ever used the words "enticing" or "tempting" when describing their own internal audit department or listening to a business client describe the internal audit department in their own words. However, "temptation" is a word used often when discussing the continuous auditing methodology because throughout the foundation, approach, and execution phases of the methodology, it can be very tempting to consider increasing the sample chosen, sample population, target objectives, scope coverage, number of tests, or even testing attributes. However, as the responsible auditor for the execution of the continuous auditing program, you must resist the temptation and recognize that the effort dedicated to creating the program is solid and represents the most effective method to test the selected control(s) linked to the audit objective.

The best way to illustrate this concept is to relate it to a nonaudit event like food shopping. Everyone always says that the worst possible thing you can do is to go food shopping when you are hungry. The reason it is a bad idea is that you end up purchasing items that you really do not need and often are not the healthiest choices. Going food shopping when you are hungry most likely will result in the purchase of things you do not need and also impact the effectiveness of your goal of selecting the items you truly needed.

Let me share a personal example. I went to the food store to purchase eggs and milk, two very simple items that should take only a moment to select and purchase. On the way to the store I realized how hungry I was and started thinking about things I would like to eat. Once I got to the store, my initial objective of purchasing eggs and milk was overtaken by the thought of having pretzels, bagels, waffles, pizza, and a childhood cereal that I have not had in years. I felt great as I cruised through the store selecting items without regard for my objective. As I returned home and am emptying my bags of food, I suddenly realized that I forgot to purchase milk. Milk was one of the two specific items I had set out to purchase. Somewhere between the selection of my shopping cart and checking out, I forgot my original objective. The moral of this story is to plan effectively and have the discipline to execute the plan and corresponding steps as designed. Now, this concept can be converted to a business process, where temptation can be the potential cause of altering the established program.

For a business example, consider account reconciliations. Account reconciliations are an effective example for illustration purposes of a continuous auditing program because most business operations personnel and auditors are familiar with completing account reconciliations. Assuming an effective foundation phase has been completed and identified, account reconciliations are the target area. It has been identified that manual entries pose a significant risk, and they have been chosen as the target objective. The foundation is completed and the approach is developed with focused steps to validate the handling of manual entries. The only remaining steps to completing the first continuous auditing program are to execute the work as designed. The sample is chosen. During testing, you notice that some account reconciliations are not approved as required by company policy. Your immediate thought is to expand the continuous auditing testing to include a step for proper reconciliation approval. It sounds like a great idea but, in reality, it is not. Remember that the continuous auditing objective set in the foundation phase was focused on manual entries, period. Changing the specific program requirements to include proper approvals will alter the testing objective and impact the effectiveness of the continuous auditing methodology to provide a validation of repeatable, reliable results for the selected control. There is also no longer an opportunity to use the results as a predictive tool because the target testing objective has been changed to include some other aspect of account reconciliations besides manual entries. Initially, altering the test program may seem like an enhancement to the audit service being performed; in actuality, it reduces the effectiveness of the continuous auditing application.

However, this is not to say that if you are executing a continuous auditing program and identify a $5 million entry that does not belong in the account, you should just ignore it. The continuous auditing methodology stresses that responsible auditors must stay focused on the specific testing objective and not expand the test program because of temptation. That is not what the concept is trying to illustrate. If you are performing testing and identify a significant weakness or blatant mistake, of course you have the responsibility to examine it and determine why it is happening. This is where the utilization of common sense becomes important. During any continuous auditing testing, there are going to be items that do not specifically comply with existing policies and procedures. However, their identification should not result in expansion or additions to the current continuous auditing program. You should note them for future work to be performed in the area unless the corresponding risk is so significant that it must be addressed immediately. The bottom line is that the continuous auditing program should be completed as designed while, as always, you should be aware of other potential areas for improvement.

The other temptation that arises, as much if not more than additions to the program is to stop performing the continuous auditing testing after the first couple of months because no reportable items have been identified during the testing. The continuous auditing methodology has been designed to examine the effectiveness and efficiency of controls over a period of time at a specific set frequency. This approach must be performed for the designated period of time for the methodology to be effective. Stopping the testing after a couple of months does not provide sufficient evidence to the responsible auditors that the selected control(s) are producing repeatable, reliable results. Stopping testing short of the agreed frequency and time period only proves that for the two or three samples selected, no reportable items were noted. Auditors who believe that, after a couple of months, they understand the business control environment and can make a conclusion based on the results gathered to date are mistaken. If the continuous auditing methodology is not fully executed as designed in the methodology requirements, it cannot be used as a predictive audit tool and does not really provide any additional assurances to the business unit that its control structure is well designed, implemented, and operating as intended for the control(s) selected during the continuous auditing foundation phase.

The key to ensuring that the performance component of the continuous auditing execution phase is effective is to have confidence in the other phases of the methodology (foundation and approach). With the focus application of this methodology, it will provide a proactive evaluation of the selected control(s) while at the same time delivering audit-tested data to support the conclusion of the effectiveness and efficiency of the control environment. The control environment represents the required steps developed by management to facilitate the execution of the business process.

 EXCEPTION IDENTIFICATION

As the execution phase of the audit methodology unfolds, the results may identify instances where the actual work being performed by business unit does not meet the business-approved process requirement standards. In this case, the gap between the actual work performed and the processing standard must be documented, sufficiently supported, and validated with business unit management before labeling the gap as an exception. This process should not vary or differ from the exception identification process used in any audit service being performed. However, identifying gaps in the process or opportunities for improvement is increasingly important in the continuous auditing model because the specific testing is focused directly on the critical one or two controls that provide stability to the business process. When the audit testing is strategically focused on a single control or two, proper documentation and support as well as validation with the client becomes invaluable to solidifying and maintaining the integrity of the audit department and the audit/client relationship. This process of exception identification has three critical steps to ensure that the exception is not only valid but also has an adequate level of detailed documentation to support the corresponding conclusion as to risk and exposure. These steps, when considered each time a performance gap is identified, will assist in the delivery of a critical message to the business client and reduce the possibility that the work performed will be questioned by business unit management for authenticity. The steps are:

1. Document potential observations
2. Document exception evidence
3. Validate

Document Potential Observations

When a discrepancy is identified between the established standard obtained from the business unit and the actual sample tested, the testing details must be adequately and fully documented to ensure that the continuous auditing results relate directly to their supporting evidence. Just as with all other audit services, the continuous auditing program requires the testing documentation to be detailed and clear. To ensure that the documentation is clear, it should contain a testing objective, source, scope, tick mark and attribute legend, and conclusion. Each one of these components provides the critical detail and explanation summarizing the testing performed.

- **The objective should explain specifically the reason why this particular testing is being performed.** The testing objective answers the question why. An independent reader needs to understand the reason for the testing and also should be able to match the actual testing attributes to the objective as the work paper review continues.

- **The source statement of the work paper should indicate where and how the information used in the testing was obtained.** The source is usually the department or system used by the target department that performs the control(s) being tested.
- **The scope statement provides the exact time frame for the testing as well as the specific control(s) to be tested.** It should spell out the exact items selected with no need for any additional explanation.
- **All work papers should contain a legend that explains the testing attributes (what was tested) and the tick marks (individual markings for each attribute tested explaining compliance or noncompliance with the attribute) documented on the work paper. The final component of the work paper document is the conclusion.** It summarizes the effectiveness of the control(s) tested and must be supported directly by the sample testing.

The most effective way to double-check the effectiveness and appropriateness level of the detail is to read the objective, verify that the testing sample was selected from the corresponding department or operation, ensure that the testing was consistently performed across the sample, and validate that the conclusion appropriately and fairly summarizes the testing results. The final verification will be to ensure that the conclusion is linked to the stated objective of the work paper and that sufficient work was performed to formulate the corresponding conclusion.

Document Exception Evidence

The second component to be discussed regarding exception identification is the documented exception evidence. The key here is to make sure that the documentation you have compiled to explain the potential exception is sufficient. There are many different ways to support a potential exception noted, but the only factor that should be considered is whether enough documentation has been compiled to adequately support the reasoning behind internal audit, identifying that there is a difference between the actual work performed and the expected department requirement standards.

When determining how much evidence would be sufficient, an effective method is for auditors performing the testing to put themselves in the place of the business owner and determine how much evidence would be sufficient to understand the potential issue being discussed. The documented evidence must be able to stand on its own and provide the necessary support for the identified discrepancy. The most effective way to ensure completeness of documentation is to take a copy of the potential exception. I like to have a copy of the documented evidence as an example of what I am labeling an exception per the testing standard that is being tested. There are two reasons to take a copy:

1. **The copy provides documented evidence of the potential exception.** It is not that the document could or would change, but I want to be sure that I capture an exception example for discussion purposes. It also shows the business owner exactly what internal audit is calling an exception or variation from the standard.
2. **The documented evidence provides a tool to increase the internal audit team's knowledge.** With the exception details in the continuous auditing files, other auditors outside the continuous auditing testing team can use the documentation to review and better understand the different business processes for which they may not have an opportunity to perform any work. The copy provides documented evidence to present and discuss with business management and provides internal audit with an effective cross-training tool.

Every internal auditor knows that the work performed and conclusions reached are only as good as the documentation that supports them. Strong documentation helps auditors in their discussions with business partners to obtain validation and concurrence that the discrepancies noted are truly exceptions and represent a deviation from the established department operational policies and procedures.

Validate

Validation is the final step in the process to complete the confirmation of exception identification. This step requires the responsible internal auditors assigned to execute the continuous auditing testing to schedule a meeting to discuss the potential exceptions with the business owner. The sole purpose of this meeting is to ensure that the information identified during the testing that the auditors are calling an exception truly is a deviation from the current processing standards. The responsible auditors are looking for business operations personnel to review the exception support data and verify that it does not agree to the processing standard. If the documented evidence supporting the exception noted is strong, it will make the validation process go smoothly. In this meeting, auditors should recap the objective of the continuous auditing program and summarize the testing approach performed. This extra explanation step provides the business partner with the necessary background to clearly understand the exception detail about to be presented. The auditors should adequately prepare for the exception discussion meeting by reviewing the foundation and approach information of the continuous auditing program as well as the completed testing results in order to facilitate a fluid discussion related to all of the work performed and the reasoning behind the specific testing approach. This additional preparation gives the responsible auditors another opportunity to examine the work to ensure it links directly to the testing objective and is appropriately supported and documented in the work papers.

You may be wondering why internal audit needs to obtain validation of the exception noted. After all, if the responsible auditor correctly followed the continuous auditing methodology in building the foundation and approach, the execution of the testing should be sufficient to conclude as to the effectiveness and efficiency of the related controls. Although this is true, because the continuous auditing program is such a targeted approach to control evaluation all apparent discrepancies of control performance must be documented and reviewed with the business owner to ensure the adequacy and accuracy of the interpretation. There are instances where a particular control appears to be broken when, in reality, supplemental or compensating controls capture the initial discrepancy and prevent it from impacting the overall product that ultimately is delivered to the customer.

The continuous auditing methodology is effective in its approach and execution but requires the additional step of exception validation. This extra step ensures the validation of results before attempting to compile the exception data in a constructive format to interpret the results. Upon validation, the responsible auditor will generate a final conclusion on the control environment to be presented to management. This validation helps to facilitate a strong working relationship with business clients; they recognize that internal audit is willing to take the time to review the exception details with them to obtain their concurrence. This simple step creates a relationship based on honest and up-front communication between internal audit and its clients while simultaneously showing that internal audit does not use some secret method to identify potential exceptions but bases it on the operational standards created by business unit management or industry standards. Remember always to set the standard with your business clients by fostering honest and up-front communications that always are based on the data.

 ## SUMMARIZING RESULTS

Once internal audit has completed the exception validation process, the testing results must be compiled into a format that will assist in the final communication of the results. It is important to organize the information in a simple format to convey a clear message that does not require any interpretation by the reader. To accomplish this, it is critical to categorize the exceptions where applicable and identify any trends or themes. Discuss the process of interpreting results by stepping back before generating any initial conclusions. Doing this helps in reviewing the data and safeguards against the responsible auditor rushing to judgment believing that the exceptions are clear and require no qualification. The final step in the summarization process is preparing to communicate the compiled results to the business client.

Compiling and Categorizing the Data

As the continuous auditing program is executed and the findings are listed, the potential exceptions identified during the testing must be arranged and organized prior to trying to interpret the results. The auditor, who performed the testing, will go through the interpretation process to organize the exceptions into specific categories and examine the supporting documentation obtained to verify that all information matches. This compilation and self-review is performed at the completion of all the sample testing and is used as an internal quality control in an effort to strengthen the data support for the exceptions identified. The organization of the testing details and exception data provides the foundation for the responsible auditor to begin to evaluate the overall performance of the selected control or controls.

Creating a disciplined internal audit environment that requires every auditor to be responsible for obtaining solid documentation to evidence the testing performed will help the internal audit department meet the evidence standard of ensuring that the work papers contain relevant, useful, and reliable documentation to support their conclusions. This process of obtaining the information and reviewing the documentation ensures that the message being derived from the continuous auditing testing data is based on facts, not a subjective opinion. Every audit department should document the specific work paper requirements for their individual audit methodologies to ensure consistency of documented evidence regardless of the type of audit service being performed. Even if the testing results noted are not included in the final report, the work papers still must provide solid documentation of the specific testing performed.

Now that the compilation of the data has been explained, let us touch on the concept of categorization. Categorization is most commonly used in summarizing continuous auditing testing because the same attribute(s) are being tested repeatedly from month to month or quarter to quarter. This type of focused testing and frequency lends itself to repetitive exception identification, which must be handled appropriately to avoid creating a very negative or condescending tone in the summary of the testing results. Due to the recurring nature of the testing, there will be a temptation to repeat the same finding over and over. There is no point to breaking down the same type of finding repeatedly in the testing results and repeating the same exception over and over. Doing this causes the business owner to believe that internal audit is not performing the new continuous auditing program to assist the business but rather unnecessarily focuses on the same item throughout the sample. If the same type of finding is occurring throughout the sample, note that condition in one sentence rather than repeating the same finding over and over. This concept of unnecessary repetition is called "piling on," and it creates a challenging working relationship with business unit management rather than improving the overall strength of the processing environment.

Focus on identifying trends and categorizing like findings so that the report summary is not only factual but also direct and clear. The goal of performing the recurring testing in a continuous auditing program is to confirm that the control environment produces repeatable, reliable results; it is not to harangue the business unit processing team about the same thing over and over.

Interpreting Results

Internal audit departments do not always have the best reputations. Because most of the work is exception based, it is no surprise that internal audit departments usually are viewed as the enemy. Contrary to popular belief, at least from the perspective of business unit management, internal audit is a valuable partner that is focused on providing its business unit clients with a value-added service to proactively identify opportunities for improvement based on independent and objective testing. In an effort to continue to provide this valuable service, internal audit must continually strive to understand the business processes and deliver a quality, useful product on every audit service performed. A huge factor that directly impacts the audit product delivery is interpretation of the testing results data. With its limited amount of experience with the business process combined with the development of the testing approach based on input from the business unit and existing policies and procedures, it is not always easy for internal audit to interpret testing results data, especially when they are generated from executing a continuous auditing program. Any time the testing is centered around one or two controls, the recurring data results must be interpreted effectively in order to deliver the quality results the business management is expecting.

One of the most common mistakes internal auditors make regarding their data interpretation responsibilities is that they sometimes rush to judgment based on initial results without validating the current situation with the business unit. This rushing is usually a result of overconfidence on the part of the responsible auditor executing the testing. The overconfidence comes from a feeling that the auditor knows enough about the existing process to create a valid conclusion and that there could not possibly be any other factors that would change the overall results identified through the continuous auditing testing. All auditors should recognize, however, that at no time during a continuous audit or a full-scope audit will they have even half of the knowledge that the operational business personnel possess. As internal auditors review their work and related findings, however, they often come to believe that they have enough information to have a risk-based discussion regarding the operational effectiveness of the control environment being tested. Unfortunately for the entire internal audit department, this miscalculation in judgment not only results in the possible incorrect interpretation of a risk exposure but also reflects poorly on the department as a whole, because the business unit now believes that all auditors rush to judgment when summarizing their findings. The only way to truly validate the results is to schedule a meeting with the operational process experts and validate the accuracy of the internal audit assumptions. This small step will save time, effort, and the audit/client relationship.

Also, another potential pitfall internal auditors are faced with is not having patience in the audit execution of the continuous auditing methodology. All auditors must exhibit patience when performing this focused testing—and any audit testing, for that matter. The saying that has been around for centuries is that patience is a virtue; nowhere is it more applicable than with audit testing, especially in a continuous auditing program. To ensure that the facts are clear, it is critical to step back and look at the results as a whole and ask yourself: What is the data telling me? This additional step will help ensure that you do not rush to judgment and that you have taken an extra moment to identify a more comprehensive, thought-out explanation of the testing rather than the apparent, obvious problem. Not all testing is clear, direct, and simple. Take the extra time and ensure that you have considered and discussed what the data is telling you. The goal of the additional step is that as the responsible auditor, you are looking for the core issue that is pervasive throughout the testing, not just one item here and one item there. Those types of issues have been identified before, but is there an overriding issue that is causing the other exceptions to occur? The only way to effectively make that determination is to review all of the data and try to determine if there is a more global issue than the one or two exceptions that have been identified during the execution of the continuous auditing program.

Once the results have been interpreted with the assistance of the business owner, where applicable, the responsible auditor can focus on developing the continuous auditing testing conclusions. Remember to formulate all conclusions on the data obtained during the testing, and not on opinion. It is much easier to discuss and defend the testing data than to try to defend the noted exceptions based on an internal audit opinion.

Generate Conclusions

After the validation and consideration of the data, it is time to develop the initial testing conclusions. Remember to base these conclusions on the data. At this stage of the results summary, you are looking to interpret the data results and create the conclusion to be discussed with the client. Generating conclusions is probably the easiest of the components under the summarizing results category; you should have completed all of the challenging efforts when compiling the data, categorizing the exceptions, and interpreting the continuous auditing testing results. One thing to keep in mind is that up to this point, the business client has been involved in the discussions and interpretation of the data. If that is the case, the generation of conclusions should just be a matter of creating a conclusion based on the validated testing results.

Using the data results, develop the continuous auditing testing conclusion that best captures the current state of the control environment for the selected control(s) tested. Once you have drafted the conclusion and prior to discussing it with business unit management, review it and verify that it is based on the testing results and is directly related to the continuous auditing testing objective. Another way to independently verify the strength of the conclusion is to ask another internal auditor—one who was not involved at all in the continuous auditing program–to review the testing performed and the conclusion. This additional review acts as an independent verification, from an individual with no prior knowledge of the continuous auditing testing requirements, to determine whether the documented work adequately supports the testing conclusion.

Once the conclusion has been created and an independent review has been accomplished for accuracy, the final step in the conclusion generation process is to review it with the business unit management. This final review provides the client with closure of the testing for this time period and completes the communication loop that began with the development of the continuous auditing objective. If the process has been performed according to the continuous auditing methodology, the client would have been included in the foundation, approach, and execution of the specific continuous auditing program and should clearly understand why the work was being performed, how the objective and testing was developed, what was going to be included in the scope, how the testing was going to be performed, and what the testing results identified as opportunities for improvement. Strong communication is absolutely critical in the summary of exceptions in the continuous auditing methodology and will greatly benefit the responsible auditor when developing the final report.

 ## SUMMARY

As the continuous auditing methodology begins to evolve and take shape, the execution provides the components that will detail the keys to performing a continuous audit effectively. Additionally, the execution phase provides guidance to resist the potential challenges of temptation, develop strong supporting work paper documentation, summarize and categorize the specific results of the testing performed, and recognize the keys to communicating during the most critical phase of the continuous auditing methodology. Adherence to the execution guidelines help to support the foundation and approach components described in Chapters 5 and 6. It is important to remember that the performance of the work must be completed consistently from month to month or quarter to quarter while staying true to the continuous auditing methodology requirements of not adding or deleting the approved testing attributes or stopping the testing prematurely. Take the time to review and consider the test results and identify what the data is telling you as you develop the exception detail and corresponding conclusion. Always remember to validate the exception detail and summary of exceptions with the client to ensure accuracy of the results. The extra time dedicated to these attributes, especially communication, will prove invaluable as you move to develop the root cause and final report of your continuous auditing program.

8

Root Cause Analysis

 ROOT CAUSE

In this chapter, we define and discuss the concept of root cause analysis. This cause-identifying approach is often used by internal audit departments around the world to describe their valiant efforts to discover the true or underlying reason why an exception exists. The ironic aspect of the concept is that many departments believe that they are attempting to find and identify the root cause of an exception but are, in reality, unfamiliar with the most effective way to obtain and recognize it. Root cause analysis is one of the most overused terms in internal audit departments; it also is one of the most misunderstood as to process and identification. Even though almost every audit department states that they use the root cause analysis, not everyone understands the process of how to find root cause nor recognizes the root cause when it has been identified. In addition to clearly explaining the concept, we discuss the keys to validating that the internal audit team understands the analysis and the supporting explanation as to why it is critical to identify the true root cause each and every time a reportable exception has been found through internal audit testing. Also, this chapter provides a practical approach and keys to learning how to identify root cause for any exception noted.

 ## ROOT CAUSE DEFINED

By definition, root cause analysis is a research-based approach to identifying the bottom line reason of a problem with root cause representing the source of the problem. The other key concept to recognize about root cause analysis is that it is a reactive method of solving a problem (or exception) that has been identified previously. If root cause analysis is being used, it is because a problem has occurred already and needs to be addressed from a detective or postevent perspective. The objective in root cause analysis is to focus on the problem, review the supporting documentation, and identify the origin of the problem.

As mentioned, root cause analysis is a research-based approach. In other words, the root cause of a problem will never jump off a page and self-identify itself as the reason that a problem exists. Unfortunately, root cause identification requires a little bit more effort. Time is needed to discover all of the components that may be contributing to the problem but may not be the real cause. Therefore, research and analysis into the process requirements will have to be done in order to identify the true reason that the particular problem exists. This research and analysis will provide the information and support for validation of the root cause once it has been identified. Any time the word "research" is used in the internal audit environment, it denotes a significant commitment of time, resources, and effort. The root cause analysis will require no less. The research aspect of root cause analysis requires:

- Effort to determine the bottom-line reason why the problem exists
- Resources to perform the corresponding analysis
- The time necessary to complete the analysis

Each one of these components plays a critical role in the success of the root cause analysis performed and the subsequent proper identification of the reason for the failure of the business control tested.

The one unfortunate aspect of root cause analysis is that it is a detective process. For this reason, all of the work to be done in the analysis will be forensic reviews of sample items processed through the control environment that did not result in the expected or desired outcome. Internal audit departments always look to be more proactive in their approaches to assist business processing units with the control environments that govern the processing functions. Even though the root cause analysis process is not proactive when executed correctly, it provides valuable results and helps business unit management strengthen the control environment by implementing the identified control enhancements. Conversely, the continuous auditing methodology is designed to be a more proactive audit service by using a recurring testing approach in the identification of potential exceptions and potentially predictive depending on the assigned frequency. However, in both continuous auditing methodologies and full-scope audits, root cause analysis is required when an exception has been identified and validated. Keep in mind that even though every business processes will generate a result, it may not generate the intended result. If the business process does not produce the expected result, a forensic review must be performed to determine why the control(s) established to guide the process did not work effectively. This forensic review to identify why a business process did not work is known as root cause analysis.

In a continuous auditing program, the selected control(s) will be tested to ensure they deliver the expected results. When the testing results are negative, the selected control(s) will be researched to identify the root cause. This research to find the reason for the control(s) failure is called the root cause analysis. Because of the focused nature of the continuous auditing methodology, it is critical to ensure that all internal auditors clearly understand not only what root cause analysis is but also how to identify root cause consistently once a problem has been noted by the continuous auditing program and validated with client management. Also, in executing a continuous auditing program, there are going to be advantages and disadvantages when it comes to root cause analysis simply based on the continuous auditing objective and timing requirements. The advantage is that the subsequent action will properly address the issue and the disadvantage is that the root cause process will take time.

From an advantage standpoint, the fact that the continuous auditing objective is so direct and focused assists in root cause analysis efforts because the research and analysis required will be confined just to the specific control tested. This type of focused continuous auditing objective provides auditors with an easier starting point to begin the analysis as opposed to a full-scope audit with multiple testing objectives, which sometimes can cloud where the root cause analysis should begin. Whether the root cause analysis is for a targeted objective, as in a continuous auditing program, or process wide, as in a full-scope audit, the requirements for researching, analyzing, and identifying the root cause remain the same.

When executing a continuous auditing program, one of the biggest disadvantages in the root cause analysis effort is time. Due to the short execution time and recurring nature of the continuous auditing methodology, the time allotted to perform the root cause analysis will be much shorter than in a full-scope audit. This time constraint puts additional pressure on auditors to complete the analysis in a relatively short period of time, especially if the continuous auditing program is being executed on a monthly basis. No matter what time pressures, restrictions, or constraints are placed on the root cause analysis process, it must be completed fully to ensure the true reason for the problem is properly identified.

 ## TEAM UNDERSTANDING

Now that the definition and basic concepts of root cause analysis have been introduced, it is time to examine the internal audit department's responsibility to perform a root cause analysis on each audit service executed for any validated issues identified through audit testing. Keep in mind that it is irrelevant whether the audit service is for a continuous audit, a full-scope audit, or even a special project; root cause analysis *must* be performed to identify why there is a difference between the business unit requirements and the actual work being completed. Root cause analysis does not apply to any one type of operational, financial, or compliance audit. It applies to every single audit service where a discrepancy has been noted as a result of testing.

If a root cause analysis must occur on all validated issues noted, why do we need a special section of the book to discuss it? The reason is that auditors do not consistently perform a root cause analysis for testing discrepancies. And it is not because the internal audit does not believe it is important to incorporate root cause into the audit process; or that root cause is not spelled out in the internal audit operations manual; or that there is a malicious reason behind not performing a root cause analysis. None of those reasons is true. Yet, more often than not, root cause is not used consistently across internal audit teams. Time, effort, and trust are three of the biggest reasons why it is not done consistently. Let us break each one down and explain the details.

Time

One thing that you will never hear internal auditors say is that they have too much time on their hands and that they wished they had work to keep them busy. Due to the amount of detail that planning, executing, and reporting on internal audits requires, time is a luxury that most auditors always wish they had more of. When it comes to root cause analysis, internal auditors are being asked to dedicate more time trying not only to understand the intricate details of a business process but also what has happened inside the process that has resulted in a discrepancy in the audit testing. If you recall from the definition, root cause analysis requires auditors to do research in an effort to identify the bottom-line reason the problem exists. In order to perform such research, auditors must allocate a sufficient amount of time. Root cause analysis, especially for internal auditors, is a process that takes time due to the level of detail required and the intense scrutiny that all audit work comes under. In addition to the added time needed for internal audit to complete the root cause analysis, extra time is required for the business unit contact to discuss and evaluate the root cause analysis components and preliminary conclusions. Root cause analysis is really a partnership between internal audit and the business unit to make the final determination as to what has caused the difference noted by the internal audit testing. Although the continuous auditing methodology with its targeted objective and selected control testing reduces the time needed for research and determination, time still must be added for an effective root cause analysis to be performed.

Effort

Effort is the second reason to be discussed regarding inconsistent root cause analysis. Let me state first that I do not believe in any way, shape, or form that internal auditors are not giving a solid effort in the execution of their audit responsibilities. It is, however, important to note that root cause analysis takes a dedicated effort if auditors are going to research, understand, determine, and discuss with the client the source of the exception noted in the audit testing. Performing root cause analysis is not overly complex or difficult; ensuring that the correct root cause actually gets identified, however, does require a dedicated effort. The research component of the analysis takes additional effort because auditors must obtain a more detailed understanding of the process intricacies in order to evaluate the potential sources of the exception. Only someone who puts forth an effort to learn above and beyond the baseline business knowledge used to execute the testing can accomplish such work. Consider the effort needed to review the policies and procedure and perform the corresponding testing. All and all, the amount of effort required to do this is not significant. In performing a root cause analysis, auditors must desire to expend an additional effort to understand the process better and interpret the results at a granular level. This effort and additional business knowledge will be beneficial even after the root cause analysis and audit have been completed. Make no mistake about it: Dedication and discipline are the two critical characteristics that auditors exhibit to show the effort of education and interpretation needed to complete a root cause analysis regardless of the type of audit service being performed. Even though the continuous auditing methodology has a targeted objective and selected control testing, the effort level for the root cause analysis does not get any less stringent or require less effort. The root cause analysis is the same exercise regardless of the specificity of the audit objective.

Some people oppose internal audit performing root cause analysis; they believe the business unit management team should be responsible for identifying the root cause and should provide it to the internal audit team for inclusion in the report. Other opponents argue that, in the end, root cause analysis may not be worth the effort (and time) to identify the source of the problem because it requires a detailed knowledge of the process the likes of which the business unit team already possesses. Thus, strengthening the argument that root cause analysis should be left to the process owners. Why waste the effort on gaining the knowledge if the business team already has it? These arguments, although cogent, do not reflect the true value of the experience and skill gained by successful performance of a root cause analysis and the corresponding value and dividends the increase in business process knowledge provides to future audits and cross-training.

Trust

Root cause analysis also is applied inconsistently due to trust issues. Trust, by definition, is the reliance on the integrity or ability of a person, process, or thing. What does trust have to do with the failure to perform root cause analysis consistently? It is a simple mistake of believing or placing reliance on an individual as it pertains to the business process being evaluated by the full scope or continuous auditing methodology. This means that the root cause determination is based on a communication of the *supposed* root cause without any validation or discussion of details. This reliance can be placed either on the responsible auditor executing the continuous auditing program or on the business unit owner who is being audited. Next we discuss two different scenarios where trust can impede the effectiveness of completing a root cause analysis on a consistent basis.

To illustrate the scenario from a responsible auditor's perspective, consider a completed continuous auditing program where the testing identified an exception. Once this exception has been validated with the business client, the auditor begins to consider the condition identified and discover why the condition exists. Once they believe they have identified the source of the exception, there is no need to perform any additional root cause analysis because the problem source has been located. However, this belief is only from the auditor's point of view; it is possible that they are not aware of other relevant circumstances at this time. The risk here is that auditors performing the testing trust that they clearly understand the issue and, more important, already possess a detailed working knowledge of the business process. They believe they can accurately identify the root cause of the exception without any additional research or client input. This potential overconfidence can lead to auditors presenting a root cause for the identified exception that is not the true source of the discrepancy. One would think that, in this scenario, the business owner, upon being asked to validate the root cause, would be quick to point out that other factors impact the process being tested and that, upon a comprehensive exchange between responsible auditors and business owners, the true root cause would be identified. But it does not work that way.

Auditors identify their version of root cause and provide it to business owners for validation. Unless the root cause presented is significantly off base, nine times out of ten, business owners accept the root cause presented and develop an action plan to address it. However, in these instances, auditors who lack a detailed working knowledge of the process required for the root cause analysis present a root cause that addresses only a symptom of the exception noted, and not the true source of the issue. Furthermore, the subsequent action created by the business owner to address this symptom will not address the real root cause. It may, in fact, result in a potentially larger exposure to the effectiveness and efficiency of business operations.

This situation leads directly into the second scenario in which auditors place too much trust on the responsible business owners to identify the root cause for the exception noted. Placing such trust in business owners seems logical, given that no other individual in the company understands the process being audited more than the business owner themselves. One of the keys to performing a successful root cause analysis is having detailed business knowledge. This should be a no-brainer. The responsibility for root cause analysis should reside with business process owners, not the auditors performing the testing. Unfortunately, business process owners may not:

- Understand the steps necessary to complete a root cause analysis.
- Be separated enough from the process to be totally objective.
- Want to drill that far down into the process because it could result in a time-consuming or expensive solution to address the source of the exception.

Also, it is important that responsible internal auditors question business owners who are providing explanations or suggestions regarding the root cause to ensure that business unit management performed all aspects of the root cause analysis.

In the end, trust between the auditors and business unit management is critical to understanding root cause, whether it is from the responsible auditor's perspective for gaining the business knowledge and questioning the business owner, or from the business owner's perspective in considering all potential reasons why the exception could have occurred prior to suggesting a root cause. The most effective approach for auditors and business owners is to work together, sharing detailed business knowledge information and the specifics of process breakdowns used to illustrate the current condition that compared the established business standard as described by the process owner to the actual audit testing performed. A strong commitment to communication and partnership leads to a successful root cause analysis.

Remember to verify that the entire audit department understands the definition of root cause and recognizes the need to perform root cause analysis any time a validated issue has been found during the execution of audit testing. If the audit team does not understand the concept or the need, train staff members to define the process and review different real-life scenarios that illustrate the challenges auditors face when trying to determine the true source of an exception. Additionally, to ensure that a root cause analysis is completed on every audit, add a step to your internal quality review which verifies that the root cause was identified and discussed with the business client prior to the development of the draft report. This extra validation will strengthen the core components of an audit issue and ensure that the audit report details do not require any interpretation.

DO I NEED TO FIND ROOT CAUSE?

The previous section raised the question of whether business owners should be responsible for finding root causes instead of internal auditors. The risks of making that assumption were already addressed, but here is another thought to consider. Regardless of who identifies root cause, the question arises of whether it is really necessary to perform a root cause analysis, especially when the exception will be reported officially in the final audit report. If this condition is documented accurately in the audit report, an action is going to be created to address it and subsequently reduce the risk to business unit operations and the company as a whole. That is true. If the root cause is not identified, however, the exception detail will not accurately portray the current state of the control environment of the business unit being reviewed. The root cause analysis provides business owners with critical information needed to determine when, how, and, ultimately, if the root cause can be properly addressed. So the question still remains: If the condition is clearly stated in the audit report, does the exception detail really need to contain the root cause? The answer to this question is absolutely. Root cause analysis is the most effective—really the only—way to provide the specific reason as to why the condition exists in the first place. Incorporating the root cause into the detailed explanation of the exception will strengthen the report and deliver a clear message of a need for action to be taken to address the identified gap. The internal audit department, business unit management, and external partners recognize the value that root cause analysis provides and the focus it brings to the business unit as well as the company overall to required actions needed to strengthen the overall control environment.

If the root cause is not identified, readers of the report either will have to believe that the source of the problem has been identified and will be addressed by the action plan or will be required to interpret the data presented and make their own assumptions as to the reason there is a stated difference between the condition (representing the actual work being performed) and the criteria (representing the business processing standard). If responsible internal auditors diligently perform the root cause analysis, each of these scenarios can and should be avoided.

ROOT CAUSE "WHY" APPROACH

By now the critical role that root cause analysis plays in trying to identify the source of exceptions noted during a continuous auditing program or any audit activity for that matter should be clear. Now we shift focus to a technique used by internal audit departments and process excellence teams to identify root cause. This process is known as the "why" approach. You may have also heard it referred to as the "five why" approach. However, I believe that the "why" technique is different from the "five why" approach because the latter approach suggests that the root cause and the solution for a problem can be identified by asking "why" five times. Asking "why" five times will help you to identify the root cause, but it does not seem likely that all root causes will magically appear after five questions. Sometimes root cause identification is much more complicated than just five questions. From my years of internal audit experience, I can tell you with certainty that no predetermined number of questions consistently identify root causes.

The best way to ensure that root cause has been identified consistently is to follow this simple and direct four-step approach:

1. After identifying a difference between the business processing standard and the actual work performed, always remember to validate this condition (what was noted during the testing of controls) with the business owner to ensure it really represents a deviation from the stated policy requirements. There is no sense in dedicating time and effort in performing a root cause analysis if there truly is no exception.

2. After validating the condition, make the effort to obtain a more detailed understanding of the process requirements surrounding the exception condition. Doing this will provide you with the knowledge to facilitate the meeting with the business partner in step 3. If you do not take the time and invest the effort to obtain this critical process knowledge, you will be unable to distinguish relevant from irrelevant facts during the root cause analysis.

3. After you have completed the continuous auditing program or full-scope testing, schedule a meeting with the business owners to discuss root cause. In this meeting, provide a background of the work performed and the condition identified during the testing. Then ask the business owners specifically: "Why do you believe this particular condition exists?" This question with the proper background should allow the business owners, who possess the most detailed knowledge of the process, to answer the question.

4. Keep asking "why" until there are no more "why" questions to be asked. Patience and dedication are needed for auditors to maintain the discipline to ask the same question over and over in an effort to identify the true root cause. At times, business owners may become frustrated, but it is important to keep reminding them of the goal of the exercise: to use this questioning approach to find the true source or root cause of the exception noted. Remember to stress that this exercise is a partnership between auditor and business owner in an effort to strengthen the overall process control environment.

 ## ROOT CAUSE KEYS

Although there are no special secrets to performing a root cause analysis to identify the source of an exception, there are ways to ensure the success of your root cause analysis efforts. These keys are listed next and are in no particular order. Each represents a different concept in the ongoing evaluation of process environments that are tested using the continuous auditing methodology or a full-scope review approach. No matter which method you used to validate the critical controls, these keys provide a useful guide to handling the challenging assignment of root cause analysis and identification:

■ The primary goal of root cause analysis is to identify the source of an exception to create effective corrective actions.
■ To be effective, auditors must dedicate the time and effort necessary to complete the research needed to clearly understand the condition and potential causes of the exceptions.
■ There is always a root cause associated with a noted exception.
■ True root cause analysis takes discipline and dedication.
■ Do not be misled by a symptom of the exception and mistake it for the root cause.
■ Do not accept the first root cause suggested by a business owner.
■ Continue to ask if this reason is the source of the condition identified.
■ Patience and strong communication skills are required to effectively facilitate meetings with business owners.
■ Keep asking "why" until there are no more whys left to ask.
■ You will not have true validation of root cause until subsequent control testing is performed and the original control weakness has been addressed. If issues remain, only a symptom was fixed, not the true root cause.

SUMMARY

The concept of root cause analysis is nothing new to internal audit departments around the world. All departments recognize the critical nature of the successful performance of root cause analysis and work diligently to maintain a high level of compliance when it comes to performing the analysis every time an exception has been identified and validated. With the increased expectations placed on internal audit departments, given scandals that have hurt the business environment in general, root cause analysis plays an even more critical role in ensuring that business units focus on the appropriate corrective actions to address breakdowns or opportunities for improvement identified during continuous and full-scope audits.

Moreover, the continuous auditing methodology has become a critical addition to the internal audit service offerings. Continuous auditing is being used not only to expand audit universe coverage and audit depth but also to assist in the validation of compliance with root cause analysis requirements. As noted earlier, the only way to truly verify that the root cause analysis was performed successfully is to complete subsequent testing on the control weakness originally identified. Instead of creating and re-performing follow-up testing on the control weaknesses noted, internal audit departments are specifically and strategically developing continuous auditing programs to validate the action plan developed to address the original control weakness identified during testing. The continuous auditing program will verify whether a true root cause analysis was completed. If the testing identifies weaknesses in action plan implementation, it will be clear that the action plan originally developed merely addressed a symptom and not the root cause. In this case, the root cause analysis incorrectly identified the source and resulted in addressing a symptom. This additional reason for incorporating a continuous auditing methodology into your audit department not only increases your current audit services but also provides a useful tool to validate the audit process requirements for consistently completing a root cause analysis for every validated exception.

CHAPTER NINE

Continuous Auditing Reporting and Next Steps

 REPORTING AND NEXT STEPS

In this chapter, we identify and discuss the two different formats to consider for the reporting phase of the continuous auditing methodology. With this type of customized audit approach, there are a couple of different options available to formally convey the results of the completed continuous auditing testing. In this chapter, both formats are identified and discussed along with the advantages and disadvantages of using each type of report. The specific nature of a continuous auditing methodology requiring recurring testing causes concern when it comes to reporting because no internal audit department wants to issue more reports. That is why this chapter also covers the creation and distribution of formal reports as well as recommended techniques to assist in the delivery and acceptance throughout the entire continuous auditing program. The other reporting component covered is the five-component approach to developing report exceptions. With the frequency of delivery coupled with the concise report format, it is absolutely necessary that the exception be well written, direct, and clear. To deliver a high-impact report, we break down and explain the five-component approach.

In addition to the reporting process, the chapter reviews the next steps for completing an audit executed under the continuous auditing methodology. Due to the unique requirements of the foundation, approach, and execution phases of the continuous auditing methodology, certain review and documentation steps must take place to ensure all the information detailed in the report are properly supported. No matter what audit is being performed, auditors tend to move onto the next project or audit without completing all of the administrative work needed for subsequent testing and cross-training. These steps include reviewing the approach, documenting testing specifics as needed, and recognizing potential process changes.

 REPORTING OPTIONS

When considering how to report the results of a continuous auditing program, there are two distinct formats to choice from: a formal report or an exception memo. The formal report format provides a more detailed account of the continuous auditing program activities and is based on the same structure as the report for full-scope audits. The exception memo format provides a summary of the continuous auditing activities and resembles a work paper summation more than a formal document used to convey issues noted during an audit. Next we dissect, examine, and explain the required components of each type of report and highlight their key differences.

Formal Report

A formal audit report is, by definition, a document that provides a detailed explanation for the work completed during the continuous auditing program. The objective of this document is to communicate the results of the specific audit work performed by documenting the purpose of the audit and assessing the level of effectiveness of the control(s) tested and the detailed exceptions supporting the overall rating that assesses the strength of the corresponding control environment. At a minimum, this report contains these components:

- Overall opinion
- Audit objectives and corresponding ratings
- Exceptions created with the five-component approach
- Background section describing the business process reviewed

Each of these required components of the formal report plays a critical role in conveying the results of the completed continuous auditing work. The detailed discussion begins with the overall opinion.

Overall Opinion

The overall opinion represents a summary statement evaluating the effectiveness of the control(s) validated during the continuous auditing testing. This opinion is probably the most anticipated and read component of the final report and thus garners the most attention even during the development and discussion phase of the report-generation process. It is important to base the overall opinion on the results of the completed testing. The importance of the overall opinion is shown by its usual location at the beginning of report; sometimes it even forms the very first statement after the report title. With this implied power, it is critically important that the overall opinion be derived from a clearly defined set of ratings that take into consideration the overall risk to the business identified during the execution phase of the continuous auditing methodology. The consistent application of the standard report ratings is one of the biggest challenges auditors face when developing the overall opinion. The goal of having standard report ratings for the overall opinion is to ensure that ratings are consistently applied based on established definitions and not applied on an individual, case-by-case basis based on the responsible auditor's judgment. When judgment becomes the deciding factor in the overall report rating, it will result in not only an inconsistency of application of overall rating but also an increase in the time it takes to generate the final report. It is much simpler to dedicate the time to creating meaningful report ratings instead of wasting the time discussing differences in perspective and judgment when it comes to how effective or ineffective the control environment really is based on the continuous auditing results. As all internal auditors know, when the discussion turns to business process judgment, it is very difficult for the auditor to convince a business owner of their interpretation, simply because the auditors lack the owners business processing experience. The overall opinion should relate back to the effectiveness and efficiency of the control environment based on the risks identified and validated during the continuous auditing testing. This is the type of fact-based discussion the responsible auditor wants to have to explain the reasoning behind the overall opinion of the final report.

Table 9.1 provides an example of overall report opinions. These opinions are the most successful at directly conveying a clear message on rating the effectiveness of the control environment in a continuous auditing report. These opinions are based on overall process risk and are characterized by color rather than words or numbers. Colors are used to direct readers to areas in need of urgent action to address the control deficiency identified during the continuous auditing testing. Also, experience has shown that it is much more difficult for business owners to accept and agree to an overall opinion stating that the business process needs improvement than to accept an overall opinion of "Yellow" indicating that the control environment needs attention to address a gap in the control tested. The use of colors in the overall opinion eliminates endless wording changes required to get business owners to accept the final message.

TABLE 9.1 Continuous Auditing Overall Report Opinions

Color	Opinion
Red	An overall unsatisfactory or unacceptable state of control. The red level of control denotes significant business risk or exposure to the company that requires immediate attention and remediation efforts. The overall control environment does not provide reasonable assurance regarding the safeguarding of assets, reliability of financial records, and compliance with company policies and/or government laws and regulations.
Yellow	A state in which the controls in place need improvement. Failure to improve these controls could lead to an overall unsatisfactory or unacceptable state of control.
Green	An overall satisfactory or acceptable state of control, where risk is minimized and managed. The overall environment provides a high degree of assurance regarding the safeguarding of assets, reliability of financial records, and compliance with company policies and government laws and regulations. Control weaknesses noted, if any, are relatively minor.

Remember that the ultimate goal of the report is to get business owners not only to recognize that there is a gap in the process that needs to be addressed but to also create and implement an action plan focused on the root cause of the problem. Internal audit uses the overall opinion to generate change. Although the explanation for each color rating contains the words most often used in opinions—unsatisfactory, needs improvement, and satisfactory—business owners more readily accept the color rating without even turning to the last page of the report to read the detailed explanation. The reason for this acceptance is that business owners and responsible auditors are focused on the facts and data used in the continuous auditing testing that identified the control weakness. This focus represents a call to action for business owners to accept and address in an effort to strengthen their overall control environment.

At the end of the day, it does not matter if the continuous auditing report has an opinion that is based on colors, numbers, words, or symbols as long as the method is consistently applied and based on the specific risks identified during the execution phase of the continuous auditing methodology. Always remember that the overall opinion given must be supported by the business unit data tested and focused on results; independent readers should not have to make any interpretations to determine the severity of the risk or the level of urgency needed in the corresponding action.

Audit Objectives and Corresponding Ratings

The audit objectives represent an explanation of why that audit was performed and specify individual areas that were jointly determined by the responsible auditor and business process owner based on risk in the foundation phase of the continuous auditing methodology. It is important to note that the audit objectives, no matter how many you have, must be developed from the business objective. There are many times during the foundation phase of the continuous auditing methodology where responsible auditors believe they have sufficient information to develop a successful audit objective when, in reality, they do not truly understand the business objective. It is not that a continuous auditing objective cannot be developed without knowing the business objective; without sufficient business processing knowledge, the corresponding audit objective will not provide the useful, relevant testing results that can be achieved by proper execution of all phases of the continuous auditing methodology. As with any type of audit service, nothing delivers a recognized benefit to the business unit management team unless it is properly planned. The continuous auditing methodology requires an investment of time in order to understand the business process to create strategically targeted audit objectives focused on the key controls supporting the operational business environment.

To ensure that the formal report is complete in its details, it is important to strengthen the overall message by including an individual rating for the each audit objective documented in the report. Doing this helps readers to understand the overall opinion given at the opening of the report. These individual ratings are scored on the same scale as the overall opinion; it is just as critical to ensure that these ratings are scored in the same manner based on risk and exposure that was identified in the testing of the continuous auditing program. Table 9.2 provides one of the most effective ways to not only separate and document the continuous auditing objectives but also provides reference to the color format used to illustrate the corresponding risk rating given to each objective. Each individual objective tested during the audit will be documented in the objectives grid. You can use word column headers as shown in the table or shade the individual columns with their corresponding color for a more impactful display.

In Table 9.2, each of the continuous auditing objectives is documented in the first column. Its corresponding rating, based on the results of the completed testing, is indicated by an "X" in the appropriate column. Again, these color ratings represent how well the business unit succeeded in achieving the listed objective. Business unit management must take a specific action for any objective that receives a yellow or red rating. The use of color in lieu of words in the rating conveys to business owners the sense of urgency needed to address

TABLE 9.2 Continuous Auditing Objectives Rating Table

Continuous Auditing Objectives	Objective Ratings		
	Green	Yellow	Red
Objective 1			X
Objective 2		X	
Objective 3	X		

the cause and reduce and/or eliminate the risk and exposure to the achievement of the overall business objectives.

Exceptions Created with the Five-Component Approach

By the time readers get to the detailed exceptions in the continuous auditing report, they should already have expectations regarding the topic of the exception along with its severity based on the corresponding color rating provided in the objectives table. The exception details must be clear and concise while linking directly to rating of the corresponding objective. Contrary to popular belief, more words do not necessarily equate to a stronger message. The purpose of the exception is not to convince readers that the specific issue should be included in the report. Its true purpose is to provide the necessary information for independent readers to understand and agree that the exception should be included in the report as a way to clarify and support the overall opinion of the continuous auditing testing. Many times internal audit report writers, in an effort to strengthen their message, provide too much detail, which ends up clouding the exception. One of the biggest challenges that audit report writers face, whether for continuous or full-scope audits, is presenting information overload in the final report that ultimately will require an independent reader to interpret. Too much information can cause a reader to miss the true exception detail. Interpretation is the biggest enemy of internal audit reports. At no time in any audit report do you want readers to have to interpret information, especially information pertaining to the overall rating or severity of the exceptions identified in the execution phase.

In order to avoid any need for interpretation, use the five-component approach to construct the exception. The five-component approach for exception development creates a complete message. As is discussed in more detail later in the chapter, the five-component approach includes the condition, criteria, cause, effect, and recommendation. Each component serves a specific purpose in explaining the results of the continuous auditing testing in a clear, concise manner. Also, the five components provide foundations for one another; each one links to the other four in an effort to develop a full-circle exception. This full-circle exception supplies the necessary details to ensure that the exception is clear and can stand independently. Also, not too many words should be required to illustrate and convey the risk and impact of the identified gap between the actual testing performed in the execution phase and the business unit standard identified in the foundation phase. If the overall opinion and the continuous auditing objectives have been rated consistently and the exceptions are built using the five-component approach, independent readers will be able to follow the information and link the exception detail to the objective rating that in turn will tie directly to the overall report opinion.

Background Section Describing the Business Process Reviewed

The final component that should be included in the continuous auditing report is the background. Background, for reporting purposes, is the section that provides a high-level overview of the business unit that partnered with internal audit on the continuous auditing program. Although the background section should be the simplest to create, it usually ends up being one of the hardest sections to draft. Internal auditors experience so many challenges as they create the background section because they tend to include every detail of the business unit function; their assumption is that such a level of detail is necessary for independent readers to understand what the business unit does. In reality, the background section does not have to be at a granular level and explain every task that the target business unit produces. Especially for a continuous auditing program, the background section should be focused on the particular objectives related directly to the controls identified in the foundation phase of the methodology.

When drafting the background section of your continuous auditing report, go back and review the foundation phase details before beginning to write. This quick refresher of the continuous auditing objectives will help you focus on what details need to be included in the background section. The background does not need to be multiple pages or even multiple paragraphs. It should be clear, concise, and focused on providing supporting information explaining what the business unit does in regard to the particular objectives identified in the objectives grid illustrated in Table 9.2. You can validate the clarity of the background by matching the operational business summary in the background to the continuous auditing objectives. Limit any additional information included in the background section to how the business unit

FIGURE 9.1 Continuous Auditing Background Format

Background

Enterprise Process:
Subprocess:
General Background:

operations link to the function or division in which it operates. Figure 9.1 provides a template for internal auditors to develop a focused background for the continuous auditing report.

Exception Memorandum

An exception memorandum is used to communicate the results of the completed continuous auditing testing. This format resembles audit work paper detail more than a formal communication of the continuous audit. The objective of this document is the same as for a formal report in that it is designed to communicate the results of the specific audit work performed. The biggest difference between the formal audit report and the exception memorandum is that the latter does not provide any formal assessment regarding the level of effectiveness of the control environment nor does it document the exceptions. The most attractive component of the exception memorandum, from the business owner's perspective, is that internal audit does not provide an overall opinion based on the work performed during the execution phase of the continuous auditing methodology.

At a minimum, an exception memorandum contains an objective statement and a listing of any discrepancies identified in the execution phase of the continuous auditing program. Each component plays a critical role in conveying the results of the completed continuous auditing work. Next we describe the two necessary components.

Objective Statement

The audit objective represents an explanation to independent readers of what testing was actually performed during the continuous auditing program. This objective statement is directly linked to the targeted area that was determined in the foundation phase of the continuous auditing methodology.

Again, remember that it is critical for the audit objective to be developed from the business objective. The objective statement is direct and usually obtained from the corresponding work paper evidencing the continuous audit work performed.

Unlike the objectives grid in the formal report (illustrated in Table 9.2), the exception memorandum audit objective statement is direct and requires no additional explanation or background. It is a pure statement that repeats the testing objective used in the work paper documentation. Also, this audit objective does not have a corresponding rating as to performance efficiency and effectiveness. It is used as a lead statement to explain specifically why the testing was performed. This is one of the main reasons that internal audit departments prefer to use an exception memorandum as opposed to a formal report to document the continuous auditing testing results: No long explanations are required to support the audit objective, and a rating does not have to be assigned and explained. Without these additional details, the audit objective should take responsible auditors only moments to create; often the testing objective can be taken directly from the work paper documentation. Whether you draft or copy the audit objective from the work papers, remember to verify that it relates directly back to the overall continuous auditing objective and the business objective.

Discrepancy Listing

The discrepancies reporting in the exception memorandum is very different from the exceptions reporting in the formal report format. In the exception memorandum type of continuous auditing report, any discrepancies, identified during the execution phase where the actual work performed does not agree with the business operational standard, are documented in a bulleted format. This summary format lists the raw results that were identified during the testing. This type of summary for exception documentation detail is also known as a laundry list. As in the audit objective for the exception memorandum, here there is no need for details surrounding the testing, sample selection, or work details. Only the discrepancy facts are listed. Also, another significant difference between the exception memorandum and the formal report is that the responsible auditor creating the memorandum does not have to write the identified discrepancies using the five-component approach. As a matter of fact, any internal auditors, regardless of their audit experience, can develop a very successful exception memorandum; all it requires is transferring the continuous auditing testing results verbatim from the work paper to the memorandum for communication to the business owner.

Although the discrepancy listing is not the most well thought out composition of writing due to its lack of supporting details, it still accomplishes the goal of communicating to business owners the results of the continuous auditing program that was executed in their area. The aim is for the discrepancy listing to provide sufficient detail for business owners to understand exactly what was identified during the testing. It is hoped that business owners have the process knowledge to understand the severity of the risk associated with the discrepancies listed in the exception memorandum. The goal, as with any internal audit report, is to convey the noted exceptions to ensure not only that business owners are aware of them but also that they recognize and agree to address the identified gaps.

At the completion of the continuous auditing program, the discrepancies noted must be communicated to business owners so that they can be addressed. Depending on business owner experience and expertise, an exception memorandum may be sufficient to communicate the information; if business owners do not have the ability to recognize the risk and the corresponding action that needs to be developed and implemented to reduce the exposure to the company, then a formal report may have to be used to convey the exception detail and request for corresponding action. There are many factors to consider when determining the type of report to communicate the continuous auditing results. Take into account the advantages and disadvantages of each type of report discussed next before finalizing your continuous auditing methodology as to the report format that will be used consistently to report and obtain the appropriate business owner actions.

ADVANTAGES AND DISADVANTAGES OF REPORT TYPE

As with any internal audit report, there are always different formats responsible auditors can use to communicate the results of the particular testing performed. The choices for the continuous auditing methodology are a formal audit report, just as would be issued for a full-scope audit, or an exception memorandum.

TABLE 9.3 Report Format Advantages and Disadvantages

	Formal Report	Exception Memorandum
Advantages	Provides overall opinion	Quick and easy to create
	Five-component detail for exceptions	Requires no ratings or overall opinion
	Identifies corresponding risk	Informal
	Requires management action	Requires no experience to develop
	Consistent report format	No distribution (usually)
	Taken more seriously	No formal management action
	Distributed	No management buy in needed
	Formal communication	
	Documents specific objectives	
Disadvantages	Requires experience to draft	Lacks detail
	First one is time consuming	Contains no ratings for comparison
	Need management buy-in	No distribution
	Requires risk knowledge and interpretation	Assumption of risk understanding by business owner
	Assigns an overall opinion	No action item accountability
		Addresses risk based on hope

To help evaluate these two distinct reporting formats, Table 9.3 lists advantages and disadvantages for each one. This table is not designed to capture every advantage and disadvantage of the two types of reports but provides a solid outline to make an informed decision. When determining which format will be the most effective for you and your company, consider the advantages and disadvantages listed before making a decision. It is hoped that this table will help you focus on the different aspects of the report formats that correspond to your internal audit department as well as your business unit clients.

REPORTING OPTIONS SUMMARY

A significant amount of information has been provided regarding the different reporting types available for the execution phase of the continuous auditing methodology. However, it is important to note that the objective of any internal audit report format is to convey a need to address a confirmed gap in a business process. The confirmed gap identified reflects a risk to the business unit and the company as a whole. The report's goal is to get an action from business owners to address the cause of the exception noted.

One quick caution regarding the exception memorandum format. I realize that this format appears to be the way to go because it is simple to produce and just regurgitates the testing performed. However, be sure to consider one of the most significant disadvantages with this method: the lack of distribution. If you do not communicate continuous auditing report exceptions to anyone but the process owners, there is a risk that the required action needed to address the cause will not get completed or at least not in a timely manner. But the continuous auditing methodology will follow the approach phase and repeatedly identify the same exceptions that could possibly grow in significance over time. Any identified risk not addressed in a timely manner by business unit management always poses a greater risk the longer the exposure goes unaddressed. Therein lies the challenge. At some point during the continuous auditing execution (month after month), there will be a need to raise the issue to another level in order to get the appropriate action to address the risk. Keep in mind that the business partner involved in the continuous auditing program is not intentionally ignoring the need for action. The business owner wants to address the cause but has many other responsibilities and problems to deal with in the day-to-day business process. And if internal audit has no requirement for a formal action plan and only the business owner is aware of the current exception, it gets reprioritized and moved down on the list of things to do. The need to raise an exception detail to another level will reflect poorly on the business owner who appears to have ignored an identified risk and also hurt the internal audit department's relationship with the business partner involved in the continuous auditing program.

All of these aspects must be considered when deciding on the most appropriate report format to use in your continuous auditing methodology. It is also possible to create a combination report that combines the formal report and the exception memorandum. From my experience, the most effective reporting format for a continuous auditing methodology always is the formal report because it is formal, requires an overall opinion, contains the five-component approach, requires management action, and is distributed. But more than any of these aspects, it keeps the delivering a consistent product out of the internal audit department and that provides a clear message to the business owners, senior management, audit committees, and external parties as to the state of risks identified and the corresponding control environment effectiveness of the business process under review.

In an effort to clarify a couple of the key distinctions in the report selection process, we are going to discuss two specific components that play a significant role in every report but have a particular impact on communicating the findings in the continuous auditing methodology. The two components are report ratings and report distribution.

Report Ratings

Anyone who has spent time in internal audit or has been a partner in an internal audit knows that the rating process is challenging. Whether it is for an overall opinion or an individual audit objective, consistent application of ratings requires a solid knowledge of the business process and associated risks. Implementing standard definitions for the ratings that are to be applied assists the auditors in consistency of rating determination. Ratings in general are a point of angst for business unit owners because the overall rating is drawing a conclusion on the business processing unit's effectiveness in achieving its objectives. Keep in mind that the conclusion being derived usually is based on a sample test performed by an outsider and represents only a fraction of what the business unit processes on a daily basis. At least that is the way business owners see it. To a certain degree, that is a fair assessment of how internal audit executes an audit plan. The details being left out are that the internal audit samples selected are well thought out after a significant effort has been spent on planning and represent testing of the most critical controls supporting the achievement of the business objectives.

All detail aside, it still comes down to assigning a rating to the work performed. In a continuous auditing program, the rating is applied to the specific objective determined during the foundation phase and is based on the results of the testing performed during the execution phase. The rating that is going to be assigned communicates to independent readers the strength of the business unit control environment as it pertains to the objective and corresponding controls tested. Most rating scales have at a minimum three possible ratings: satisfactory, needs improvement, and unsatisfactory. Each rating must have a definition that specifically explains the risk represented when receiving that particular rating.

With all of the details and documentation required for ratings, audit departments have to determine if it is really worth evaluating control environments to this level and then having to explain it to business owners. Except when a satisfactory rating is achieved, responsible auditors will have to expend energy explaining why business owners receive a less-than-satisfactory rating. Providing these explanations is a challenge, especially with continuous auditing reports, because they are completed on the established recurring cycle. To ease the communication and ultimate business unit acceptance of the rating details, some internal audit departments have switched to rating with colors instead of words. The color scale for this type of rating system would be green for satisfactory, yellow for needs improvement, and red for unsatisfactory. Believe it or not, this quick switch helps reduce business owner discussion by a significant amount. It is much easier for a business process owner to accept that their control environment is yellow than to say that the control environment needs improvement. So much time is wasted when it comes to reporting because specific words are being debated and interpreted differently. If you are having those types of discussions, consider making the switch to color ratings instead of words.

A stated rating in the report, whether it is words or colors, provides a specific conclusion from the internal audit department as to the current effectiveness of the control environment in which the continuous auditing testing was completed. This rating can be used by the internal audit department and other internal groups, such as enterprise risk management, to evaluate the overall risk and control effectiveness of the particular business unit reviewed as well as the department, division, or company. Providing a rating on the continuous auditing report also drives consistency from a service delivery standpoint and can be used to summarize and categorize risk across the company.

The alternative of not providing a rating is so attractive because it removes the most contentious component of any internal audit report from the equation. But there are risks to issuing a report without any rating. These risks include, but are not limited to, informal communication, work performed with no conclusion, unknown risk level of process tested, and an interpretation factor of control environment effectiveness. Probably the biggest risk is the interpretation factor that an independent reader is required to apply to the continuous auditing results because no overall opinion has been rendered by the company's control evaluation experts: internal audit. This can be very dangerous. Allowing independent readers to reach their own conclusions can go one of two ways. They can interpret a result as bad when in reality it is not, or they can interpret a result as good when in reality it is not. The challenge is not just in a mistaken interpretation; the bigger exposure is that independent readers could make business decisions based on erroneous interpretations and could cause significant exposure to the business unit or the company. To ensure that there is no opportunity for misinterpretation of continuous auditing testing results, consider including an overall opinion based on risk in your report format.

Table 9.1 can assist you in incorporating color ratings in your continuous auditing report. This is the color rating format that I use for both my continuous auditing methodology and for my full-scope reviews. If you prefer not to use colors, you can still use the explanations included in Table 9.1 since they include the standard satisfactory, needs improvement, and unsatisfactory definitions with each corresponding color. However, I recommend utilizing the color rating system as it is easier on business owners and more versatile in high-level reporting.

Report Distribution

Distribution is the other specific component to be discussed in relation to the continuous auditing report. Distribution is the process by which the report is sent out to other parties in addition to the business process owner. Distribution seems straightforward and easy to understand, but often it is not performed during the execution phase of the continuous auditing methodology. Many internal audit departments believe one of the best ways to gain acceptance of the continuous auditing methodology is by telling business owners that the report will not be distributed to anyone other than themselves. The responsible auditor and the business owner agree to discuss discrepancies identified during testing and not to discuss the results externally.

Although this may seem like a good approach, it can cause significant challenges long term. To illustrate the point, consider this example. A continuous auditing program has been launched in a department, and the business owner and the responsible auditor make an agreement that the report will not be distributed to anyone other than the process owner. Note that it does not matter what type of report the continuous auditing methodology is slated to issue. The only item to focus on in this example is that the final report will *not* be distributed. Also, for this example, consider that we are dealing with a continuous auditing objective that has transactions occurring multiple times every day and that the testing frequency will be "6-9-12," as described in Chapter 5. This frequency requires testing to be executed for the first six consecutive months and then at the end of month 9 and month 12. In our example, testing in the first month reveals no reportable issues. The continuous auditing report is issued and indicates no reportable issues; everyone is positive about the results. However, in month 2, the testing identifies a reportable control weakness. The weakness is supported by the testing and validated with the business owner. Everyone agrees it is an exception, and it is documented in the report and provided to the business owner for remediation. In month 3, testing shows the same exception noted in the prior month. This is not uncommon; it usually takes 60 days to recognize a change in the continuous auditing testing results. The month 3 report is issued and accepted by the business owner. In month 4, the responsible auditor expects that the testing results will show an improvement. After completing month 4 testing, however, the responsible auditor not only does not see any improvement but also notices that the exception has gotten worse. After discussing the results with the business owner, the responsible auditor realizes that control improvements are not going to be coming anytime soon and the exception details need to be communicated to the next level to ensure the risk gets properly addressed. With this recognition, the responsible auditor must now tell the business owner that the prior results are going to be communicated to a distribution, which will include additional parties outside the business unit to assist in obtaining the proper attention to address the issues noted. This "betrayal" (from the business owner's point of view) will cause a significant relationship problem between internal audit in general and the business unit.

Unfortunately, in this example, expanding the continuous auditing report distribution is the only way to ensure that the control exception will be addressed. It is difficult for any process owner to commit to an action plan without formal accountability and the knowledge that other individuals in the company are aware of the issue and are expecting a remedy to be created and implemented. Undistributed continuous auditing reports do not receive the proper attention due to lack of accountability.

A secondary challenge arises when continuous auditing reports are not distributed. Other independent readers, especially senior management in the business area being reviewed, are going to wonder why this is the first time they are hearing about the continuous auditing work and report being performed in their area. This newly revealed audit activity causes stress not only in the internal audit department but also in the targeted business area. Relationships across the board suffer as a result of the newly distributed continuous auditing results, especially because the report will identify three consecutive months of unsatisfactory testing pertaining to a critical process control.

The best way to avoid this reporting dilemma is to communicate with business owners up front and let them know that the continuous auditing methodology requires that a report be created and distributed to business owners and at least one level above to ensure that there is strong communication surrounding the newly implemented continuous auditing activity. To ease business unit owners' distribution concerns, let them know that in the "6-9-12" frequency model, they and one level above receive a report each month; a full distribution, such as that which occurs with a full-scope audit, takes place on a quarterly basis. If you prefer, you can distribute the continuous auditing report fully only twice a year, at midyear and year-end. Whatever you decide, you must clearly document the full distribution requirements in your continuous auditing methodology and follow them consistently for all continuous audits executed under the "6-9-12" frequency model.

It should not be surprising that the two critical components that we have discussed in detail are the ratings and distribution of the continuous auditing reports. These are the two components of any audit report that business owners fear the most. If you told business owners you were going to rate every audit report you gave them but would never tell anyone else, they would be fine with receiving a red or unsatisfactory on every audit. If you told them every audit report would be fully distributed but not rated, they would be fine with that as well. However, once audit reports are rated and then fully distributed, business owners become increasingly concerned about every word used to describe the state of the current control they own. It is understandable that business owners are concerned about how their department or operation is portrayed in the continuous auditing report, especially given the frequency at which the report is scheduled to be generated. To reassure business owners, let them know that the continuous auditing methodology is designed to deliver proactive audit results that are focused on partnering with business units to identify opportunities for improvement. Reports are critical components of delivering quality results. Remember to say that all continuous audits are reported in the same fashion so business owners recognize that one business unit could never be treated differently from another.

FIVE-COMPONENT APPROACH

The five-component approach is the most effective way to describe and explain the details surrounding an exception identified during the execution phase of the continuous auditing methodology. When properly explained, the components convey a complete message to all readers, regardless of their knowledge of the subject or involvement in the continuous auditing program that was executed. In addition, the five-component approach provides the appropriate level of detail so that readers do not have to interpret the results. As mentioned, the five components to be explained are the condition, criteria, cause, effect, and recommendation.

Condition

In the five-component approach, the condition, which should be one of the more straightforward components to document, often poses a challenge to internal auditors. In its simplest form, the condition is a statement of pure fact that details exactly what was identified during the execution phase of the continuous auditing methodology. Condition represents a captured moment in time that documents the results of the testing specifics from the scope detailed in the approach phase. The condition statement should repeat almost verbatim whatever was identified in the testing. For example, a condition statement for account reconciliation testing should read: "There was no evidence of supervisory approval for 10 of the 25 account reconciliations tested." The condition is straight-forward and direct.

Think of the condition as the data results of the testing. This statement should focus on the data. Auditors should not have to interpret how to present the condition. The condition is in no way an opinion. Its sole purpose in the five-component approach is to document the specific, validated exceptions revealed during the testing.

Many times internal auditors struggle with writing the condition because they are using the condition statement to convince readers that the exception should be in the report. By the time responsible auditors are preparing to draft the audit report, however, there should be no reason to do so. Auditors should have discussed and validated why an exception is in an audit report during the execution phase of the continuous auditing methodology. The draft report is a formality that documents all of the completed work previously reviewed and validated with the process owner.

Criteria

Criteria makes up the second component of the five-component approach, and is by far the easiest to document. The standard or process requirement, established by business unit management detailing how the current process is supposed to be performed, makes up the criteria. The criteria is the easiest to document because it is the same exact standard that was identified in the approach phase of the continuous auditing methodology when the testing criteria was developed. The criteria represents the specific standard that the selected sample tested was verified against. Without knowing the processing standard, the continuous auditing program could not have been executed. When developing the criteria component for the exception detail, review the work paper documentation and use the criteria that was incorporated in the testing to determine the effectiveness and efficiency of the processing control environment.

Another point to remember regarding criteria development is that the criteria can be established only from one of two places: internally as a result of a business management decision regarding processing needs or externally as a result of a local, state, or federal regulation. Beware of adjusting the processing criteria or standards of an externally set regulation or rule to be more stringent than the current rules require. If the business unit adjusts the criteria of an external rule, that new criteria becomes the standard and must be adhered to in the processing requirements. As an example, consider an external rule that mandates three days to complete a specific financial transaction. The business unit processing these types of transactions would like to set a higher standard; accordingly, it sets the internal policy and procedure at two days to complete the specific transaction. Then two days becomes the criteria that must be validated. Even though it is not a federal violation to process the same type of transaction in two days, it is still an exception to the established standard for both internal audit and external regulators. The lesson here is to accept externally generated criteria and not change already stringent requirements. If a company would like to complete the transaction in a shorter period of time, you can track the efficiency, but there is no need to change the criteria.

As you develop criteria, remember that it will become the standard to which testing is executed in determining compliance with the current policy and procedures. The criteria will be plainly stated in the exception detail in order to provide readers with the benchmark that the condition statement should be measured. Think of the criteria as the acceptable range of performance that the business process must comply with to achieve satis-factory results.

For example, the criteria statement for account reconciliation testing condition noted above should read: "Account reconciliations must be reviewed and approved by a supervisor according to company policy 210." The criteria statement should be as detailed as possible and when available, include the actual policy or regulation details.

Cause

The third component of the exception documentation is the cause. Cause represents the specific detailed reason why the condition exists. In even simpler terms, cause answers the question of why the condition was found. As I write this explanation, it appears to me that to document cause, the auditor should apply logic to determine why something else occurred. But the cause component remains one of the biggest pitfalls in the documentation of exception detail. Cause is the most difficult component to identify correctly. During any audit service—whether it is a continuous auditing program or a full-scope audit—all parties involved appear to know the exact reason why the condition exists. The responsible auditor believes the cause is clear based on the testing results; business owner believes the cause is something totally different. What is the best approach to finding the cause or reason that the condition exists?

The first lesson in determining the specific cause of the exception is to stop trying to identify the reason why condition exists and focus on identifying the *root cause* of the exception. "Root cause" is a frequently misunderstood term that is used by internal audit departments when discussing the documentation of audit issues. Root cause by definition is the bottom-line reason why a particular condition has been identified. Determining root cause takes time and discipline. Business owners often become frustrated when auditors try to identify the true root cause for the condition. Make no mistake: Root cause analysis is not a quick or easy process.

Determining the root cause of a condition requires auditors to dedicate effort and time to work with business owners to understand the condition statement and discuss the potential reasons why condition exists. Both responsible auditors and business owners must commit to identifying the true root cause. Root cause identification is such a significant challenge because many times the data tested appear to reveal the cause although business owners provide alternative reasons why the standard was not achieved. The most common way to verify that the root cause has truly been identified is to apply the "why" methodology. The "why" methodology requires participants to question the condition statement repeatedly until there are no more "why" questions to be asked. Once there are no more "why" questions, the root cause has been identified. Discipline is required to keep questioning until you find the root cause. It is easy just to accept the answer to the first question and assume that is the root cause; more often than not, however, the first answer is never the root cause of the condition that was found. It is probably obvious why the process to find root cause can be frustrating to business owners; at times during the questioning it will appear that the auditors do not believe anything that the business owners are saying. That is not the case. The key to avoiding frustration is to take a moment before beginning the questioning to explain the "why" methodology, what it entails, and the reason it is such a critical step in identifying the root cause.

Focus on the root cause and continue to question business owners in an effort to find the true bottom-line reason why an exception condition exists. The continuous auditing methodology is unique because the established frequency component naturally validates the performance of the root cause analysis. As the testing is repeated, subsequent testing should begin to produce more positive results. If the future tests do not provide validation that the condition has been addressed, it will signify that an incomplete root cause analysis was performed. This confirmation further validates that only a symptom of the condition was addressed by the business owner's original action plan and not the root cause. Remember to stay focused and dedicated to identifying the root cause and use the continuous auditing methodology to verify the effectiveness of the root cause analysis.

For example, the cause statement for account reconciliation testing condition noted above should read: "Supervisors were not reviewing the reconciliations on a consistent basis." To truly determine the validity of this cause statement, the responsible auditor must determine if there were any specific reasons for the supervisors not complying with the established company policy.

Effect

The effect component of the exception detail is what is called the validation statement. Without an effect statement, there is no reportable issue. The effect component validates the reason that this particular exception is being included in the final report. This component is also the factor considered when trying to determine whether an exception is truly reportable or just should be communicated to the business owner. Exceptions that are documented in the final continuous auditing report are those that provide significant risks or exposures that could be realized based on the testing results.

By definition, the effect component is the specific response to the question "So what?" The moment the responsible auditor approaches the business owner with a validated exception, owners will ask: "So what?" Auditors must be prepared for this question and provide an adequate response as to the risk and exposure to the process based on the testing data and not an opinion. The effect statement should never be based on an auditor's judgment but rather the specific testing data that led to the discussion of risk. Remember to use the continuous auditing testing data to drive the discussion. It is very difficult for business owners to dispute their work, and that is exactly what the testing data represents. The results of testing discrepancies supporting the condition must indicate an exposure and impact on the process controls being evaluated. Focus the discussion of effect on how the condition impacts the execution of the process, whether it is related to timing, accuracy, or another reason. The effect component must be specific and when possible quantified. Contrary to popular belief, not all effect statements have to be quantified in dollars. A significant effect can be directly related to performance accuracy that has no direct dollar impact but prevents the timely completion of a process and results in a dollar loss.

In the five-component approach, although, the cause component requires the most diligence and discipline, the effect component is the most contested because auditors are trying to describe the potential impact that the condition may cause while business owners are providing alternative reasons why it is not as significant. Ensure that the effect is well thought out and clearly links to the condition and cause component of the exception detail. Remember that without an identifiable impact on the business process, there is no effect; in such cases, the exception should not be included in the continuous auditing report.

For example, the effect statement for account reconciliation testing condition noted above should read: "A lack of supervisory review could result in inaccurate account reporting and possible misappropriation of funds." The impact statement identifies the possible outcome of the process risk not being addressed.

Recommendation

The recommendation is the final component of the five-component approach and represents a suggestion as to how to address the identified cause. The recommendation does not represent an exact action plan that the business owner is going to take to address the cause (root cause). The recommendation component must address the root cause. Too often, internal audit departments and sometimes business owners try to create both a recommendation and an action plan to eliminate root cause. The goal of the recommendation is to address the root cause, not eliminate it. Elimination is not the goal of the recommendation or subsequent action plan developed because usually it is not feasible or cost effective to eliminate the root cause. In the recommendation component, auditors address the root cause in an effort to bring the corresponding risk to an acceptable level. This step also communicates the corresponding benefit to business owners so they clearly understand why the specific recommendation is being presented. It is important to explain to business owners that the recommendation is a guide to assist the business owners in creating an action plan. Ultimately, the development of the final action plan to be proposed to address root cause is up to the business unit as they are the group with the most intimate process knowledge and thus more qualified to create the appropriate action.

 NEXT STEPS

Internal audit departments all over the world struggle with finalizing the details of file completion especially once the final report has been formally distributed. However, some significant steps are required to complete the continuous auditing methodology. These steps, in addition to the usual documentation requirements for the file, include three key components that are different and unique to a continuous audit as opposed to a regular audit. The required steps are an approach review, testing nuance review, and process changes review. Each step has a specific objective linked to the continuous auditing methodology and is required on every continuous audit executed, even if it is being performed monthly.

Approach Review

Upon completion of the continuous auditing testing, the specific testing approach is reviewed (especially during the first month of testing) to ensure that the testing approach created is directly linked to the continuous auditing objective developed in the foundation of the methodology. The first month of testing is critical because all subsequent continuous testing performed is executed with the same program, which only increases the reliance on the dedicated performance of the business process validation targeted by the continuous auditing program. The goal of the approach review is to ensure that there is a direct link among the critical components of the continuous auditing methodology: objective, scope, sampling, testing attributes, and results.

The approach review validates the value of the continuous auditing methodology phase requirements in an effort to deliver a quality, useful product to business owners. If built correctly (which the approach review will verify), the continuous auditing methodology will confirm to business owners that the selected control(s) tested are operating as intended as long as the work is performed in accordance with the phase requirements.

Testing Nuance Review

The objective of the testing nuance review is to document any anomalies identified during the first few months of executing the continuous auditing methodology. There are instances when the sampling, information or data gathering, or testing execution requires a distinct process or technique. Another example of a testing nuance that should be identified is if business owners have a particular request or challenge the method or even location where the continuous auditing testing takes place. Any of these testing nuances should be formally documented in the continuous auditing work papers so that the next responsible auditor to execute the testing is aware of any potential challenges with performing the work. The goal of the testing nuance documentation is to compile a detailed profile of testing requirements in an effort to become more effective and efficient in subsequent months of continuous auditing testing. This simple step does not take a significant amount of time but provides a huge value to the audit department over the course of the continuous auditing program.

Process Changes Review

One of the most significant differences between the continuous auditing methodology and a full-scope audit methodology is the frequency of the testing. Since the planning for a full-scope audit happens every 12 to 18 months for a high-risk area, there is always a review of the process to ensure that the existing documentation represents the current operational process. Conversely, the continuous auditing program is executed on a monthly basis for the "6-9-12" frequency audit. To ensure that the work performed provides the value as promised, it is critically important to verify each and every month that the control(s) being validated have not changed in any way. If the targeted key controls have changed since the previous month, any subsequent work executed will not provide valid the effectiveness of the controls. Always remember to take a moment to verify, prior to testing execution in the following period, that no significant process changes occurred that could impact the source or objective to be tested. The good news regarding the process change verification step is that if the continuous auditing foundation phase was executed in accordance with the methodology, there should not be a change to the testing because only rarely do key controls change. Because of the importance of key controls in a business process, it is not likely that they will be changed. However, it has happened; so you must be diligent to verify each month to ensure that the continuous auditing testing approach is still valid.

SUMMARY

Two different formats to communicate audit results were discussed in this chapter. The two options provide internal audit departments with a choice on how to convey what was identified during the execution phase. Both formats have advantages and disadvantages; each internal audit department will have to determine which report format will complement its current audit methodology and clearly communicates what was identified during the continuous auditing testing. The recurring testing requirements of the continuous auditing methodology causes immediate concerns with internal audit groups because no audit team wants to issue more reports than are absolutely necessary. The frequency at which the continuous auditing report is issued and distributed is up to the discretion of each individual group. Once the internal audit department has adopted a specific report format, frequency, and distribution for its continuous auditing methodology, it must apply it consistently for all business owners. There can be no deviation from the approved execution phase requirements; inconsistency of application will prove detrimental to the effort to build audit/client relationships.

The supporting topic to report format discussed in this chapter was the five-component approach that is required for high-impact continuous auditing report development. The five-component approach provides the necessary discipline for communication of confirmed critical process risks. Without the five components, the exception detail does not describe the exception noted and leads to interpretation from independent readers. As stated, interpretation is the biggest enemy of audit reports. Due to the required frequency of delivery coupled with the concise report format, it is absolutely necessary that the exception be well written, direct, and clear. To achieve the delivery of a high-impact report, the five-component approach must be used to detail all reportable issues noted. Be careful not to include in a final report exceptions that do not have a specific impact to the business process. In order to be reportable, there must be a recognized risk, as detailed in the condition statement, and a corresponding impact, as documented in the effect statement.

The temptation to move on to another project always exists once any type of final report has been issued; however, it is a continuous auditing methodology requirement that the post audit steps detailed in this chapter be performed. The approach review, testing nuances, and process change validation steps do not require a significant amount of additional time but are necessary to ensure not only the completeness of the continuous auditing file but also to provide coaching notes for any auditor who performs subsequent testing. The unique requirements of the foundation, approach, and execution phases of the continuous auditing methodology dictate the necessity for these review steps to ensure completeness and strength of supporting documentation. This supporting documentation impacts both the work that has been performed and the work that will be performed to complete the continuous auditing methodology requirements.

CHAPTER TEN

Action Plans

 ACTION PLANS

In this chapter, we identify and discuss the keys to obtaining focused action plans from the business process owners at the conclusion of the execution phase of the continuous auditing methodology. So much time and effort is spent developing, planning, and executing a detailed continuous auditing program that is it critical to remember to partner with the business process owner to create a specific action plan designed to address the root cause of the exception identified during testing. There is nothing more frustrating, disappointing, and disheartening for an internal audit team than being pushed to complete the continuous auditing work and then not having business unit management held accountable for delivering an action plan focused on the root cause.

If a formal action is not required as part of the continuous auditing methodology, it will be very difficult for the responsible auditor and the internal audit department to develop, implement, and maintain a successful continuous auditing methodology. Even if in the most obvious testing scenarios where the continuous auditing program repeatedly produces negative results, sometimes no formal action plan is developed until the problem is elevated to a senior management level. Although the action plan eventually is developed, no internal audit department wants to have to go to senior management each time it needs a formal action plan to address exceptions.

To ensure that appropriate action plans are obtained on every completed continuous audit, include a specific requirement in the execution phase of the continuous auditing methodology. Also be sure that the methodology details and expectations are shared, in advance, with the business unit management team. With this detailed exchange of the process requirements, there should be no doubt regarding the expectations of providing action plans to address validated process improvement opportunities. To assist in facilitating these audit/client discussions, this chapter highlights the keys to obtaining true actions on your continuous auditing programs. The topics to be covered included a root cause refresher, action plan development, real action components, and suggestions for actively following up on existing action plans.

ADDRESSING ROOT CAUSE

Although root cause analysis had a dedicated chapter (Chapter 8) and was discussed as part of the five-component approach in Chapter 9, it is important to provide one more aspect to complete the knowledge transfer regarding the critical nature of this concept when it comes to the development of a focused action plan. As discussed, the action to be developed must address the root cause. This section spends a moment discussing the concept of "addressing" rather than eliminating root cause.

During a continuous auditing program when discrepancies are identified, business process owners look for a solution to eliminate or get rid of the reason for the exception. This is a common response because process owners do not want to have exceptions in their process and truly believe that they will be judged based on the accuracy and performance of their respective teams. Although this may be the case, it is almost impossible for any process owner to totally eliminate all exceptions from a process, especially a process that requires any human interaction. A zero exception rate is nearly impossible and not the way business processes operate. So why would someone want to try to come up with an action plan to eliminate root cause when, in reality, the responsible auditor is looking for an action plan that will address the root cause focused on bringing the corresponding process risk into a more acceptable level. The goal of addressing root cause is to find the acceptable level of processing efficiency, not to try and eliminate root cause. Process risk is normal and expected. The goal of a true action plan is to address the root cause while maintaining a strong control environment focused on consistently achieving the stated business objectives effectively and efficiently.

As discussed in Chapter 8 and 9, root cause is a critical component of the continuous auditing process, and this is a reminder to focus the corresponding action plan on addressing the root cause to a level that is acceptable not only to business process owners but also to the responsible auditor who will provide an independent, unbiased opinion of the suggested action. Keep in mind that the responsible auditor is accountable for reviewing and challenging any proposed action to validate that it will address the root cause. If the planned action is not complete or adequate, the responsible auditor must reject the action and work with the business process owner to develop a more appropriate action. Internal auditors do not really want such responsibilities, but they are in the best position to honestly assess suggested action plans because they have just completed the continuous auditing program and are intimately familiar with the exception details.

 ## CREATING THE PERFECT ACTION

When faced with the responsibility of developing an action plan, there is always a temptation to try and create one that is so complete that it will address every possible business scenario. Sometimes business process owners and even auditors become so focused on different exception details that directing their efforts toward finding a root cause solution becomes extremely difficult. This attempt to develop a perfect action is counterproductive and ultimately ends up wasting a significant amount of time. Imagine the time and effort it would take to discuss and review multiple action plans to address a root cause identified from the testing of one key control. At what point does the repeated discussion of possible actions plans become an exercise in futility? Due to the specific time requirements of the continuous auditing methodology, there is not a significant amount of extra time available to consider multiple different action plans. Also, if you are ever in this situation, it will become apparent that the different action plans are very similar (and possibly the same); the necessary steps just may be in an alternate order. If you realize you are in that type of discussion, take a stand to ensure that the similarities are revealed and direct the focus back to addressing the identified root cause.

From my experience in six different internal audit departments over 20-plus years, I can tell you without hesitation that there is no perfect action to address any identified root cause. The perfect action does not exist. Sometimes business owners argue that a new system will correct all of the processing exceptions noted during the continuous auditing review. The special system that fixes everything also does not exist. Trust me. I have heard business owners say this it many, many times; each time something is supposed to fix the noted exceptions and the corresponding root causes, it fails. Why? Because each business process is unique and has its own risks that require the business process to be analyzed and then strategically addressed. If a perfect system fix or ultimate action was available, it could signal the end of the internal audit profession as we know it. However, we auditors know that due to the strategic differences in company objectives, cultures, and risk tolerances, no perfect action plan or system can cure every business exception. Work to keep your business process owners focused on the requirements of the continuous auditing methodology; by doing so, they will develop and implement the appropriate actions.

To ensure that business process owners stay focused on addressing the root cause with their corresponding targeted action plans, there is no need to search and develop the perfect action especially during the execution of a continuous auditing program. The continuous auditing methodology has a built-in validation process to ensure that the suggested action is working as designed. That validation is the continuation of the planned recurring testing. The testing will be executed according to the methodology. If the proper root cause analysis and corresponding action were completed as described, subsequent testing will prove it. Conversely, if the root cause analysis was flawed or the business owner tried to implement a "perfect" action, subsequent testing will indicate that the problem's root cause has not been properly addressed and the risks identified during the execution phase are still apparent in the subsequent months of testing. At times the apparently "perfect" action gets implemented and initially appears to address the identified root cause but ultimately ends up impacting process effectiveness, efficiency, or accuracy farther down in the process details. Auditors must challenge all action plans suggested by business owners to verify their appropriateness. This extra step will help ensure that the action plan is appropriately linked to the root cause.

The continuous auditing methodology is a targeted approach to testing the key control(s) supporting a business process. With such an approach, the action taken to address the exception details noted should be just as focused as the selection process was for the key controls tested. Therefore, when it comes time to evaluate the root cause and build an action plan, do not look for the most comprehensive action which supposedly will correct every problem. Identify the most appropriate action to address the root cause and implement it.

Symptom Fixes

Just like creating the perfect action is a temptation, the rush to implement a quick fix is even more of a temptation. Every person, especially from the business unit, believes they understand what it will take to correct the exceptions noted during the continuous auditing program. The development of action plans that address symptoms of the exception rather than the root cause identified during testing are very common and the direct result of incorrect assumptions. The information and data compiled during the specific phases of the continuous auditing methodology provide the necessary background to describe the exception characteristics as well as the five-component detail for the development of the corresponding action plan. However, if the compiled information is not used to discuss and create the action plan, assumptions will be made as to how to fix the problem. These assumption or quick fixes will address only symptoms of the root cause, not the root cause itself.

Believe it or not, symptom or quick fixes are more common with continuous auditing programs than with other typical audit services. This occurs because the continuous auditing methodology requires the development of a targeted focus on one or two key controls and the corresponding exceptions noted appear to require an obvious solution to address the issue. Contrary to popular belief, there are no shortcuts in identifying the root cause or the associated action plan needed because the execution phase tested only a single control. Regardless of the number of controls tested or the type of audit executed, the action plan must not focus only on the root cause; it must be examined to ensure it is not a quick fix to address a symptom and not the true root cause, which more appropriately represents the reason the exception(s) exist. Unfortunately, often both business process owners and responsible auditors alike believe that they both have the remedy to the noted exception. This assumption of solution knowledge usually is attained without the proper level of research and analysis of the supporting documentation. Remember that action plan development is a combined effort between responsible auditors who executed the continuous auditing program and business process owners. Their aggregate knowledge of the exception details (from the responsible auditors) and intimate business knowledge (from the business process owners) will ensure that the proposed action plan adequately addresses the root cause, not just a symptom of the overall problem identified during testing.

Another unfortunate aspect of a symptom fix, as opposed to the true root cause action plan, is that subsequent testing may not immediately reveal that the symptom fix did not address the root cause. It may take a couple of months of recurring testing to reveal that the exception originally noted still exists. In addition, it is quite possible that the symptom fix has exacerbated the risk associated with the original exception. In these cases, the symptom fix not only masked the existence of the original exceptions but also created a more complicated issue that will require additional time, effort, and resources to examine. Additional effort is necessary because the auditors must review the current situation along with the supporting work papers that initially identified a similar problem. Symptom fixes appear to be appropriate action plans but ultimately end up resulting in additional risk and exposure to the business process.

Missing Cause for Condition

The condition and cause were identified and explained in detail in Chapter 9 during the five-component discussion. Both of those components play a key role in determining the action plan to be developed. Remember that the condition represents the pure statement of fact describing exactly what was identified during the execution phase of the continuous auditing methodology; the cause represents the bottom-line reason why the particular condition noted exists. In reviewing internal audit reports, regardless of the type of audit executed, it is sometimes difficult for independent readers to differentiate between the condition and the cause. That is why the five-component approach is so critical in the communication of the results of the continuous auditing program.

However, there is always the risk that an action plan is developed that addresses the condition, not the root cause. This is a common mistake and often is the result of not taking sufficient time to understand the five-component approach before discussing exception specifics with business process owners. The condition is the component that initiates the discussion surrounding root cause and the corresponding action plan. However, sometimes during initial discussions of root cause—discussions that should occur only after process owners confirm that the condition is truly an exception—potential solutions start to be introduced. Somewhere in the discussion of the condition component of the exception and root cause considerations, the focus switches to action plan development. When this shift in topic occurs so early, the action plan being developed is likely to be linked directly to the condition, not to the root cause. This exact scenario is common, especially with business unit owners who do not have a significant amount of experience with internal audit and with the introduction of a new audit approach, such as the continuous auditing methodology. The main reason the problem occurs with inexperienced owners is that auditors do not spend a lot of time explaining the audit approach require-ments regarding development of the most effective action plans and how critical it is that they address root cause. As we know, if the root cause is addressed, the condition will be eliminated or reduced to an acceptable level of risk. As opposed to the reason it happens with the introduction of the continuous auditing methodology is that the approach being so much shorter and direct in execution easily links to the action plan being directly focused on addressing the specific exception identified by the responsible auditor.

Remember that no matter what audit methodology was executed, how long it took for an exception to be identified, or how big or small the reportable issue appears, the action plan to be developed must link directly to the root cause, not to the condition. Creating an action plan that addresses the condition will provide a temporary solution to the exception but will not address the root cause or the associated risk. Sometimes auditors make recommendations linked to the condition, not the root cause; such situations result in a domino effect of business process owners creating an action plan that addresses the condition, not the root cause. Internal audit departments must be aware of the importance of the five-component approach and its impact on not just the reporting responsibility of communicating the exception but also the action plans that will be developed to address the specific issues noted as a result of the continuous auditing testing.

Management Buy-in

Since the internal audit department is not responsible for developing and ultimately building the action plan, the business process owners must buy into the documented exception component details. The most effective action plans are the ones where business process owners and responsible auditors work in partnership to ensure that the plans are appropriate.

To facilitate this partnership and obtain management buy-in of the action plan development process, it is critical that responsible auditors have a solid understanding of the continuous auditing methodology requirements. This understanding is crucial because the partnership development between audit and client is not just about looking at the cause and asking business process owners what they are going to do about the problem found during continuous auditing testing. The partnership is based on a high level of communication and sharing. This communication begins with a review of the continuous auditing program that was just executed in an effort to provide a foundation for discussing the condition. The condition statement facilitates the process of identifying the root cause. Without the root cause, it is not possible to create an appropriate action plan. Without a root cause discussion, action plans get incorrectly linked to the condition and not the root cause. Once the root cause has been identified and jointly agreed between auditors and owners, the process of determining how to address the root cause can begin. Only with this type of dedicated discussion regarding the continuous auditing methodology and five-component approach can true action plans be created with the right level of business unit management support.

Without business process owner support and buy-in, the action plan developed, no matter how well thought out or detailed, ultimately will fail. This lack of agreement or commitment by the business process owner is probably the only facet of the internal audit process where the end result cannot be helped by the auditors assigned to complete the continuous auditing program. Any auditor on any audit assignment can never be involved in the business process owner's implementation of corrective action. The internal audit department must remain independent in its execution of audit services and report deviations from standards and practices as well as the corrective actions created to address those deviations.

Remember to work in partnership with business process owners to obtain their buy-in for all action plans developed. Doing so will facilitate the timely implementation of the appropriate actions needed to correct the exceptions noted. The goal of action plan development focused on the root cause and management buy-in is to ensure that only real actions are created by business process owners as well as reviewed and approved by the responsible auditor who completed the continuous auditing testing.

COMPONENTS OF A REAL ACTION PLAN

Action plans are a critical aspect of every internal audit and play a crucial role in the continuous auditing methodology because of the recurring nature of the testing and the targeted focus on the testing performed. Given the challenging time frames associated with the execution phase of the continuous auditing program, the action plan, provided by business process owners, must be developed specifically and implemented accurately to ensure that the subsequent continuous auditing testing will produce positive results. To obtain the type of action that will ensure that the root cause gets addressed properly, the action plan must contain the key components of real action. Action plans that contain these components are called real actions because, when implemented as designed and approved, they produce real results. There are three components of a real action plan: a true owner, cause-specific action, and a realistic, achievable target date. The challenge to business process owners and responsible auditors are whether the partnership between the two is strong enough to stay focused and dedicated to produce a real action plan. The discussion begins with the true owner component.

True Owner

Every action plan ever developed as a result of an internal audit has an individual identified as the owner of the action plan; this person also is specifically identified in the final audit report as the responsible party for overseeing the implementation of the corresponding action plan. The question that should be asked is whether the responsible party assigned as the owner can truly implement the specific action plan requirements in the final report. If responsible owners can implement the action plan as it was designed in a timely manner, they would be considered a true action item owner.

The true action item owner has two distinct characteristics: ability and authority. A true action item owner has the *ability* to make the action happen. Many times the person initially assigned as the owner does not understand all of the steps that may be required to implement the action. This person usually ends up being overwhelmed with the task and ultimately does not accomplish the goal or interprets the action in his or her own way and implements a different version of the originally agreed-on action. This new or revised action will not address the root cause properly and will result in at least a repeat exception in subsequent testing and possibly an increase in the associated risk. It is the responsible auditors' job to ensure that action item owners identified in the report clearly understand the corresponding action as well as the details surrounding the exception requiring it.

True action item owners also must have the *authority* to make the action happen. This means that they have the power to assign resources, prioritize assigned work, and identify other business process team members who must participate in the implementation of the corrective action. Without this level of authority, plus strong communication and organization skills, the action plan will not be implemented by the target date and possibly not ever depending on the support at the top of the company hierarchy. Too often individuals on a business processing team are assigned an internal audit action item when they do not have the authority to bring the action from the drawing table to reality. Authority is just as important as ability when it comes to successful implementation of an action plan.

The combination of ability and authority are particularly important for action item owners who are responsible for a continuous auditing program action plan. The ability and authority of the assigned owner indicates that the business process management team is engaged and has accepted the core objectives of the continuous auditing methodology. It also shows that the team wants to partner with internal audit to proactively address opportunities for improvement. Also, remember that continuous auditing testing must be performed according to strict time frames. With such tight time frames, it is imperative that action item owners clearly understand the exception detail and recognize what it will take to make the action real.

Cause-Specific Action

Although it has been mentioned a couple of times so far, it is important to note once again that the specified action plan must address the root cause. Having an action plan that is focused on the true root cause (jointly identified by business process owners and responsible auditors) is the second component of a real action. Symptom fixes or condition-focused action plans may appear as viable solutions to the noted exception details, but, in reality, their implementation will not produce improved results in the subsequent testing performed. And even though the continuous auditing methodology will identify that the implemented action plan was not focused on the root cause. Under this scenario, it could take a couple of months before the incorrect, incomplete, or inappropriate action is discovered. Also, this detective discovery will require additional time to be dedicated to the forensic effort needed to research and review previous work and root cause analysis.

It cannot be stressed enough how important it is for you, as the responsible auditor, to spend time explaining exception component details to business process owners when requesting the associated action plan. Also, remember to challenge process owners when you feel that the suggested action plan may not fully address the root cause component of the exception. All responsible auditors should ask business process owners if this suggested action plan is implemented, will it address the root cause and bring the corresponding risk to an acceptable level. Any response other than yes must be challenged to ensure an effective action plan gets developed.

Achievable Target Date

The final component of a real action plan is an achievable target date. All action plans require a date that indicates the final date of full implementation, but the dates provided by business process owners are not always realistic. The target date for action plan components must provide the parties involved with sufficient time to complete the required tasks. It is not unusual for an action plan target date to be too aggressive or too long for the corresponding action plan commitment. The one positive aspect of the target date component is that when the action plan is required as the result of a continuous auditing program, the action plan details are focused on the one or two controls tested that usually indicates an adjustment to an existing key control in an effort to address a small defect or design flaw in the control originally tested as part of the continuous auditing program.

When requesting the target date for a continuous auditing exception, ensure that you review the details of the proposed action to verify that the documented action is strategically focused on addressing the root cause of the testing exception noted. Validate the action details again when examining the target date component of the action plan; you must understand the action plan details before you attempt to validate the corresponding action plan timeline until completion. Responsible auditors are required to examine the proposed target date and determine whether it is reasonable. Even though the definition of "reasonable" is subject to judgment, it is unfortunately the best way to describe the consideration that must be applied to the submitted target date. Responsible auditors must examine the suggested target date while considering the details of the action plan and assess the feasibility of completing all of the required tasks in the time frame proposed. If there is any question as to whether action plan owners can implement the action plan by the target date, you must challenge the business process owner for a more realistic time frame. Because of the uniqueness of the continuous auditing methodology and its aggressive execution schedule, most often business process owners suggest aggressive target dates with deadlines that are too short for proper implementation. Only very rarely is a continuous auditing action plan target date 6 or 12 months from the report date. Any action plan needing this type of time frame usually represents that a significant design weakness was identified that required the entire process to be reworked. Remember that the continuous auditing program is focused on the key controls and should not require a total process redesign. Specific action plans usually are implemented within a 30- to 60-day window due to the targeted nature of the continuous auditing testing.

Keep in mind the three components of a real action plan while recognizing the nuances to the action plan development process in the continuous auditing methodology. The real owner and action plan focused on the root cause play a critical role in the evaluation and subsequent acceptance of the realistic target date proposed by business process owners. There is no sense in challenging or accepting an action plan target date if the action itself is not specifically focused on the root cause component of the exception detail or if the action plan owner does not have the ability or authority to make the action real.

 ## ACTION PLAN TRACKING

It is highly unlikely that the internal audit department will have to track outstanding action plans when executing the continuous auditing methodology. Since almost all suggested action plans for continuous auditing programs have an implementation within 30 days of identification, the control adjustment is applied before the subsequent month's continuous auditing program has been completed. The status of the previously noted exception and corresponding action plan should be identified in the subsequent report to highlight the implementation and document the business process owner's action.

If the action plan will require an implementation schedule longer than one month, responsible auditors will have to track and communicate the action plan status. A high level of oversight is needed to ensure that the action plan does not become a delinquent item. Such a case would result in multiple subsequent reports detailing the absence of specific action on behalf of the business process owner as evidenced by the repeatable poorly rated continuous auditing reports. These poorly rated audit reports would be the result of the continuation of the "6-9-12" methodology. In reality, action item tracking is critically important to any action plan submitted to the internal audit department, but it should be recognized that in the continuous auditing methodology, there is not as significant a need since validation testing is being performed to track the implementation of the originally proposed action plan in the subsequent months of testing. Unfortunately, if the continuous auditing action requires formal tracking of the corresponding action plans, there may be larger issues with the process requirements or business process owner that were not identified initially during the month in which the exception was first reported.

For examples of action plan tracking reports, see the appendix.

SUMMARY

Action plans are critical requirements in any audit service provided to ensure that the root cause component of the exception noted is addressed appropriately. Action plans required in the continuous auditing methodology should be focused specifically on adjusting the control detail tested. The targeted approach of the continuous auditing program makes the action plan development process easier not only on the business process owner but also on the responsible auditor attempting to validate the appropriateness of the suggested action plan and its components.

The other unique factor of the continuous auditing methodology, as it pertains to action plans, is that subsequent testing provides real-time validation that the implemented action plan properly addressed the root cause. If the subsequent months of the continuous auditing methodology testing reveals the same or similar exceptions as previously noted, this immediately indicates that the appropriate root cause analysis was not done and the discrepancy identified in the continuous auditing program's execution phase was not properly addressed. If the action plan and its components were designed effectively, the continuous auditing program will provide positive results within 60 days of the implementation of the control fix. Remember to link the action plan to the root cause, validate the owner, and challenge unrealistic time frames. If you follow these recommendations to action plan development, the continuous auditing methodology will provide verification of successful implementation.

CHAPTER ELEVEN

Continuous Auditing Conditions

 CONDITIONS

In this chapter, we define and describe the critical conditions that assist in the creation, implementation, and maintenance of a successful continuous auditing methodology. In addition, we break down in more detail specific conditions regarding business unit management, internal audit department, and technology. Although the identified conditions provide an outline and support to ensuring the success of a continuous auditing methodology, all conditions do not have to be present in order to begin developing the specific methodology requirements. The conditions provide a baseline guide to the details needed when discussing and developing the continuous auditing program components with the audit team and potential business unit partners. Because of the amount of time and effort required to develop, plan, and execute a detailed continuous auditing program, it is critical to recognize and understand the current state of the conditions to be discussed as you begin considering the custom components of your own continuous auditing methodology. With this

171

knowledge, you will be able to identify potential pitfalls in the creation process and potentially avoid them.

The condition discussion is divided into three different sections: business unit management, internal audit, and technology. In each section, we discuss specific conditions as they pertain to each owner. Even though the discussion begins with business unit management, it does not mean that the business unit is more important than the internal audit department. It is just that it is important to recognize the questions and challenges that will come from the business process personnel when this new audit approach is introduced. With this condition knowledge, it will be easier to develop, incorporate, and address the business process concerns into the continuous auditing methodology requirements. Doing this will help to ensure that the methodology is fully developed and includes not only the specific phase requirements but also the detailed process knowledge that must be communicated to business process owners to adequately explain the objectives, process, and reporting of a continuous auditing program.

After examining the business management conditions, the discussion focuses on the internal audit conditions. The conditions for internal audit review and reinforce the importance of having buy-in from the entire internal audit department as to the requirements of what a continuous auditing program is and the keys to its successful implementation and execution.

The chapter wraps up by reviewing the conditions for technology. Although technology can certainly be useful and complementary to a continuous auditing program, the specific identified conditions ensure that unnecessary time is not wasted trying to understand the complex system environment unnecessarily unless it is specifically related to the continuous auditing objective that is to be tested. The technology system details can be helpful if properly understood and focused on the continuous auditing objective; often, however, the sheer magnitude of the systems involved makes them misunderstood. Knowledge of the critical systems could impact the overall effectiveness of the continuous auditing program.

To ensure that the continuous auditing methodology is created appropriately and implemented successfully, the conditions must be understood clearly and addressed adequately in the supporting documentation. The discussion begins with the conditions specific to business unit management.

BUSINESS UNIT MANAGEMENT CONDITIONS

Whenever the internal audit department decides to introduce a new audit approach or even change a process, business unit management always is naturally apprehensive. Now consider you are about to introduce another methodology to perform audits, and it contains the word "continuous." That word alone will conjure up a vision of the internal audit department having a constant, daily presence in the business unit. In an effort to address the immediate concerns that will be raised during the introduction, we outline the key topics of the business unit management conditions and present corresponding questions every internal auditor must answer when discussing this new approach.

The business unit management conditions to be discussed include education and understanding, buy-in, commitment, and ownership of action plans. We define and explain each condition and identify the direct questions that will be asked by the business unit management in their effort to understand the objective and process requirements for a continuous auditing methodology.

Education and Understanding

Every person fears the unknown, no matter who the person is or what the situation. Nowhere could this statement be truer than when someone is trying to describe the challenging relationship between an internal audit department and its business management clients. Internal auditors must focus on educating their business counterparts to ensure that there is a clear understanding of the purpose of the continuous auditing methodology and, more important, of the differences between a full-scope audit and a continuous auditing program. To accomplish these communication objectives for education and understanding, responsible auditors must be prepared to answer the next questions adequately and eloquently.

What Is a Continuous Audit?

The first question to be asked will require the responsible auditor to explain what exactly a continuous audit is. This is the critical point in the internal audit and business unit relationship in which the foundation of trust will be formed.

The success of relationship foundation development hinges on whether auditors are able to provide a sufficient answer to this simple question. The other issue that impacts the effectiveness of the communication is the consistency of the message from all members of the internal audit department. Each internal auditor must have a clear understanding of the way to communicate exactly how the continuous auditing methodology works.

When asked what a continuous audit is, internal auditors must confidently explain that it is another audit technique used by the internal audit department to validate that the control environment, for the targeted controls selected, is operating as intended. Additionally, the continuous auditing methodology provides the internal audit department with another service it may deliver to its clients when the specific validation of a critical control is required. In such situations, the continuous auditing program strategically selects the key control(s) to be tested and accurately concludes on its effectiveness through a series of recurring audit tests.

The other significant clarification that must be made during the explanation of what is a continuous audit is that the word "continuous" does not mean that audit testing will be performed every single day from the start of the testing until the end of time. The term "continuous" is misleading. From an internal audit definition standpoint, "continuous" means that the corresponding testing will be executed on a recurring basis for a set period of time. It is critically important to make this distinction; otherwise, your business management clients may not want to discuss any details of a continuous auditing program.

The key to answering the "What is a continuous audit?" question is to remain clear, concise, and consistent and be sure to explain that it is another audit service provided to validate that specific controls are operating as intended. Then add that this is accomplished through recurring testing to conclude that the process control is providing repeatable, reliable results. Keep in mind that even if the internal audit department is strongly committed to having a consistent definition of a continuous auditing program, there is no guarantee that business process owners will be ready and willing to accept this new approach.

The other factor that greatly impacts the success of the explanation is to ensure that the internal audit department takes the time to plan, develop, and implement a formal continuous auditing methodology. Translated, a formal implemented methodology means that there is a formal document that defines and details each phase of the continuous auditing methodology, including, but not limited to, the foundation, approach, and execution phases. If you planned and strategically write out these phases, chances that you will provide an incomplete or inaccurate definition to business process management are significantly reduced. Take the time not only to develop and document your formal continuous auditing methodology but also to communicate the methodology details to the entire internal audit team.

After explaining what a continuous auditing methodology is, the responsible auditor is going to have to address how this new audit approach is different from any other audit. To the business process owner, an audit is an audit, is an audit. So it will be very important for the auditor to be able to address the specific differences.

What Is the Difference between an Audit and a Continuous Audit?

The natural follow-up question to the previous question is: "What are the differences between the normal audit (which I as a business process owner am used to) and a continuous auditing program?" Since a continuous auditing program will appear to be just another audit to a nonauditor, you must provide clear information as to why it is not. The responsible auditor and everyone on the internal audit team should be prepared for this question as it is a natural qualifier to properly explain the continuous auditing methodology. Note that we assume that regardless of the topic of the internal audit/ business process owner meeting, you have dedicated the time to prepare for it adequately. This preparation should include, at a minimum, a clear understanding of the meeting objective, the approach to be taken to address business process owner needs, and responses to any secondary or supporting questions that may be asked. More often than not, business process owners ask this follow-up question when first presented with the concept of the continuous auditing methodology.

To provide the right level of explanation, auditors must explain the continuous auditing methodology components that distinguish it from a full-scope audit. These component differences include, but are not limited to, testing approach, frequency, sampling, scope, and planning. Next we discuss these differences in order to ensure that there is no confusion.

The term "testing approach" is used to describe the objective development of the auditing methodology and focus of the audit to be completed. In the continuous auditing methodology, the approach focuses on validation of the performance of the key control selected, not validation of the entire control environment supporting the business process under review. In addition, the testing approach is a proactive examination of controls as opposed to a reactive review. The continuous auditing methodology is proactive because the testing results sometimes are used as predictive tools, once the continuous auditing program has been completed, as opposed to the reactive aspect of a full-scope audit. These two specifics of testing approach specificity and proactive testing of controls truly separate the continuous auditing testing approach from the full-scope approach. Both of these points need to be addressed when discussing component differences between the two methodologies.

The term "audit frequency" is used to describe the cyclical nature of the testing performed as part of the execution of the audit program. A significant differentiator about the continuous auditing methodology is that it is performed on a much more recurring basis than a full-scope audit. The foundation phase, as discussed in Chapter 5, recommends that the continuous auditing program should be performed using the "6-9-12" testing frequency. This testing frequency specifically requires the corresponding control testing to be performed for six consecutive months and then again at month 9 and 12. In contrast, full-scope audit testing usually takes place once every 12 to 18 months for higher-risk auditable entities. Despite the increased testing during the continuous auditing methodology, business process owners probably will see responsible auditors less often than during the execution of a full-scope audit. As long as the continuous auditing program is planned and executed as required, the audit testing can be performed strategically with minimal client disruption. Business owners could misinterpret the high frequency of testing required as meaning that auditors will be in the business processing area more often. Be sure to explain how the higher frequency of the continuous auditing methodology does not automatically equate to a constant internal audit presence in the business processing area.

The term "audit sampling" is used to describe the method in which the transactions being tested were selected. The approach phase, as discussed in Chapter 6, identified the three different types of sampling: random, judgmental, and statistical. Due to the unique planning objective of the continuous auditing methodology, the purpose is focused strategically on a selected key control(s). To support that objective adequately, the sampling technique used in the continuous auditing methodology is judgmentally to ensure that the transactions being tested specifically link to the objective developed. The sample selection is targeted to ensure all items to be tested related directly to the continuous auditing objective of what control(s) are to be validated. Conversely, a full-scope audit can use multiple different sample techniques, depending on what the testing being performed requires. Recognizing that the continuous auditing methodology operates most effectively and provides the most value-added results while using judgmental sampling techniques consistently is a key to separating the continuous auditing and full-scope auditing approaches. Just be sure to explain the primary reasoning for using only one type of sampling technique is to provide the most representative transactions that match the control components being tested.

The term "scope" is used to describe what is going to be covered during the audit service being performed. This is another significant difference between the continuous auditing methodology and the full-scope one. As detailed in Chapter 6, the scope statement for continuous audits must detail specifically what is included in the testing and also what the continuous auditing program will not cover and conclude on. While a formal scope statement should be developed on full-scope audits, their scopes tend to be very broad and often do not exclude any aspect of testing due to the inclusive nature of the testing being performed. To clarify with the business process owner, stress that the continuous auditing scope targets a very specific control(s) while a full-scope audit validates all controls implemented from start to finish. Additionally, the typical scope in a continuous auditing methodology is uniquely focused on current data (as current as can be selected—the most recently completed month) as opposed to the historical nature of full-scope audits. Remember to point out the reason for the specific scope statement details, in the continuous auditing methodology, is to strategically support the corresponding requirements of the continuous auditing methodology.

In any audit, the term "planning" describes the effort put forth to gather the necessary details and information required to effectively perform the audit service. This is one of the easier differences to explain. In a continuous auditing methodology, planning focuses on key controls identified in the process under review. The planning is further narrowed down to the most critical of the key controls, and those are the controls in which the corresponding planning is focused on to meet the continuous auditing methodology requirements of validating a selected control(s). As a result of this targeted planning approach, the planning phase in continuous auditing methodology is usually shorter in duration than in full-scope audits. Full-scope audits require a planning phase that discusses, documents, and understands the entire process from start to finish. That type of detailed planning requires a significant amount of time and resources to complete properly. The best way to explain this difference concisely is to state that because the continuous auditing methodology is a very targeted approach to validating the control environment, so is the corresponding planning that supports it.

What Is the Purpose of a Continuous Auditing Program?

The final question to be addressed as part of the education and understanding component is communicating the purpose of the continuous auditing methodology. Before attempting to answer this question, it is important to recognize what the word "purpose" means. When discussing "purpose," the underlying focus is on why the continuous auditing program is being performed. For this discussion, "purpose" always represents the reason for the testing. To articulate that message, responsible auditors should reaffirm the objective development process of the continuous auditing methodology and further explain that the custom audit approach is designed to test the selected controls proactively to validate their effectiveness. Additionally, the work completed in the continuous auditing program will be leveraged going forward not only for future audit services in the business area but also to educate the internal audit department regarding the key control details identified during the testing.

In any communication meeting, keep in mind that more words do not necessarily represent a more effective message. When more words than are required are used, often the message becomes cloudy. Let the continuous auditing methodology speak for itself, and be sure to stay consistent in how you communicate the documented methodology. If you have a solid understanding of the department-approved continuous auditing methodology, you will be effective in communicating the education and understanding component to your audit clients.

Buy-in

After navigating the education and understanding component of the business process management conditions, you are ready to focus on buy-in. The buy-in component of the conditions is a fairly straightforward discussion and does not require too much clarification. The reason why this is true is that the questions related to buy-in have direct answers that ultimately do not allow for much debate. Nevertheless, sometimes responsible auditors are nervous as they communicate with business process owners. There is no need to be nervous if you effectively prepare and are armed with a clear understanding of the documented continuous auditing methodology. Confidence in these initial introductory communications is critical to the overall success of the implementation of the continuous auditing methodology. Here are the questions that you will be presented with and expected to answer consistently. Once again, the business process owner will be studying and examining every word in your explanation. Remember to stay focused and use your existing audit methodology for support.

Is This Continuous Audit Optional?

Without a doubt, this is probably the easiest question that you will be faced with. The answer is a simple yet polite no. However, as entertaining as it might be to just say no and move on to the next question, you must explain why the business process owner cannot choose to participate or not. Business units are selected to be audited based on a formal risk assessment process. Take a moment to explain how the risk assessment process works but do not get into a detailed discussion; doing so will only confuse the business process owner and take away from the answer to the question of why it is not optional. Explain that once an area has been selected for review, it is up to internal audit management to determine the type of audit service to be performed in an effort to validate the target area's control environment. The audits to be completed for the year and their corresponding risks have been reviewed by the internal audit management team, and the most effective audit methodology has been chosen to validate the corresponding control environment.

From a straight operational perspective (do not share this point with the audit client), internal audit provides a service that validates the effectiveness and efficiency of the target areas tested. At no point does it direct process owners how to operate and run their business units. The same can be said about the internal audit department that there are no outside business unit influences on what audit techniques the internal audit department should use to review and test a control environment. Unfortunately, it is not up to the individual business units to decide what areas get audited and what type of audit service will be used. Those audit-related decisions are the responsibility of internal audit management. In summary, business unit management does not have the final say on whether a continuous auditing program is optional.

Can I Select the Area to Be Reviewed?

The next question that often follows when business process management is told that the continuous auditing program is not optional is whether the business owner can select the target area for the continuous audit. You probably will be surprised by the response to this question, especially given the matter-of-fact way we addressed the previous question. The answer is absolutely. Almost everyone who hears this response during a conference or seminar does not understand or initially even agree. But here is why the answer is absolutely.

Remember how important relationship development is for internal auditors with their business process clients. In an effort to strengthen that relationship, it is critical to have excellent communication skills. Unfortunately, listening often is one of the most overlooked communication skills. The value that internal audit adds during any audit, not just a continuous auditing program, is that the work executed is focused on the evaluation and effectiveness of the control environment.

This is the perfect opportunity for responsible auditors to learn and understand the control environment detail from the expert: the business process owner. So when business owners ask whether they can select the target area, say yes. The business process owners do not need to know that they can suggest focus areas for the continuous auditing program, but the ultimate decision rests with the responsible auditor based on their evaluation of process risk. This statement seems to contradict the previous statement that business process owners can select the target area. Owners can provide guidance as to where the highest risks are to the process; audit resources will not be used and wasted evaluating a low-risk control. Sometimes business owners will try and direct the internal audit efforts to process components with a smaller risk. This is where the responsible auditor needs to use the business process knowledge obtained during planning to make educated decisions of true process risk to be tested.

When going into a meeting to discuss the upcoming continuous auditing program, auditors already have an idea of the targeted audit objective, based on the completed background preparation as described in Chapter 4. With that knowledge, responsible auditors can more effectively engage in a process-level discussion; as mentioned, auditors will never possess the level of operational business knowledge that business owners have. In the final determination of the continuous auditing program objective, responsible auditors must listen and evaluate the corresponding risk in the suggested target area provided by process owners. If a high level of risk is not associated with the suggested topic, auditors must discuss their understanding of the process risk in the business unit and state the objective for the continuous auditing program.

Sometimes responsible auditors complete their background planning and truly believe that they have appropriately identified the most critical controls in the target area process based on risk only to discover, after a discussion with the business process owner, that other controls have a higher level of risk and impact on the operational effectiveness. Understanding and accepting a different continuous auditing program objective is more than acceptable once the risks have been identified, understood, and validated. Ensure that you use your experience and judgment when selecting the final objective, but remember always to allow business process owners the opportunity to provide some guidance during the selection phase. No matter how much audit experience internal auditors have or how long they have performed audits in a particular area, they will never have the depth of knowledge of business process owners.

All audit services, especially the continuous auditing methodology, are partnerships between internal audit and business process owners. To succeed, both parties involved in the partnership must be open and honest and have a willingness to listen and respect the expertise that each party brings to every discussion. Use this partnership to strengthen the value of the audit service and to expand your business process knowledge.

What Is in It for Me?

When it comes to getting any individual to buy in to a new concept, there is always going to be the question of what is in it for them if they choose to participate. The good news is that this question has a variety of answers because the continuous auditing program provides a couple of significant benefits. Here are just a few examples of how business process owners will benefit from participating in a continuous auditing program.

First and foremost, the continuous auditing methodology has been structured to provide an almost real-time validation of the effectiveness of the selected controls tested. This validation is accomplished by executing the work on a recurring basis, and that work is selected from the most recent transactions processed by the business unit. This approach does not require an examination of the past 6 or 12 months, just the last completed month prior to the start of the testing. This testing approach provides a more effective and efficient way to identify potential control deficiencies and to validate the strength of the existing control environment.

The second benefit is that the nature of the recurring testing increases auditors' business knowledge; they become more familiar with the operational business process requirements each time the testing is performed. This increase in knowledge translates directly into the more efficient planning of subsequent audit services and a reduction in the amount of time business process owners have to spend explaining operational procedures every time an audit is initiated. It is important that all responsible auditors participating in a continuous auditing program take the time to review the planning documentation and objectives in order to increase their business process knowledge on every audit.

The final benefit is that all information and knowledge obtained during the execution of the continuous auditing methodology will be leveraged and used during all other future audit activities in the target area. There also is a potential, depending on testing results, that the successful execution of a continuous auditing program results in a reevaluation of the corresponding risk of the targeted business unit. One potential outcome in such a reevaluation is that the timing for the next full-scope audit is extended based on positive results identified during the continuous audit. Unfortunately, there is a flip side to this benefit. If the results of the continuous auditing program indicate significant weaknesses in the control structure, the timing of the next full-scope audit may be accelerated in an effort to fully dissect the control environment deficiencies noted.

During the potential benefits discussion with business process owners, be certain to discuss all possibilities, including the rare but not impossible situation in which the continuous auditing program results in the initiation of an immediate full-scope audit. This may not seem to be a benefit, but in reality it is; the continuous auditing methodology performed exactly as it was designed by proactively identifying a control environment weakness that needs immediate attention.

Will There Be a Formal Report Issued?

The final question the responsible auditor will face in explaining the buy-in component of the business unit management conditions is whether a formal report will be issued. From my perspective, this is a no-brainer; a formal report will be issued, and it will require formal action plans where applicable. Experience has shown that when audit services are provided but there is no formal communication of exceptions noted, the required corresponding actions to address control deficiencies ultimately never get done. This lack of action is not caused by business process owner malcontent or lack of concern. Once an audit is over, process leaders go back to managing the business operation. Without the accountability provided by a formal audit report, exceptions never get addressed properly. Stand firm on this question and communicate to the business process management team the critical objectives for creating a formal audit report. The purpose of the report is to provide a formal communication of the objectives of the work performed and the results of the testing. Any opportunities for control improvement should be documented using the five-component approach as explained in Chapter 9, and an action plan(s) specifically to address their root cause should be created by business unit management to adequately address the issues identified during the testing. If a formal report that requires business process owners to acknowledge the exceptions and develop a plan of action is not completed, the risk will never be addressed properly.

Commitment

Once you have discussed the buy-in component of the business unit management conditions, it is time to address the next critical component:

commitment. Commitment can be effectively summed up in one question, and that is when business process owners ask what is it they have to do to make the continuous auditing methodology successful. Thankfully, the strategic development of the continuous auditing methodology does not require a significant investment of time or resources from business process owners. From a commitment standpoint, initially it is important for business partners to spend time (usually 30 minutes) discussing the new audit approach to ensure that all participants fully understand the continuous auditing methodology requirements and objectives. After that initial investment of time, the auditors ask the business management team to identify a subject matter expert with whom auditors can meet to finalize and verify the specific details of the approach phase, as discussed in Chapter 6, to ensure that the testing details agree with the objective. The detailed process review with the processing expert usually takes from 30 to 60 minutes. As a standard, I always request an hour meeting, but it never takes the full amount of time allotted.

Other than the time dedicated to understand the continuous auditing methodology details and finalizing the testing approach, the only remaining commitment request will be permission to access the business-level data to complete the testing requirements. The commitment component is a formality once you have adequately explained the education, understanding, and buy-in components. At this point, business process owners recognize the value of the continuous auditing methodology and just need to understand the specifics of what needs to be provided from a management perspective.

Ownership of Action Plans

The final component to be discussed regarding business unit management conditions is ownership of action plans. This condition as it pertains to the continuous auditing methodology should be no different from the way the ownership of action plans is for any other audit where an exception was identified in an audit report. The information to be highlighted here ties directly to the action plan requirements discussed in detail in Chapter 10. The specific questions to be addressed focus on the reporting process and the handling of outstanding action items.

Will the Report Be Distributed?

The two aspects of an audit report that business process owners fear the most are the overall rating and the distribution. If the report carried a rating but only process owners were told, there would be no problem or challenges issuing audit reports. The challenge with issuing audit reports is that the business owner would prefer to keep their issues within the business unit and not have it communicated to the company and executive management that there are opportunities for improvement in the operational unit. The same could be said if process owners knew the report would be issued to a full executive management distribution but it did not contain an overall rating; there again would be no delay in getting approval from the business unit management to allow internal audit to issue the final report. However, continuous auditing reports do carry a rating, as discussed in Chapter 9, and require distribution to ensure that proper attention and resources are applied to complete the documented action plan.

Besides serving as a driver to implement the action plan detail, report distribution also documents the effort and resources that the internal audit department has expended to plan, execute, and report on the completed continuous auditing programs. Unless there is a confidentiality issue (potential or confirmed fraud), there should never be a reason not to report on the products generated by the internal audit department. When process owners ask about report distribution, stress that the continuous auditing methodology is handled no differently when it comes to the reporting of validated exceptions noted and the subsequent formal communication of the issues in a continuous auditing report. Whether it is a continuous audit or a full-scope audit, the corresponding report is designed to provide an independent, unbiased summary of the identified process risk and applicable business unit action plan(s).

Will Action Plans Be Required and Tracked?

As mentioned in the response to the previous question, even though the continuous auditing methodology is a customer audit service, the tracking and follow-up on outstanding action plans will be handle the same way regardless of the type of audit performed (continuous or full-scope). Any time a continuous auditing program identifies a reportable exception, an action plan to address the root cause must be developed by the business process owner and accepted by the responsible auditor to verify that it will address the root cause satisfactorily. Without a formal requirement to provide an action plan, the root cause almost never gets properly addressed, resulting in an increase in operational processing risk.

As for tracking outstanding action plans, this internal audit department responsibility is not as complicated or time consuming as it would be in a full-scope audit when dealing with the continuous auditing methodology because the action plan required specifically addresses the individual control tested. Usually process reengineering or multiple control enhancements are not needed to solve the problem. Most actions associated with exceptions noted in a continuous auditing report require a particular enhancement to the existing key control. With their direct linkage to the control structure, most action plans are implemented before the next month's continuous auditing program testing is executed. This focused action plan approach allows for the newly enhanced control to be tested immediately for effectiveness and efficiency of design that will be validated in the 60 days following the formal implementation. This validation occurs as the execution phase of the continuous auditing methodology continues even after an exception has been noted. This methodology has a built in verification of action plan effectiveness.

To ensure communication success when discussing the ownership of action plans, focus on the unique nature of creating an action plan that directly links to the control tested and the fact that the corresponding action proposed will be tested immediately as part of the continuous auditing methodology to ensure its effectiveness. This validation eliminates the need to go back and perform additional testing in the coming months, as in a full-scope audit, to ensure that the action plan was implemented properly while at the same time fulfills the requirements of the execution of the continuous auditing methodology, which requires the testing to continue even after exceptions have been identified, validated, and addressed.

Overall, the business unit management conditions focus on the critical communication needed to support the implementation and rollout of the continuous auditing methodology to business unit management. The education and understanding conditions, which define the continuous auditing methodology and set the tone for the foundation of the audit/client partnership, must be fully developed to provide the proper foundation for the remaining three conditions to be successful. Only through the dedication and attention to the methodology details coupled with a clear understanding of the continuous auditing phase requirements will responsible auditors be able to communicate the key requirements effectively to business owners. Every member of the internal audit department must have a clear understanding of the continuous auditing methodology in order to effectively communicate to the business unit management team the requirements and benefits of the new audit approach.

INTERNAL AUDIT CONDITIONS

Now that we have completed the discussion on business unit management conditions, we can turn our attention to the conditions pertaining to internal audit. The internal audit conditions review and reinforce the importance of having the entire internal audit department clear regarding just what a continuous auditing program is and the keys to successful program implementation and execution.

The successful introduction of the continuous auditing methodology is the responsibility of each member of the internal audit department and places a significant amount of pressure on the auditors. Everyone fears change, but change coming from the internal audit department creates an extra level of stress for all parties involved. To ensure the successful introduction and roll-out of the continuous auditing methodology, it is critically important that everyone in the internal audit department recognizes and understands these conditions. These conditions are focused on the continual development of internal audit business knowledge throughout the continuous auditing program as well as being aware from planning through reporting that this methodology is unique. Without a conscious acknowledgment that this approach is drastically different from a full-scope audit, the implementation and recognition of the continuous auditing methodology will never be achieved.

The specific internal audit conditions to be discussed include knowledge of the target area, information technology expertise, unique review, and timely reporting. Not only is each condition defined and explained, but we also identify the supporting components that clearly link to the objective and process requirements for a continuous auditing methodology.

Knowledge of the Target Area

Nothing is more valuable to an internal auditor than a detailed knowledge of the business. The important lesson in developing business knowledge its that all auditors must realize that they are never finished learning about the business processes. They must challenge themselves continually to stay motivated and learn about the business operations that they audit on a daily basis. In addition to obtaining business knowledge from the process owner, auditors responsible for executing a continuous auditing program must also look inside their own department for a different perspective on the business knowledge that impacts the continuous auditing program phase details. The additional knowledge resource starts with their own individual audit experience.

Use Previous Audit Experience

When trying to expand your knowledge of the target area being tested using a continuous auditing methodology, consider the different audits you have been involved in prior to taking on this new approach. As you review your own experiences, determine if any of the other audits you have completed relate to the topic that you are going to build the continuous auditing program to complete. This review process allows you to examine the target area to decide what additional questions, risks, or potential critical controls could be involved in the test plan you are creating.

Also, when planning any internal audit activity, you should always leverage previous experiences with the particular team that will be partnering with you on the auditing program. If you have worked with them previously, you are already aware of the type of business unit management team you will be dealing with (barring any turnover since your last audit) and more importantly how they view the internal audit department in general. This kind of knowledge of business operations is invaluable when conducting the continuous auditing program because you are familiar with the business unit management communication style and their expectations from the internal audit department. Use this knowledge as you address the specific questions posed in the business unit management conditions section of this chapter to ensure a smooth transition from the typical audit to the continuous auditing methodology and its phase requirements.

Experience of the Audit Team

To be successful in the internal audit department, you must be an excellent communicator, which means that you must be able to actively listen, write effectively, and speak intelligently. Strong communication skills are required when dealing with different levels of management throughout your company. More specifically, the ability to exhibit your communication skills when dealing with your peers and other department team members in internal audit is even more critical. Without strong communication skills, you will be unable to work effectively with your audit teammates to discuss the continuous auditing program you are beginning to develop.

Every successful continuous auditing program must be planned effectively; this planning is the result of an inquiry to the audit department asking if anyone has had experience with the targeted business unit. The auditor will have to provide teammates with a clear understanding of the preliminary objective when requesting additional information on the target business area. This background will help ensure that only relative information is discussed and that the time dedicated has been well spent. Once all information has been obtained from your audit teammates, ensure that it is included in the planning of the continuous auditing program where applicable.

Audit Management Input

The last time I checked, the audit management team was part of the audit department, yet the team is separated into another section apart from the audit team experience section. Audit management is listed separately because its members must be asked a different question as you build your knowledge of the targeted business area. Include internal audit management when you are meeting with any teammates who have performed audits in the target area. To complete the internal audit discussion requirements, it is important to approach the audit management team and ask them if they have heard anything regarding the targeted business unit. Often managers throughout the company, including the internal audit department, are sent to leadership or management development training. Usually attendees are encouraged to share the challenges they are currently facing in their own departments. This type of information often does not get discussed in an internal audit or business process owner meeting. In order to identify potential barriers in the development or execution of your continuous auditing program, it is important to ask the management-related question to verify that no specific challenges or initiatives impacting the target business unit could prevent or distract business unit management from actively partnering in the continuous auditing program.

Remember that internal audit management may have knowledge of other challenges to the target department that could impact implementation of the continuous auditing methodology. More often than not, internal audit managers are not able to make the linkage immediately when the information is first presented to them from a peer in the company. But when the responsible auditor asks if they have heard of any challenges facing the targeted business unit, they may have some relevant information that could reduce and possibly eliminate wasting time and resources on a continuous auditing program trying to be implementing in a business unit in a state of change. A state of change could represent a business unit updating operational policies and procedures, planning a new system implementation, or even addressing previous full-scope audit recommendations. No matter what the change is, internal audit would not want to try and launch a continuous auditing program into an area while the operational unit is in a state of flux.

Outstanding and Closed Action Plans

To ensure that you have considered all available internal audit information pertaining to the targeted business unit, it is important to review the open and closed action plans related specifically to that business unit. By examining these action plans, you will be able to determine the current status of initiatives that the target department is working on implementing. The action plan reports generated by the internal audit department provide a good starting point to begin researching the specific action plans applicable to the business operation.

If the action item detail identifies a number of open action items being worked on by the business being considered for a continuous audit program, it is probably not the best time to dedicate resources to a business unit area already in the process of implementing change. Internal audit will be unable to effectively implement a continuous auditing program in an area where change is currently underway because there will be no consistency of data and/or operational procedures to compare as required in the continuous auditing methodology. Also, if there are a number of recently implemented (closed within the past 60 days) action plans, it is also not the most opportune time to launch a continuous auditing program for two specific reasons.

1. The business unit is still getting familiar with the new process requirements and is experiencing growing pains with the revised controls.
2. Due to the recent control enhancement, not enough transactions have been processed using the new process for the responsible auditor to select a representative sample, as required by the continuous auditing methodology.

Some internal audit departments use the action plan tracking reports to identify areas to target for their continuous auditing methodology. They do so by identifying all high-risk areas for which full-scope audits discovered significant control deficiencies requiring the business unit to implement new controls. To ensure that the enhanced control addresses the root cause, the internal audit department will create a continuous auditing program to validate the new control's effectiveness and efficiency. To ensure there is an appropriate population of transactions to choose from, the internal audit department will not implement the targeted continuous auditing program until the new control has been in place and operating for at least 60 days. Use of the continuous auditing methodology to validate the implementation of critical control improvements has increased since 2008. Internal audit departments believe that the most effective way to adequately test new controls is over a period of time to ensure that the control produces repeatable, reliable results.

Information Technology Expertise

Although the continuous auditing methodology does not require any specific technology tool to generate value-added results, technology can provide assistance in certain circumstances. However, using technology in conjunction with the continuous auditing methodology has associated risks. Here we introduce technology and the continuous auditing program so that you understand how technology can help in the execution of the continuous auditing program. The discussion focuses on the need for a specific technology, potential technology uses, and potential hazards of incorporating technology inappropriately.

Use Existing System Tools

There is a misconception that says that in order to implement the continuous auditing methodology, the internal audit department must have a technology solution to perform the execution phase requirements. This could not be further from the truth. There is no legitimate reason why the continuous auditing methodology cannot be implemented quite successfully without any technology tool. In truth, technology can be used with a continuous auditing program, but it is certainly not required.

The key aspect to using technology with continuous auditing programs is to ensure that you use technological tools that your department already possesses. The secret to using your technology to assist with the continuous auditing methodology is in how you use the technology, not the specific type of software that is being used. One data-sorting software rather than another is not going to guarantee a more effective continuous auditing methodology. At the end of the day, there is no reason that your current department tools cannot be used to meet the needs of your continuous auditing programs.

Some internal audit departments do not use any technology to perform their continuous auditing programs. All of the three phases of the continuous auditing methodology can be built with zero technology. However, if the internal audit department contains technology tools to perform computer-assisted auditing techniques as well as auditors who understand how to use the tools effectively, some specific uses for technology can enhance the continuous auditing methodology.

Technology Uses

If the decision is made to use the internal audit department's existing technology to complement the continuous auditing program, it is important to be aware of the areas in which technology can be used most effectively: in data analysis and sample selection. To understand how to incorporate the technology tools, we explain each one, beginning with data analysis.

The most common use of technology in the continuous auditing program is to create an automated routine that compares the established standard to the actual work performed for the selected transactions. In reality, the technology is performing the data analysis that has been designed in the approach phase of the continuous auditing methodology. It is critically important to ensure that the automated routine has been designed properly before relying solely on the system-generated results. The most effective way to determine the accuracy of the technology testing performed is to select at least two individual transactions to run through the automated test. Once the two test transactions have been processed, review the results and verify that the automated test performed the approach phase requirements appropriately as designed. If discrepancies are noted, refine the technology tool parameters and rerun the validation testing until all aspects of the continuous auditing program requirements are met successfully. If no issues were identified during the validation test of the technology tool, process the continuous auditing sample as designed and evaluate the results.

Another primary use for technology is to assist in the execution phase requirement of the continuous auditing methodology by selecting the sample transaction to be tested. Custom technology programs are created to select transactions that meet the exact criteria of the testing requirements of the control that the continuous auditing program is verifying. Since the recommended sampling technique required in the approach phase, as discussed in Chapter 6, is judgmental, the sampling technique is more effective if a technology tool can be used to identify the sample transactions that most accurately match the test requirements. Because the judgmental sampling technique strategically identifies corresponding testing components, it is helpful to use an automated solution to expedite transactions matching the testing objective components.

Technology Cautions

It is easy to get carried away by technology's apparently limitless power and try to implement a technology solution across all phases of the continuous auditing methodology. Technology is not the enemy of the continuous auditing phases, but it can pose some challenges to consistent execution of the methodology requirements. This temptation to increase the use of technology has to be validated to ensure it is warranted and benefits the continuous auditing program. To assist in the validation process, we have compiled the most common technology mistakes for internal audit departments to consider when implementing a continuous auditing methodology with a technology-supported solution. These mistakes include, but are not limited to, increasing the number of samples selected, increasing the individual sample sizes to be tested, and selecting a 100 percent sample.

When an internal audit department has both the technology tools and the auditor knowledge to use the tools effectively, there is a feeling that the continuous auditing program would be even more effective if the approach phase contained more samples then what was originally identified. This is a very common mistake, but again it represents another example of when more does not equate to better. The continuous auditing methodology phases were strategically built to use the understanding of the critical controls of the business operations in an effort to specifically test the most significant control(s). This is evident through the validation of the continuous auditing objective to the specific sample selection and verification of control effectiveness. Increasing the number of samples to be tested defeats the purpose of the strategic approach to the methodology. To ensure that the execution phase requirements are followed properly, resist the temptation to add more samples. There is no corresponding benefit to selecting additional samples. The only outcome of adding additional samples will be an increase in the time and resource commitment needed to complete the work required.

Another common mistake, probably made more often than increasing the number of samples tested, is increasing the size of the testing samples to be verified during the execution phase. Due to the recurring nature of the continuous auditing methodology, the total number of transaction items that will be tested far exceeds any sample size requirements used in the execution of a full-scope audit. The total transactions tested in a continuous auditing program usually are three to four times the number of transactions tested than in any other audit.

To illustrate this point, consider a transaction that is processed multiple times every single day. According to most suggested sample size charts, for a transaction with this type of processing frequency, the recommended sample size will be anywhere from 20 to 30 transactions. Now, if you are using the recommended "6-9-12" frequency when executing a continuous auditing program, assuming the monthly testing sample size is 15, you will have tested 120 transactions over the life of the continuous auditing program. A full-scope audit would test 30 transactions while the continuous auditing program would test 120. With this number of transactions being tested in the continuous auditing execution phase, there is no need to increase the sample size of the monthly transaction testing. But there *is* a temptation to do so. Most of the time this temptation is evident when the testing is being performed using a technology tool. Logic says that if it is an automated test, does it really matter if we increase the monthly sample size? After all, the technology can handle the volume easily. Unfortunately, you must analyze the results of all the testing and research any potential deviations identified during the execution. In the end, the time and resources that could potentially be needed to interpret all of the testing results may not be worth it. When determining sample size, trust in the continuous auditing methodology requirements. Select a sample size that will provide an adequate number of transactions that are acceptable based on transaction frequency as well as feasible to adequately test and evaluate on a recurring basis. The transaction frequency and volume guide the continuous auditing sample selection. If the operational process generates transactions multiple times every day, sampling 15 in the "6-9-12" frequency is more than sufficient to conclude on the effectiveness of the selected control(s).

One final mistake related to technology has to do with selecting all of the items in a population for testing (performing a validation of 100 percent). The risks of testing an entire population relate back to the risks when considering increasing the sample sizes. Unless you are using a technology tool, there is no way to test an all-inclusive sample on a monthly basis. But the most significant risk to testing the entire population is that the responsible auditor would spend so much time examining potential exceptions that there would be no time to work on anything else.

There are only two times in which it is recommended that an all-inclusive testing approach be used: in payroll validation tests and in fraud examinations. In a payroll validation test, the continuous auditing program is validating that every paycheck is created and distributed only for legitimate company employees. In this instance the payroll file is matched by Social Security number for every employee in the company. The objective is to ensure that there are no fictitious names on the payroll receiving money inappropriately. And all fraud investigations require an all-inclusive sample to identify which transactions are appropriate and which ones are fraudulent. However, other than these two specific examples, there is no need to test 100 percent of the population on a continuous basis.

Any time you have technology tools and the expertise to use them, it is easy to get distracted and increase samples, but doing so does not always provide any additional benefit. Resist the temptation, and use your technological expertise most effectively to complement your continuous auditing methodology. If you do not, you will increase the time, effort, and resources required to perform the required work on a recurring basis. This is because you will spend more time researching false positives than anything else, and the time requirements of the continuous auditing methodology do not allot any extra time. The unfortunate consequence is that once you fall behind while executing your continuous auditing program, it is nearly impossible to catch up, unless you change the frequency or somehow alter the methodology requirements. Follow the methodology as designed and be confident in your planning of the execution phase requirements. If you do that, you will not make any mistakes and will effectively use your existing technology.

Unique Review

Another critical internal audit condition is ensuring that the entire internal audit department recognizes that the continuous auditing methodology is drastically different from a typical full-scope audit in all aspects of planning, fieldwork, reporting, and wrap-up. If there is any confusion regarding the uniqueness of this approach, the specific requirements supporting the continuous auditing program and full-scope audits will become indistinguishable. Every individual in the internal audit department must recognize the differences between the continuous and full-scope audit approaches. Without accepting and understanding the differences, it will be impossible to effectively use both methodologies to execute the internal audit plan. If that occurs, the true benefits of the continuous auditing methodology will never be realized, and every audit executed will contain the full-scope audit phase requirements. It is important to reaffirm the differentiating factors to the audit team to ensure that they clearly understand the requirements. These are the two points on which to focus:

1. Recognize that the continuous auditing methodology is not an audit.
2. Recognize what the continuous auditing methodology requires to be integrated successfully into the internal audit department.

This Is Not an Audit

The primary component of this internal audit condition is always to remember that continuous auditing is not an audit. Recall the specific differences discussed when continuous auditing was being defined in Chapter 1. Use those differences as the foundation for understanding that the continuous auditing program is distinctly different from any other audit service provided. The phase requirements establish those key differences. Any time there is a doubt about the objective or phase requirements of a continuous audit, refer to the chapters related directly to the point in question to verify that you are following the requirements as designed. One deviation from the methodology requirements can cause responsible auditors or business process owners to misinterpret the objective of the testing being performed. If that occurs, the benefits of the continuous auditing methodology will not be realized.

Keep the continuous auditing methodology requirements clear. Use the foundation, approach, and execution phase details to explain the objectives and components of the methodology to business process clients to ensure that all parties are clear regarding expectations and deliverables. The key is to remember that more than one type of audit technique can verify the strength of a control environment. There are distinct differences between the techniques as well as specific instances in which each one is more effective.

Requires Experience, Discipline, and Dedication

Any time the word "unique" is used to describe a process, especially an audit service, other adjectives will be used to describe the responsible auditor who will be most successful at adapting, implementing, and using the unique technique. The continuous auditing methodology is no exception. To be successful with this enhanced audit approach, the personnel involved must be experienced, disciplined, and dedicated to the specific requirements identified in the three phases.

Experience is required because in the foundation phase, described in Chapter 5, the responsible auditor will be required to identify not only the potential target area to perform the continuous auditing program but also, the corresponding critical control to be tested. Doing this will require audit experience; only experienced auditors will be able to examine a business process and effectively identify the most critical controls that support the operational process. Additionally, experience in the current company would also be helpful in the identification of critical controls. Also, most experienced auditors have strong communication skills, which are a must in order to discuss the continuous auditing methodology objectives and phase process requirements with business owners. Auditors can sell this methodology only if they have a detailed working knowledge of the corresponding requirements and the ability to communicate them.

Discipline is required because in the foundation phase, responsible auditors must exhibit patience not to change the established testing objectives once they have been created. The testing objectives were developed strategically based on research into the target business unit and detailed planning. Attempting to make changes once the continuous auditing program has begun violates the methodology requirements. Also, discipline is needed to resist the temptation to add additional components to test. Once the testing attributes have been established, new ones cannot be added after the first month of testing has been completed. Adding attributes would not link to the continuous auditing objective, and the testing frequency would have to begin again to ensure that the same components were being evaluated throughout the established frequency. Any deviation from the established testing approach also would render the continuous auditing program useless as a predictive tool due to the inconsistency of what was being tested from month to month. Responsible auditors must be disciplined and trust in the methodology requirements to provide the validation that the control(s) being tested are producing repeatable, reliable results.

Dedication is required to perform the continuous auditing methodology as designed through all three phases while adhering specifically to the requirements. After the first couple of months of successful testing, auditors will be tempted to conclude on the adequacy of the control(s) being evaluated due to the misconception that performing subsequent testing will not provide any additional benefit. This is an incorrect assumption. To realize the benefits as designed, the continuous auditing methodology must be completed for all cycle testing requirements as established in the foundation phase. If the phase requirements are not completed, the continuous auditing program cannot be used to assess the adequacy of the control environment and it most definitely will not be able to be used as a predictive tool. Even when the testing results are not positive, the subsequent months of testing must be performed to ensure not only that the exception has been completely identified and understood but also that the specifically developed action plan has been implemented and adequately addresses the root cause of the exception noted.

Timely Reporting

There is no substitute for the timely completion and distribution of an internal audit report, and the continuous auditing report is no exception. Just as with any other audit product, the continuous auditing report has to be completed and reported in a timely manner; otherwise the overall impact of the message and communication of the exceptions is diminished. There is really no good explanation for the late delivery of an approved continuous auditing report. Most auditors can provide many reasons why audit reports do not get issued in a timely manner, but here are a few reasons why it is a bit easier to issue continuous auditing reports on time. In the continuous auditing methodology, a final report is considered timely if it is issued within one week of the completion of the testing.

Immediate Results

Due to the unique characteristics of the continuous auditing methodology and its targeted objective, the corresponding report provides immediate results of the completed testing since the information can be summarized efficiently and quickly. With this type of targeted testing approach, the draft report should be available for business process owner review within a few days of the completion of execution phase requirements. This advance delivery of the draft report provides time for discussion of the exception details, if necessary, as well as the specific wording used in the report to describe the overall effectiveness of the control(s) tested. The results are immediate because they are obtained from each month of testing completed and communicated on the same recurring basis to business process owners. With this type of focus testing approach, the results direct any required action to the specific control that was tested.

In addition, the subsequent testing and reports will provide immediate validation regarding the adequacy of any newly implemented action plans.

Consistent Communication

One of the biggest challenges to issuing internal audit reports on a timely basis is that each audit presents a unique situation and is directed to a unique business process owner. These two components provide the perfect storm of customization requirements even for the internal audit departments that use a standard internal audit report format. The reason this is true is because every exception has specific details, and every business process owner has different communication styles and expectations of how the final audit report should be written. Experienced internal auditors can provide numerous instances when final report issuance was held up due to differences in wording or overall opinions in a draft audit report.

However, because of the recurring nature of the continuous auditing program and the established report format, as discussed in Chapter 9, there should not be any delay in meeting the completion and delivery requirements of a continuous auditing report. The continuous auditing report should be drafted within two days of completion of testing and provided immediately to the business process owner after internal audit management review and approval. In order to ensure that a consistent message is being provided to business process owners regarding the effectiveness and efficiency of their control environment, the completion, timing, and distribution must be accomplished on each recurring continuous auditing program executed. Once the initial month of the continuous auditing program has been completed and the corresponding report has been issued, only the results section of the continuous auditing report will have to be updated for subsequent months of testing; all of the other report components will remain the same until all testing has been completed. After the first month's report has gone out, there is absolutely no excuse for a report delay in any other month.

Targeted Action Plans

Action plans usually are one of the primary reasons that final audit reports are delayed. Whenever business process owners are presented with a control deficiency exception pertaining to a process that they own, there is going to be some discussion as to its validity as well as the action plan necessary to address the root cause. These discussions take time because so many factors are involved in exceptions identified during a full-scope audit. Conversely, because of the focused nature of the continuous auditing methodology, when an exception is identified, there are no significant discussions because the control deficiency identified links directly to the control tested. It is difficult for process owners to debate the data tested pertaining to the targeted control selected. Therefore, action plan development is much more focused and usually can be implemented without requiring a significant amount of resources or time. This is because the control deficiency identified usually requires only a small adjustment to become fully effective. Most continuous auditing action plans require an adjustment to the tested control and can be corrected in the following month of testing. The other advantage to the continuous auditing methodology is that the subsequent months of testing will validate whether the corrective action was appropriate. There are only two reasons why subsequent testing does not improve: (1) No root cause analysis was performed and the implemented action plan addressed only a symptom of the exception, not the true root cause; and (2) the proposed management action plan created and implemented by the business process owner did not effectively address the root cause since the subsequent testing is still providing negative results.

Overall, the internal audit conditions focus on the business unit knowledge for the targeted area. This knowledge should translate into a continuous auditing methodology that is more effectively planned. Also, this knowledge coupled with the clear understanding that this alternate auditing testing methodology is distinctly different in all aspects of planning and execution will provide a strong foundation for the internal audit department to implement a continuous auditing methodology that will complement its existing audit approach.

 TECHNOLOGY CONDITIONS

Now that we have completed the discussion of the business unit management and internal audit conditions, we can turn our attention to the final conditions pertaining to technology. The technology conditions point to important considerations that must be examined as you encounter the specific systems used in the business units targeted by the continuous auditing methodology.

Since the continuous auditing methodology detailed in Chapters 5, 6, and 7 did not specifically address technology as it pertains to each one of the phases, it is important to identify how technology is used in every business unit as part of its everyday processing. Because we rely on technology in all aspects of business operations, it is critical to validate that the system-generated reports that often are used in sample selection or specific testing in a continuous auditing program and provide a comprehensive portrayal of all business unit activity being processed during the scope period.

The specific technology conditions to be discussed include applicable system identification, authorized access, and reliable systems. Not only do we define and explain each condition, but we also identify the supporting components that clearly link to the objective and process requirements for a continuous auditing methodology.

Applicable System Identification

As this book is being written in 2010, it is amazing how dependent companies are on technology in ensuring that their financial statements are accurate, that operations are operating effectively, that calls are being routed and answered in a timely manner, and that customers are receiving a consistently high level of service. These are just a small fraction of examples as to how every company relies on technology to work effectively every minute of every single day of every single year. Internal audit relies on the business unit technology to produce accurate reports that will be examined for effectiveness or even used to select testing samples for the continuous auditing methodology. To further clarify the continuous auditing requirements for system identification, it is important to focus the system research on the ones specifically associated with the corresponding continuous auditing objective.

A huge number of systems are used not only in the business unit process being evaluated but also across the company. It is important to remember that the continuous auditing program is concerned only with the specific controls identified in the foundation phase. That being stated, to ensure that responsible auditors maintain focus and perform the applicable research on the appropriate technologies, the only time dedicated to examining the systems used in the targeted business process are the ones that are specifically used to process the transactions being tested. The continuous auditing methodology requires an examination of the technology that is directly linked to the control(s) being tested and not all technology solutions used in the business unit. There is no need to or recognized benefit in examining all systems used in the business process being reviewed. At the end of the day, the responsible auditor may have gained a small increase in system knowledge for that business unit, but no any additional benefit in completing the continuous auditing methodology requirements will have been derived.

When you are assigned a continuous auditing program to execute, stay focused on the specific objective that was developed and dedicate the time to understand any systems used to process transactions directly related to the continuous auditing objective. Any other research will result in wasting time trying to understand systems that have no role in the processing of the transaction details being validated with the continuous auditing program. Once you have identified the applicable systems needed to execute the transaction, you can request access.

Authorized Access

The security that surrounds most systems is designed to prevent unauthorized access to the system information and to restrict approved users from processing unauthorized or inappropriate transactions. Established procedures and protocols must be followed and adhered to when trying to gain access to system data. Keep in mind that data is restricted for the specific prevention items noted previously as it pertains to critical field and client information and this restriction provides the foundation for a strong control environment to safeguard critical data. However, for internal audit to perform its job effectively, it must be given temporary access to data if it is needed to validate a particular control process.

To gain the necessary access required to complete the continuous auditing program, responsible auditors must request permission from business process owners. This usually entails completing a form and submitting it to business process owners for review and approval. Request access only for the specific system that needs to be accessed to follow the transaction through the process control environment being tested. Responsible auditors have no need for access to all the business process systems that an operations person needs to perform all aspects of their job. The access must be an inquiry-only access user ID. If inquiry-only access cannot be granted and only live processing access is available, request that a business process team member assists you in obtaining the system-related information to complete the continuous audit methodology requirements.

We recommend auditors obtain inquiry-only access because there is too much risk associated with obtaining a live system ID when performing internal audit testing. Inexperienced users using a live system ID can impact the actual production data in the business unit. The associated risk of having a live system ID is not worth the potential impact to the production data if a mistake is inadvertently or unintentionally made. Request inquiry access only; if that is not available, identify other procedures to complete the required testing.

Reliable Systems

When initiating a continuous auditing program in a business unit that is highly automated, responsible auditors have to place some reliance on the effectiveness and accuracy of the systems being used in the business process being reviewed. Unfortunately, system reliability is difficult to judge, but it is critically important to consider when performing a continuous auditing program. A couple of suggestions to be used when evaluating system reliability for the corresponding systems operating and processing the transactions being tested as part of your continuous auditing methodology are presented next. These suggestions can be used when evaluating any system as part of an internal audit service.

System Produces Dependable Results

It is extremely difficult to determine if a business processing system is producing dependable and reliable results, especially if auditors have never worked with the system in the past. But a few general questions may provide some insight as to how dependably the system performs. You can ask the business unit processor how often the system involved in the continuous auditing program goes down and becomes unavailable. An important follow-up question is to verify if there are formal manual procedures to follow in the event that the processing system becomes unavailable. This does not mean that if the system has not gone down in the past 12 months, everything generated by the system is accurate and reliable. It just means that the technology appears to be working since the business processing unit has not experienced any downtime in the past year.

Another procedure to perform is to contact the corporate help desk and ask how many help desk tickets have been received for the applicable system involved in the testing over the past month, quarter, or year. This type of detailed information could provide a profile of the challenges that the business processing personnel face on a day-to-day basis.

Keep in mind that the answers to either of these questions does not in any way shape or form provide conclusive evidence, or even an indication, that the system used to process the transactions is delivering reliable and accurate results. The opposite could be true; even a system with availability issues or open help desk tickets still can produce accurate information that is used on a daily basis. The only thing that this information provides is an indication of potential challenges with processing transactions on a consistent basis.

Perform an Independent Audit Validation

The only proven audit technique used to verify the reliability of the information generated from a business processing system is to create and run an independent report that matches the information produced by the applicable source business system being relied upon as part of the continuous auditing methodology. This will require that an independently generated report be created to validate the information contained in the report provided by the operational business unit. For example, if the business system report is being used to identify all transactions processed over $5,000 for the most recent completed month, the generated report should be inclusive of all transactions over that dollar amount processed between the two specified dates. To verify that the business system has produced a reliable and accurate report, responsible auditors would use their approved access to the business process data and run an independent report using the internal audit department software to extract all transactions over that same dollar amount for the same exact time period. Once the internal audit data extraction has been completed, it is compared to the business system report generated. The two report totals should match. The only time there would be a potential discrepancy would be if there was a timing difference in the report parameters. Other than that, both reports should have produced the same results. If the internal audit generated report matches the business system report provided, then the business processing system is producing reliable results. Keep in mind that just because the report totals matched, it does not mean that the information represented in those totals was processed accurately in accordance with the current policies and procedures. Only the detailed continuous auditing program will validate that level of compliance.

Review Independent Information Technology Reports

The final suggestion for evaluating business processing systems is to request and obtain any independent audits or assessments that were completed on the systems involved in the continuous audit program being executed. These assessments could be the result of a corporate information technology review, a federal or state information technology examination, a regulatory review, or the general controls review completed by your external audit partners. All of these reports would provide insight into the effectiveness and reliability of critical company systems as well as any deficiencies noted that are currently being addressed by business process owners.

Overall, the technology conditions focus on the systems being used in the business units to process their corresponding transactions. It becomes increasingly more important for responsible auditors executing the continuous auditing program to recognize the role that technology plays in any business processing unit and to ensure that system controls are documented appropriately in the continuous auditing phase requirements. This system knowledge, whether it pertains to access or reliability, is required only for the specific systems being used in the particular business activities linked to the continuous auditing objective. Leveraging this system knowledge with the phase requirements will ensure the continuous auditing results are valid and focused on improving business processing effectiveness and efficiency.

 SUMMARY

In this chapter, we discussed the critical conditions that assist in the facilitation of the creation, implementation, and maintenance of a successful continuous auditing methodology. The identified conditions provided an outline and suggested supporting information to ensure the successful implementation of a continuous auditing methodology. Remember that even if all of the conditions are not present, it does not mean that you cannot develop a successful continuous auditing methodology. Use the corresponding conditions as a guide to assist in the formalization of your continuous auditing methodology. The condition knowledge also provides you with the potential mistakes that can be realized if the methodology is not documented formally with the condition components in mind.

Remember to review your continuous auditing methodology to ensure that it was created appropriately and that the corresponding business unit management, internal audit, and technology conditions have been addressed adequately in the corresponding supporting documentation. The specific conditions and their supporting components are the backbone that supports the successfully implemented continuous auditing program.

CHAPTER TWELVE

Selling Continuous Auditing

 SELLING

In this chapter, we identify and discuss key participants involved in the marketing of the continuous auditing methodology as well as potential partners who may be contributing to the success of this audit methodology. Plus, we review identified benefits to business unit management in an effort to validate the values of a successful partnership that are realized from this strategic proactive audit approach. We also examine a marketing plan guideline that will provide guidance as to the required deliverables to be included and the necessary steps to ensure that your continuous auditing program pilot is successfully developed and implemented.

Also included in this chapter is an internal audit department profile that examines the steps needed to create your formal continuous auditing methodology. This methodology outline profiles the specific section requirements with the associated contents and a corresponding communication plan to ensure that all members of the internal audit department clearly understand the objectives and expectations of the continuous auditing program being developed. In addition, the benefits recognized by both large and small audit shops after implementing a continuous auditing methodology are compared.

The chapter wraps up with a discussion of how the continuous auditing methodology impacts external clients as well as any potential benefits and reliance that can be placed on completed continuous auditing programs. The major benefit recognized from external clients is the expansion of coverage and the use of the continuous auditing work in lieu of additional testing that may have needed to be performed. External clients can range from your external audit firm to regulatory agencies. The discussion begins with the keys to working with business unit management and getting them to recognize the power and benefits of a successfully implemented continuous auditing methodology.

BUSINESS UNIT MANAGEMENT

Business unit management plays a critical role in every aspect of the continuous auditing methodology because this group represents the partner who is going to provide responsible auditors with the business processing education knowledge needed to effectively prepare and the transaction-level data that is required to complete the associated program. To ensure that business unit management is comfortable with the new internal audit testing approach, responsible auditors must be able to convey effectively the specifics of the continuous auditing methodology along with an explanation as to why it is a proactive auditing approach. The discussion begins with the identification of a willing business partner.

Partnership

Every internal auditor would agree that it is very difficult to perform any audit service without the participation of a willing partner. This is especially true when the internal audit department decides to develop another auditing technique that is not only a drastic deviation from the current audit methodology but also requires testing to be performed throughout the continuous auditing life cycle. The thought of this change alone will send shivers down the spines of every business process owner for fear that the internal audit function will become a permanent fixture in every operational department.

However, the silver lining is that when the continuous auditing methodology is developed and implemented properly, it can be planned and performed with minimal distractions to business unit personnel. And depending on the results, the entire continuous auditing program can be planned, executed, and reported without any time commitment from the business process owner with the exception of the initial meeting to explain the continuous auditing methodology and its benefits. That is assuming no exceptions were identified (that required validation) and no reportable issues were noted in the final report (that required a business action plan).

Imagine an audit that includes recurring testing that can be executed from start to finish with minimal, if not zero, business interruption over a period of time. It sounds silly, but once the continuous auditing methodology has been implemented in well-controlled business processing units, there is no need to disrupt the business unit personnel in order to complete the methodology requirements. However, this type of audit execution would not be possible without a strong commitment on the part of both the business process owner and the responsible auditor to partner in the creation and implementation of the continuous auditing methodology. The commitment would include the business unit owner setting aside the time to meet with the responsible auditor to explain the current critical processing environment of the business operations. Only after this knowledge sharing would the auditor be able to create a continuous auditing program to evaluate the strength of the control environment of the specific controls selected. This joint effort provides the foundation for the execution of the continuous auditing methodology phase requirements. To ensure the long-term success of the continuous auditing program, the responsible auditor must provide a detailed overview of the continuous auditing methodology as well as of the expectations and deliverables of the foundation, approach, and execution phases of the program to business unit management. If either party involved in the partnership does not possess adequate knowledge of the process or fails to communicate objectives and tasks effectively, the continuous auditing methodology will not be able to provide consistent value-added results. Without the partnership working in unison toward the same goal, the program will be unable to validate that the selected controls are producing repeatable, reliable results. Keep in mind that the key to any successful business relationship is strong, consistent, honest, and upfront communication.

Proactive Audit Approach

One of the major selling points of the continuous auditing methodology for business unit management is that the executed program results can be used as a predictive tool. When the "6-9-12" frequency methodology, detailed in Chapter 5, is being performed, the concurrent months of testing can provide a forward-looking view based on the results of the previous tests. However, in order to ensure that the continuous auditing program can be used proactively, there must be an absolute certainty on behalf of the responsible auditor that the continuous auditing testing objective and corresponding attributes were not altered at any time during the execution phases. If all of the testing programs were exactly the same, as required in the execution phases, the results can be compiled to create a picture that proactively identifies potential trends throughout the year. If for any reason the testing approach or specific attributes were altered during monthly program execution, it would not be possible to identify any trends because the source data did not match from one period to the next. If the testing plan requires a change once the continuous auditing methodology has begun, the required number of periods to be tested resets and starts again each time the program is altered.

Another unique concept with the proactive nature of the continuous auditing methodology is that the focus is totally different from that of a full-scope audit. A full-scope audit examines historical transactions from months of previously processed data; the continuous auditing methodology is focused on the current process and does not go back farther than the last completed month. The continuous auditing methodology selects transactions in this manner to ensure that they are being processed with the most up-to-date policies and procedures. This recent activity is tested for compliance with the established standard.

To maximize the value of the continuous auditing program, the sample selected must be the most current transactions in order to create a current baseline to develop the predictive side of the approach. If historical data is used, there is no way to ensure that all of the data tested over the course of the methodology execution is consistent and held to the same exact processing requirements. Anytime the data is older than the previous month, there is no way to validate the established control environment at that time.

The final selling point for the continuous auditing methodology as it pertains to being proactive is that it is not concerned with how bad or good the control environment used to be. The goal is to validate the strength and effectiveness of the current control environment. The only way to do so is to obtain and verify the current business process requirements and select current transactions on which to perform the evaluation testing.

Marketing Plan

All new processes that require a custom development process must have a corresponding marketing plan to ensure the success of the rollout and subsequent pilot program. However, when the internal audit department is announcing a new audit procedure, even more scrutiny will be applied from anyone outside of internal audit than if the new process was from just another business unit. Internal audit departments always seem to be held to a higher standard, probably because internal auditors move from business unit to business unit pointing out potentials areas for improvement on a daily basis. When there is opportunity to review, examine, and provide constructive feedback on an internal audit process, it seems like everyone has something to say.

Before the internal audit department can even consider a marketing plan and rollout strategy, it must formally document the continuous auditing methodology with the objectives, phase requirements and their corresponding activities, and the results reporting process. Once the methodology has been drafted, it will go through a review process to ensure that it is comprehensive, provides adequate processing details explaining the objectives and deliverables, and documents the continuous auditing process flow from start to finish.

Once the methodology has been documented and approved, it is time to create a marketing plan that will allow internal auditors to begin formally introducing the new process to the company. While the marketing plan is being drafted, internal audit management must introduce and explain the new methodology to the entire internal audit department at a formal department meeting. This meeting must be mandatory to ensure that all internal auditors are fully aware of the new process and its required procedures. All members of the internal audit department must clearly understand the continuous auditing program requirements; without such understanding, it will be impossible for the auditors to market the new approach or answer questions regarding the new audit product. The education and understanding component for the internal audit team can be accomplished either prior to marketing plan development (preferred method) or at the same time as the marketing plan is being created. If left to after the marketing plan has been developed and business units are being educated on the new approach, internal audit may never be educated in the process. Keep in mind that communication should come from within, especially for this delicate situation. Any time a process enhancement or change is being introduced in internal audit, it is paramount that the proper communication be executed to ensure all team members are on the same page. This is critical because the enhancement or change directly impacts business unit management and how their control environment will be tested. Internal auditors should *never* learn of a new auditing technique from a business process owner before hearing it from their own team. Such a scenario would be uncomfortable for the auditors while also portraying the internal audit department as a functional unit lacking in the critical competency of communication. Avoid the potential embarrassment and set the standard for communication by ensuring that all new methodologies and enhancements are adequately and timely communicated to the entire audit team before being made public to business process owners. Also, even if you have never had any communication issues with your team, ensure that communication is identified as one of the core competencies for all internal audit team members.

The effort to develop a successful continuous auditing marketing plan should begin with a discussion objective describing the purpose of the marketing plan and what it is designed to accomplish. The purpose is to clearly communicate the definition of a continuous auditing methodology and provide not only the specifics of the process but also the key distinctions that separate it from the normal full-scope audit that business process owners are used to receiving. Additionally, the new approach has been designed as a targeted audit technique that will focus on the performance of selected key controls and determine their strength after examining the control operations over a set period of time.

Once the plan has been outlined, the next step is to identify a willing business process owner to be a partner in the first continuous auditing program ever done by the internal audit department. Doing this can be a more complicated decision than it appears to be on the surface. The selection of a business partner seems simple: just pick a business process owner with whom you have had a good relationship with during previous audits. What this usually means is that you choose a business partner for whom you have never issued anything but a satisfactory audit opinion. However, the business owner who has never received anything but positive results is not necessarily the best partner for the continuous auditing methodology pilot. The reason this is true is because a business owner willing to participate in the introduction of a new audit approach is usually one who recognizes the value and the benefit that the internal audit group provides; in other words, the business owner who has received internal audit reports that identified controls gaps requiring formal action plans. Although internal audit has been critical of this particular business process, history has shown that this business partner recognizes the value of the audit report issued even if it did not show the targeted operational business process in the most positive light.

Once the appropriate partner has been selected, it is time to lay out the details of the continuous auditing methodology. During this conversation, it is important to explain how the continuous auditing program works from start to finish. The most effective way to navigate through this discussion is to start with the program objective and then outline the foundation, approach, and execution phase details along with their requirements. To prepare for this meeting, use the business management condition questions discussed in Chapter 11 and integrate the answers as you explain the methodology. Remember that it is critical that you have a firm grasp of the continuous auditing methodology requirements and the phase requirements before you attempt to market the audit approach. Business process owners surely will recognize whether the person facilitating the marketing discussion meeting does not understand how the program actually works. To ensure success, prepare for the meeting adequately and use an outline or an agenda to facilitate the discussion.

To provide the selected business management partner with a validation of the commitments made by internal audit during the marketing meeting, make sure that responsible auditors executing the continuous auditing program truly include the business owner as a partner throughout all three phases of the methodology. To accomplish this, create an environment based on consistent communication and details as each component of the phases are planned,

TABLE 12.1 Continuous Auditing Marketing Plan Outline

Marketing Component	Description
1. Internal Audit Department Announcement	Communicate the launch of the new auditing technique during a formal meeting. Use the meeting to explain all phase requirements of the methodology.
2. Marketing Plan Objective	Communicate the continuous auditing methodology definition and objectives to our business partners.
3. Partner Selection	Identify an audit partner who truly recognizes the value and benefits that internal audit provides.
4. Methodology Meeting	Facilitate a meeting with the selected partner to review the detailed phases of the continuous auditing methodology.
5. Partner Development	Include the partner in all aspects of the methodology with strong communication each time that you meet with them. Be prepared for every meeting.
6. Continuous Auditing Pilot	Select a noncomplex business process for the first continuous auditing program.

developed, and executed. If the continuous auditing program is completed without much communication with the business partner until the draft report, the relationship and any future audits are going to be a struggle. Remember always to focus on a high level of communication and adequately prepare for every meeting.

Table 12.1 lists the key steps as well as some additional suggestions for a successful roll-out of your continuous auditing methodology. This outline also includes suggestions for communicating the methodology to the internal audit department and the business management partner.

 AUDIT TEAM

As discussed in Table 12.1, responsible auditors will be unable to sell the continuous auditing program effectively without having a clear understanding of the methodology as well as its objectives and corresponding phase requirements. That is why is it critical for the audit management team to have their own plan to formally develop the specifics of the continuous auditing methodology. To assist in the introduction, internal audit management will have a formal introductory meeting for the team to communicate all the details of the new audit approach. At this meeting, management will stress the importance of adhering to the methodology requirements as they have been designed in order to maximize the value of the continuous auditing methodology.

Methodology Development and Communication

The first step in getting the audit team on board with the new approach is to formally document the methodology requirements. As previously discussed, it would be a very difficult task for any internal audit team member to market the continuous auditing methodology without truly understanding its objectives and requirements. To ensure that your methodology contains the proper level of detail and explanation, refer to Chapter 3 to guide you through the development process. Remember to include the purpose, objectives, and phase requirements as outlined in Table 3.2. You can also review the continuous auditing methodology template in the appendix.

The key to a successful roll-out to the internal audit department is to have an internal communication plan to ensure there is not only a formal introduction of the continuous auditing methodology but also supporting information and resources readily available to provide guidance if any of the internal audit team members have specific questions as to the continuous auditing methodology objectives or phase requirements. This internal plan should include, at a minimum, a documented formal methodology that is provided to all internal auditors, a mandatory meeting to communicate the approach and illustrate the internal audit department's commitment to the methodology, and an identification of the internal audit resources available should anyone have questions regarding the concept, objectives, or phase requirements. The internal audit department resources are usually the team members who were involved in the development and formal documentation of the methodology. If you stick to this basic plan and provide ongoing support at both the individual and the department level, you will introduce the continuous auditing methodology to your department successfully.

The next step in the internal marketing of the new approach is to communicate to the team the benefits to incorporating the continuous auditing methodology into the department as a complement to the formal audit methodology currently being used.

Department Benefits

One important distinction must be made when it comes to developing and implementing a continuous auditing methodology in an audit department. Although formal documentation of the methodology is paramount, it is even more important to ensure that every person in the department clearly understands that the methodology has been created to complement the existing risk-based audit approach, not to replace it. A continuous auditing methodology is an alternative testing approach that can be used to gain increased audit universe coverage or increased depth of a selected control to determine effectiveness and efficiency. The aim of the new methodology is not to streamline audits or just increase the number of audits completed annually.

To ensure that your department recognizes all the benefits that a successfully integrated continuous auditing methodology can provide, auditors first must realize that it is another audit technique to be used when appropriate. That message should be communicated to the entire team by internal audit management during the formal introductory meeting. This message is a critical component to ensuring the success of the methodology. Always focus on the continuous auditing methodology objectives when explaining how the approach should be used and the most effective methods of execution.

Table 12.2 illustrates the potential benefits that the internal audit department can gain from the continuous auditing methodology.

Audit Shop Benefits

It is important to note that the potential benefits identified in Table 12.2 can be realized by all internal audit departments regardless of their size. However, the table breaks down the benefits into categories that are most often recognized

TABLE 12.2 Audit Department Benefits

Large Audit Shops	Small Audit Shops
Business Education	Audit Depth
Cross-Training	Expanded Audit Universe Coverage
Business Monitoring	Project Participation
External Audit Assistance	Regulatory Compliance

by larger and smaller shops. Understand that the table does not set a defined list of benefits for large and small audit departments. Next, we briefly explain the benefits for the internal audit departments listed in the table.

The benefits of incorporating a continuous auditing program in larger audit departments (usually above 15 auditors) could include, but are not be limited to, the items listed in Table 12.2. When it comes to business education, the continuous auditing methodology provides an opportunity for all individuals to be exposed to areas in the company that they normally do not audit. Larger audit shops tend to be organized by business line and often keep auditors in their assigned lines of business to develop their business expertise. The continuous auditing program provides them with the opportunity to participate on the recurring testing in an area that they normally would not audit.

This benefit of business education links directly with the next potential benefit of cross-training. The continuous auditing methodology provides an effective and efficient way to cross-train internal audit team members on the different business units in the company, whether auditors are assigned to that business unit or not. The additional exposure helps team members develop their business knowledge and provides them with the opportunity to learn about areas outside of their specialties.

Business monitoring is another benefit that can be realized using the continuous auditing methodology results. This is the one and only time that the term "monitoring" is used in conjunction with the continuous auditing program. Recall Chapter 1, where continuous auditing was defined and specifically differentiated from continuous monitoring. However, business monitoring is not to be confused with continuous monitoring when it comes to a benefit. Business monitoring, from a benefit perspective, uses the continuous auditing program results to share business-level information with all members of the audit team. This sharing provides an effective way for the internal audit department to monitor the different audit activities that are being performed so that any internal audit team member can consider these results when planning their own individual audits. Sharing of business-level data provides valuable background when internal auditors are considering risk at the company level rather than the individual audit level. This additional knowledge allows the internal audit department to plan more effectively.

External audit assistance is the final benefit listed under large shops. This in no way means that only large shops work with external audit partners. That could not be further from the truth. The only reason it is listed under large audit shops is because larger shops have more opportunities to dedicate resources to develop continuous auditing programs to satisfy external audit requirements.

The benefits of incorporating a continuous auditing program in smaller audit departments (usually fewer than 15 auditors) could include, but not be limited to, the items listed in Table 12.2. When it comes to audit depth, the continuous auditing methodology can provide an approach that drills down into the critical controls of a business process and repeatedly tests them to verify whether they have been designed and implemented properly to produce repeatable, reliable results. Due to the limited resources available in smaller internal audit departments, this testing approach can be implemented to test critical controls in higher-risk areas without dedicating a significant amount of time and resources.

Internal audit departments with limited resources must rely heavily on their risk assessment documentation to ensure that they are managing their resources effectively to cover the highest-risk areas in the company. Smaller audit departments can audit only so many business units on an annual basis. However, with the proper implementation of the continuous auditing methodology, the department would be able to manage the audit plan more effectively and possibly increase the number of high-risk areas to be audited annually. Each time you develop or review an audit plan, consider whether there are any opportunities to incorporate a continuous auditing program. Remember, the continuous auditing methodology is integrated into existing audit departments, regardless of their size, to complement the risk-based audit approach. The strategic use of the continuous auditing methodology will help manage the annual audit plan more effectively.

It seems almost daily that business units are requesting that internal audit participate in company-wide and even department projects. Everyone wants an audit presence on their team to get an up-front assessment of the initiative from a control perspective. Unfortunately, there are only so many internal audit resources available to participate on projects. To try to address all of the requests, implement a continuous auditing program to track the deliverables associated with each project and identify whether projects are meeting their commitments. This is not the typical use of the continuous auditing methodology, but it can identify opportunities to assign audit resources where needed.

Regulatory assistance is the final benefit listed under smaller audit shops for the simple reason that such shops do not have the resources to dedicate to assisting compliance departments. The continuous auditing methodology is the perfect audit technique for compliance-related issues because there is no risk of interpretation or judgment when it comes to developing the specific testing requirements. Because the regulatory rules have clear guidelines for compliance, it is easier to identify and define the testing attributes for the continuous auditing program.

EXTERNAL CLIENTS

Selling the continuous auditing methodology to business partners in your company will not be the most challenging marketing that you will face when peddling the new audit approach. The biggest sell just might be to potential external clients, such as regulators and your external audit firms. However, the good news is that you should use the same approach to marketing the methodology to your external partners as you used with your internal business clients.

Commitment to Sell

The foundation for the marketing plan remains consistent regardless of the target audience. Always remember that you need to explain the methodology objectives and deliverables with one added dimension for every external partner you engage at the marketing level. Before any of them will accept a continuous auditing methodology as an approved method of audit control evaluation, you must spell out the details at a granular level for each phase of the methodology. This painstaking process requires the internal audit marketing representative to exercise patience when reviewing the continuous auditing methodology. Business process owners will have many questions why the audit department is using this approach rather than a full-scope audit. This is one of the main reasons why we stress how important it is for all internal audit team members to have a strong foundational knowledge of the continuous auditing methodology before attempting to engage a potential partner or external client in a continuous auditing program. To help facilitate these marketing discussions, keep a copy of the formal continuous auditing methodology document with you so that you can refer to it during the meeting. This shows meeting attendees that you have prepared adequately for the discussion and that the internal audit department has taken the time to fully develop and document the methodology.

Do not underestimate the time it will take to prepare adequately for the discussion with your potential external partners. During the discussion, it is also helpful to have examples of completed continuous auditing programs to illustrate how the methodology works and the value-added control environment improvements that were found using this approach.

Relied-on Work

The ultimate goal for any internal audit department is to get its external partners to fully understand the continuous auditing methodology so that those partners recognize and accept all of the hard work, dedication, and resources applied to complete the programs. Whether your external audit firm or regulatory agency is relying on the continuous auditing testing, it is strongly recommended that you review and explain the continuous auditing methodology to them prior to implementing the approach for work that your external partners are going to rely on in lieu of additional testing.

From my experience, both external audit firms and regulatory agencies recognize that internal audit departments are developing and implementing continuous auditing methodologies to assist in the effective management of the annual audit plan. In this recognition, external partners usually will accept work that was performed using a continuous auditing methodology as long as they are familiar with how the work was executed and the specific testing objectives that were achieved. Thus, the responsible auditors will have to review with the external partner the details of the completed continuous auditing program and every aspect of the testing from inception, to objective development, to sample selection, to testing attributes, to exception identification and verification, to reporting and communication, and finally to disposition of noted issues. If all of these components of the testing can be explained, the work will be accepted and the continuous auditing methodology will continue to provide benefits to the internal audit departments and its many clients.

 **SUMMARY**

In this chapter, the key participants involved in the marketing of the continuous auditing methodology were identified and discussed along with potential partners who must participate and contribute throughout the continuous auditing program process. The marketing further describes the importance of the partnership and the roles each party will play to ensure program success. Remember to stress the commitment aspect to the internal audit department while at the same time communicating the benefits of this proactive approach to the targeted partner.

Also described in this chapter were the specifics surrounding the creation of your marketing plan. Remember to use the components listed in Table 12.1 when researching and developing your formal marketing plan. Not only does the table provide an outline for the process but also continues to stress the importance of the high level of communication required, especially internally with the audit department, to implement the methodology successfully.

Successful marketing and ultimate incorporation of the approach leads to many benefits in every company. The key is to use the benefits described in this chapter, for both the internal audit department and the external partner, to champion the impact that the continuous auditing methodology will have on the company as a whole. And finally, remember that the chapter provides only a short list of potential benefits that could be recognized from the continuous auditing methodology. You must adapt your marketing plan to focus on the benefits that your department and business management teams will realize through successful implementation. Stay focused on the goals and objectives of the program, and remember that communication must be the cornerstone of support for your marketing efforts.

CHAPTER THIRTEEN

13

Continuous Auditing Challenges

 CHALLENGES

In this chapter, we identify and discuss the challenges that the internal audit department and the business unit management face when developing and executing the continuous auditing methodology. The key is to understand that you need to recognize and address obstacles as you plan, create, and implement the continuous auditing methodology most suited to complement your current risk-based audit methodology. As you design your custom continuous auditing methodology, use these verified challenges to ensure that your methodology includes the appropriate level of detail for each challenge described. The more details that you include in the formal continuous auditing methodology, the lower the likelihood that you will come across one of these challenges during testing. These obstacles have been broken down into two categories: the ones that challenge the internal audit team and the ones that challenge your business unit partners. The discussion begins with internal audit challenges.

INTERNAL AUDIT DEPARTMENT

Every internal audit department has challenges; they just come with the territory of being in internal audit. However, once you decide to create and implement a continuous auditing methodology, you must identify and discuss a few more challenges because any one of them could result in the continuous auditing methodology not operating as it was intended. The specific challenges to be discussed are the understanding of objectives, rush to implementation, and recognizing limitations. It is important to understand each challenge so that you can execute the continuous auditing program without significant processing issues.

Understanding the Objectives

There are not enough pages in this book to stress how critically important it is for every member of the internal audit team not only to recognize but also to clearly understand the objectives of the continuous auditing methodology. Many times auditors just beginning to use the continuous auditing program think that they understand its objectives when, in reality, they treat it like just another audit with a smaller scope. The continuous auditing methodology tries to accomplish specific objectives. The objectives focus on using a custom audit approach that validates the strength of the selected control environment through a series of targeted, recurring tests. Moreover, when the continuous auditing methodology is followed exactly as it was designed, it can also be used as a predictive approach. This predictive ability occurs because the critical control testing is performed on a recurring basis for the most current months of production during the scope period of execution. The month-after-month testing of current data allows the responsible auditor to use the continuous auditing testing results to potentially predict activity based on the testing results.

Additional continuous auditing methodology objectives include:

- Expanding the current coverage of the risk-based audit universe
- More effective management of internal audit department deliverables
- Drilling down into specific control activities that have been identified as key to the success of the operating department
- Validating the implementation of management action plans

There is no additional audit universe coverage gained by completing full-scope risk-based audits. The scheduled audits are completed as designed, but their coverage of the audit universe remains unchanged. With the strategic implementation of the continuous auditing methodology, it is possible to increase the audit coverage of the current audit universe. As the audit year passes, the current audit plan activity gets reassessed every quarter. With an implemented continuous auditing methodology, the audit department has the opportunity to increase coverage of the audit universe by using continuous auditing elsewhere, where time and resources permit. This additional work can be incorporated because of the targeted approach of the continuous auditing methodology. However, this increased coverage can be accomplished only if the internal audit department members recognize and understand the specific objectives of the methodology.

The implementation of the continuous auditing methodology also can provide more effective management of internal audit department deliverables. As the audit year progresses, it always seems that around the middle of the year, internal audit management realizes that the department is behind schedule on the audits that it is supposed to complete that year. In this case, audit management usually reviews the current audit plan and reassesses the remaining audits to determine how the department is going to complete the audit plan which was originally committed to at the beginning of the year. However, implementation of the continuous auditing methodology would give the audit management team another effective audit approach to apply to the remaining audits, possibly preventing any audits from being reassessed and placed in the following year's audit plan. Additionally, if the approved audit plan is examined carefully at the start of the audit year, the work can be managed more effectively by determining up front which audits can be completed by using the continuous auditing methodology and which ones require a full-scope risk-based audit. It is more expeditious if this audit plan review and audit type determination is accomplished at the beginning of the year before any audits are kicked off, thus eliminating the need to scramble midyear to try and determine how to meet the audit plan originally communicated. Effectively managing the full-scope and continuous auditing approaches will greatly benefit the productivity of the internal audit department.

Specific control activity performance validation is yet another objective of the continuous auditing methodology. Any time during a full-scope risk-based audit or at the request of an outside party, an individual control can be identified for testing. The decision or request to validate a specific control can be based on risk level, a hunch, or the significant volume that the key control processes on a daily basis. No matter what the reason for the request, the continuous auditing methodology is the perfect audit technique to validate the performance of an individual control. However, before jumping in and starting the continuous auditing program, remember the need to plan. Even if it is a single control that is going to be evaluated, that does not mean that no planning is necessary. After you document the control to clearly understand what the control objective is, you can create the testing to validate the control effectiveness. The target approach of the continuous auditing methodology can be implemented more effectively and efficiently to handle custom requests rather than trying to use a full-scope audit approach to address an individual control or identified gap in the process. When internal audit cannot dedicate the time and resources to initiate and execute a full-scope audit to address a control issue or concern raised by an outside party, use the continuous auditing methodology to create the necessary testing to validate the control in question.

The final objective of the continuous auditing methodology to be discussed has been responsible for its recent increase in use over the past 18 months. The objective is to validate the implementation of management action plans. Internal audit departments are using this approach to verify that business unit management has appropriately implemented agreed-on action plans as documented in the final audit report. The usual audit process is to send the responsible auditor who performed the initial work back to the business unit to verify that the action plan has been implemented. Although that is an acceptable process, it does not always guarantee that the implemented action plan truly addresses the risk identified during the audit. Even if the brief follow-up testing appears to prove compliance with action plan implementation requirements, it is usually too soon to conclude that the control enhancement is totally effective. It is recommended that the business unit have at least 60 with the revised control to ensure proper time has been allotted for the operational business team to adapt to the process enhancement. The only way to determine whether the implemented control is operating as intended in addressing the noted process risk is to use the continuous auditing methodology, which will provide the evidence that the control is producing repeatable, reliable results. The continuous auditing methodology is more effective at determining the appropriateness of action plan implementation because it tests the specific control enhancement *over a period of time* instead of just at the initial point of implementation. Anytime a control enhancement is made, everyone is complying with it because it is new. However, control enhancements can be proven effective only if they can stand the test of time and repeated transaction processing.

Now, we are not recommending that you use the continuous auditing methodology to validate implementation for every management action plan. The best practice for using continuous auditing for verifying action plan implementation is to focus only on the high-risk-rated exceptions. This is becoming a best practice as a result of replacing the subsequent control testing happening as a one-time event as opposed to the continuous auditing methodology that validates the control performance over a period of time. For these types of critical controls, it is paramount to ensure that the action plan created by business unit management adequately addresses the root cause identified in the report and that the corresponding risk has been mitigated properly.

Rush to Implementation

One of the most significant challenges to the effective development and execution of a continuous auditing methodology is when the internal audit department rushes through planning to get to implementation. This could consist of insufficient planning in methodology development or for individual continuous audits. Insufficient planning impacts the overall effectiveness of the continuous auditing methodology results and possibly the reputation of the internal audit department. Insufficient planning related to the methodology development will have a negative impact on the effectiveness of the documentation and the quality of the continuous auditing results. Chapter 3 describes the steps necessary to build a complete methodology, but you cannot complete any of those steps satisfactorily without a dedicated effort to research and plan the objective and phase requirements.

As described in Chapter 12, methodology development and marketing are associated with significant responsibilities. Documenting the critical steps is vital to program success. Plus, a considerable commitment has to be made to communicate the continuous auditing methodology to the internal audit team and prospective business unit clients. The most common mistake regarding the methodology is almost never related to the documentation; it is usually on the communication side. Many audit departments assume incorrectly that their team members do not need a formal introduction to the continuous auditing methodology because they are auditors, and this is just another way to do their job. Internal audit management feels that the transition to the continuous auditing methodology should be simple for any internal auditor on the team. Regardless of the experience of the internal audit team members, everyone needs to be told what the continuous auditing methodology is and what is required of them to execute it successfully. Truth be told, the more experienced the auditors, the more important it is to explain this new audit approach to them in detail. More experienced auditors sometimes are so set in their ways of auditing that they find it difficult to grasp and adjust to new concepts.

Another significant risk arises if the internal audit department rushes to implement the methodology without dedicating the time and resources to communicate the new approach to business unit clients. Trying to accelerate the implementation with the business partner on a continuous auditing methodology will result in an uneasy feeling on the part of your business client because they will feel like they are in the dark throughout the entire audit process. At no time during any audit activity should the business unit be unaware of what is going on or why it is happening. The communication of the continuous auditing methodology should be transparent to the business partner and foster an open exchange of critical information. Conversely, allocating appropriate time to communicate requirements with business unit clients but rushing the implementation stage of the execution of work will impact the quality of the continuous auditing report as well as take longer to execute the continuous auditing program due to the lack of sufficient planning. Nothing takes the place of planning and building the operational business knowledge. Without the proper planning, the continuous auditing objective may be incomplete or inaccurate, the wrong control may be targeted for testing, or there may be a lack of general business knowledge of the process to test it effectively.

It is critically important not to rush through the development of the continuous auditing methodology or shortcut the communication require-ments of its marketing rollout. Also, do not rush the planning of the individual continuous auditing program, as doing so will result in a non-value-added audit. Unfortunately, responsible auditors and clients will not realize that there was no value in the work performed until the report is being developed. The bottom-line reason that the non-value add will not be recognized until the report generation will be that the internal audit department did not understand the business unit operations or objectives. There are no shortcuts when it comes to developing or executing a continuous auditing methodology. To be successful, dedicate the time and resources to plan effectively.

Recognizing the Limitations

As was discussed and detailed in Chapter 5, certain business areas and processes are not conducive to the application of a continuous auditing methodology. The most important aspect of this challenge is to recognize that it is truly a challenge that, if ignored, will impact the effectiveness of the continuous auditing program. Through research and years of experience of successful implementation and execution of continuous auditing methodologies, the limitations have revealed themselves. The limitations identified in Chapter 5—judgment and operational complexity—are not the only ones, but they are two of the biggest ones. When planning an auditing program of a highly complex operational process, such as financial statement generation, or an operational process requiring a significant amount of judgment or interpretation, such as underwriting, consider whether the continuous auditing methodology is the best approach to test these control environments.

This is not to say that you could not execute a continuous auditing program in either one of these areas; it can be done. The challenge lies in determining the most critical controls to test in either scenario. Remember that anytime you incorporate judgment or interpretation into a process, there is a significant amount of variation in the processing requirements because of the latitude given to people working in these areas. The judgmental areas rely on team members' experience to interpret the information and make risk decisions. Because there are no set control limits for satisfactory performance, auditors find it difficult to create effective continuous auditing methodology phase requirements for such areas.

When evaluating the type of audit to execute for any business process, take the time to plan adequately. Adequate planning will provide the right guidance to ensure that you do not overlook a limitation that will impact the effectiveness of your continuous auditing methodology.

CLIENT

All internal audit departments are very aware that even though business unit management (the client) plays a critical role in every aspect of the continuous auditing methodology, they can pose challenges to the successful execution of the program. The challenges that the client presents directly impact the responsible auditor's ability to perform the phase requirements as designed. Unfortunately, internal audit can only try to communicate the fundamentals of the continuous auditing methodology and convey the partnering responsibilities to the client in an effort to avoid the challenges. This open, upfront communication of responsibilities of each party involved in the continuous auditing partnership helps to eliminate the potential pitfalls that may be encountered. The specific challenges include a lack of understanding, unwillingness to partner, and full-time request for service. It is important to understand each of these challenges so that the continuous auditing methodology can be executed effectively.

Lack of Understanding

The challenge that internal audit encounters often is that their business unit partner (the client) does not fully understand internal audit in general. It can be that the client does not understand what internal audit does or why; or the client may not understand why the audit work is being performed in the first place, let alone the specific objectives of a continuous auditing methodology. This challenge all comes back to the communication that should be the cornerstone of every internal audit department.

The problem arises when the client does not understand the continuous auditing methodology, its objectives, or the benefits that can be recognized from using this audit approach. Unfortunately, lack of understanding arises directly from an insufficient amount of communication from the internal audit department regarding the methodology. This challenge can be compounded by the fact that it is not easily identified unless you are really looking for it. It is not that easy to interpret a client's facial expressions or responses to mean that they have no idea of why internal audit is there or what audit type they are going to execute. Most auditors attribute such expressions to disappointment that people have to participate in the continuous auditing program. Internal audit meetings are not high on most clients' lists of things they like to do at work. However, like it or not, internal auditors have a job to do, and the meetings are a necessity, especially during the introduction of a new audit methodology.

The most effective technique to use when trying to identify if there is any issue with understanding of the continuous auditing methodology is to ask qualifying questions. If the questions result in an acknowledgment of under-standing, follow them up by stating specifically what will be expected from the client during the foundation, approach, and execution phases of the method-ology. Once the commitments have been discussed, again ask clients if they clearly understand what they will be expected to contribute to ensure the continuous auditing program is successful. If both questions receive a positive acknowledgment of understanding, summarize the methodology one final time and be sure to include the benefits that clients may see at the end of the audit.

If this challenge is realized where there is an uncertainty as to what is to be expected during a continuous audit, not only do clients not truly understand the continuous auditing methodology or its potential benefits; but they also may not want to participate at all. This attitude does not mean that clients will prevent the continuous auditing program from being executed in the business unit; however, the responsible auditor may have to pursue the business unit avidly to get the clients to participate actively in meetings and provide the required documentation to complete the phase requirements. Remember, internal audit has some culpability in this scenario; the root cause usually leads back to ineffective communication on behalf of internal audit.

Unwillingness to Partner

Another challenge that significantly impacts the continuous auditing meth-odology is an unwillingness to partner on behalf of business unit management (the clients). It is not that the clients refuse to work with the responsible auditor who has to complete the continuous auditing program. It is a more subtle problem that is usually exhibited by actions more than an outright refusal to work with internal audit. The actions to be on the lookout for are lack of participation in meetings, being late or not attending meetings, or ignoring initial and follow-up requests for critical documentation.

The most difficult problem for auditors is when clients ignore repeated attempts to obtain sample documentation for testing. This problem confirms that clients are unwilling to partner on this program and should trigger an immediate reaction from the responsible auditor. After repeated (at least three attempts) have not resulted in the sharing of any business-level documentation, the responsible auditor must meet with the client as soon as possible and emphasize the critical nature of the documentation delivery. Failure to receive documentation in a timely manner begins a domino effect; without this documentation, it will be next to impossible for the responsible auditor to meet the aggressive phase requirement timelines or perform the testing required in the following months. The continuous auditing methodology is based on recurring test programs being executed on a very tight schedule. To meet those strict deadlines, clients must be willing to partner. Once the auditor falls behind during any phase of the continuous auditing methodology, especially the execution phase, it is not possible to catch up.

The key to addressing this challenge is to recognize the signs quickly and take immediate steps to identify why a client is not cooperating with the requirements of the continuous auditing methodology. Sometimes it is an easy fix; all you may need to do is review the methodology with the process owner again and reaffirm the phase requirements as well as the benefits that a completed continuous auditing program can provide. Other fixes may require significant effort. Whatever the reason for the challenge, the responsible auditor must identify its root cause and determine the best way to address it. If additional resources are needed to assist in the determination of root cause or to implement an action plan to address the challenge, talk to your management team for suggestions or help; surely they have dealt with other difficult clients.

Full-Time Request for Service

The final challenge to be discussed is the opposite of the last one. Here the client is very pleased with the continuous auditing methodology and the results. In fact, the client has recognized such benefits from the continuous auditing methodology that it wants the internal audit department to partner with the business unit on an ongoing basis. Translated, the client would like the monthly recurring testing to be performed indefinitely. I realize that this seems outrageous; what audit client would want work to be performed in a business unit until forever? Although the situation may sound unbelievable, it happens more often than you think. Internal auditors are used to clients asking how much longer internal audit will be in their area, not how much longer internal audit can stay and perform this work.

Internal auditors cannot imagine that any client would want a full-scope risk-based audit performed in perpetuity, and that is absolutely right. But remember, this is *not* a full-scope audit; it is a continuous auditing program that does not cause the same level of disruption in daily business unit operations. Plus, once the continuous auditing methodology has been established, the responsible auditor does not even have to be in the business unit area to complete the testing. This lack of auditor intrusiveness only adds to the benefit and allure of the work being performed on an ongoing basis. Clients would benefit from an in-house quality assessment program over a key control(s) and receive validation of the strength of their control environment every single month.

Although this may sound like an excellent opportunity to partner with clients, after stepping back and realizing what is being asked, internal auditors understand that the request is not feasible. No internal audit department wants to turn down a request from a client. Everyone believes that internal audit has been established to help the business units especially in the evaluation of the control environment and this request for service would seem to fit very nicely into that assumption of expected service from internal audit. While it may appear to fit nicely into one of the primary objectives of the internal audit department, it is not feasible for a couple of reasons. First and most obvious, the internal audit department does not have the time or resources to dedicate a full-time continuous methodology auditor to any one particular business unit. Second, from an internal audit definition standpoint, this full-time auditor assignment would appear to impact the independence component of the internal audit definition. To be effective, audit services must remain totally objective and independent of the business area being audited. If an auditor takes a full-time responsibility for one client, it would impact his or her ability to remain independent.

 ## SUMMARY

In this chapter, we identified the internal audit department and business unit management (client) challenges that may be recognized when creating and executing a continuous auditing methodology. Any time a new audit approach or technique is developed, there are always going to be challenges that need to be overcome. The important aspect of challenges is identifying and addressing them adequately and timely when they are revealed.

As you begin the process of developing and executing your custom continuous auditing methodology, keep these challenges in mind so that you recognize signs that could indicate potential trouble. The more detailed the planning phase of the methodology development is, the more effective the communication of the requirements and expectation will be, which should result in fewer challenges impacting program implementation. When it comes to addressing challenges, it is critically important to keep your manager aware of the current situation, all the details of the challenges, and any steps that have been taken so far to address them. The best way to develop steps to address them is to focus on their root cause and create a strategic action plan to address the root cause. When dealing with challenges, it is important to recognize that they are going to happen; it is inevitable. However, it is important to understand the reasons for the challenges, take any lessons learned from each challenge encountered, and ensure that they are not repeated on subsequent audits.

Again, remember how important it is to communicate at a high level and keep a keen eye out for signals that may indicate a potential challenge is about to be realized. Using your continuous auditing methodology knowledge to facilitate key client discussions will reduce the likelihood that these particular challenges will be realized.

CHAPTER FOURTEEN

Continuous Auditing Uses and Users

 ## USES AND USERS

In this chapter, we identify and discuss some examples of specific uses and users of the continuous auditing methodology. Every company and its audit department, compliance division, or enterprise risk team have objectives that they have committed to completing during the year. Those objectives contain specific deliverables usually tied to the evaluation of the control environment as it relates to federal, state, and local rules and regulations; internal company policies and procedures; or the individual risk assessment of a particular operational business function. Regardless of the objective detail, multiple users use the continuous auditing methodology to evaluate risk and the effectiveness and efficiency of the corresponding control environments in which these identified risks are present. This chapter is divided into two sections so that there can be a clear distinction between the suggested uses for the continuous auditing methodology and the individual users who implement the approach to meet their own objectives. The discussion begins with the proposed uses of the continuous auditing methodology.

USES

The continuous auditing methodology is unique in that not only does it provide internal audit departments with an alternate approach to complete control evaluation testing but also can be used by any other business unit that wants to ensure that processes it has developed and implemented are performing according to established standards. Even though the continuous auditing methodology, by name, appears to be a pure audit-specific application, in reality it is not. This creative approach is designed to strategically identify and evaluate critical control process points over a period of time that is determined on a case-by-case basis. The other unique factor of this approach is that it can be customized to meet specific needs of users. The key components of the continuous auditing methodology—objectives, target areas, frequency, testing techniques, scope, sampling, testing attributes, and reporting—are all customizable to fit the needs of the developing area. Because of this customization, there is no limit to the number of uses in which the continuous auditing approach can be applied. The next sections identify and explain the most common uses. However, keep in mind that this is not an all-inclusive list; the methodology is flexible enough to evaluate any control-related process. The only rule, when using a custom-developed continuous auditing methodology, is that the formal process must be documented and adhered to consistently when executing the continuous auditing program.

Some of the most common uses for the continuous auditing methodology include:

- Compliance with regulations
- Policy and procedure adherence
- Increase coverage and depth
- Action plan implementation
- Sarbanes-Oxley testing
- Control self-assessment development

Compliance with Regulations

Perhaps the most common application of the continuous auditing methodology is to verify compliance with a federal, state, or local law. The main reason why this is one of the most popular uses of the targeted approach is that compliance rules and regulations are very specific regarding the control requirements that dictate satisfactory performance. This definition of satisfactory performance relates directly to the acceptable performance of the continuous auditing testing criteria detailed in Chapter 6 that explains the approach phase requirements of the continuous auditing methodology. Acceptable performance is identified, defined, and obtained as the testing criteria is being developed.

The acceptable parameters of satisfactory performance often are specifically spelled out in the explanation of compliance rules and regulations. This type of detailed explanation makes the continuous auditing methodology much easier to create. As mentioned in Chapter 13, one of the limitations of the continuous auditing methodology was the use of judgment when evaluating areas to test. When determining the best areas to use this custom approach, think of compliance first because of its detailed performance requirements and the very limited amount of judgment needed to perform the operational tasks.

Most internal audit departments usually select a compliance-related control for their continuous auditing methodology pilot. Compliance controls are so attractive for this testing approach because of their clear definition of satisfactory performance. The less judgment or interpretation required for the control test, the easier it is to develop the corresponding testing parameters. Also, because of the risk associated with compliance-related issues, business unit managers are anxious to address any potential compliance exposures in their operational unit.

Policy and Procedure Adherence

Another fairly common use of the continuous auditing methodology, especially from the internal audit department perspective, is to validate compliance with internal policies and procedures. In this case, it is critical to be certain that the approach phase requirements—specifically the criteria and attributes—have been identified appropriately. The common mistake made in conjunction with the approach phase requirements is that the criteria to be validated during the testing is taken directly from the policies and procedures. Although these areas may appear to be the most appropriate source for documenting the process requirements, sometimes policies and procedures do not represent the most current operational procedures being used on a daily basis by business unit personnel. The testing criteria must be validated against the current operational procedures to be sure that they match before the methodology phase requirements can be set.

Once this is done, the continuous auditing testing criteria can be finalized. One additional step should be performed before the execution phase begins: Review the select control and verify that it truly represents one of the critical controls supporting the existing control environment. This additional review step is more effective now than during the approach phase of the methodology; due to the responsible auditor now having a more in-depth knowledge of the process as a result of the policy and procedure verification and can double-check the control choice more easily. Because of the commitment of resources and time to perform the complete continuous auditing methodology, it is important to continue to verify the control selection all the way up to the execution of monthly testing.

Increase Coverage and Depth

One of the primary reasons that continuous auditing was developed was for internal audit departments to increase the number of audits they perform each year and to focus on evaluating control effectiveness. Today, it is one of the most sought-after new techniques that internal audit departments around the world are researching, developing, and implementing as a strong complement to their existing risk-based audit methodology.

As a result of this increase in adoption of the continuous auditing methodology, the expansion of audit universe coverage is definitely one of the more significant uses of the customized approach. When created in accordance with the guidelines outlined in Chapter 3, the continuous auditing methodology can be incorporated into the annual audit plan to validate critical controls across the company. Doing so will allow audit departments to increase the amount of control validation testing they perform annually. When using this audit approach, the limiting factor is that despite the increase in coverage, not all controls in the business process are verified from start to finish. The methodology is a targeted examination of key controls, not a validation of all controls involved, as in full-scope risk-based audits. However, even though the continuous auditing methodology does not verify all controls in a process, it still tests and confirms that the key control(s) are producing repeatable, reliable results. This key control validation on business processes, which would not have been audited in the first place, results in an increase in coverage of the audit universe that provides a benefit.

Another use of the continuous auditing methodology is to drill down into a particular high-risk control. Many times during full-scope risk-based audits, controls are tested. Even though the results appear to be satisfactory, the responsible auditor would like to add to the initial sample. Although that is an acceptable approach, the continuous auditing methodology provides a different approach that will validate the particular control's effectiveness over a period of time. This alternate testing technique is more effective because it proves that the control strength is adequate as long as the testing results do not identify any exceptions over the life of the testing. The continuous auditing methodology provides a stronger validation of control effectiveness than an additional 25 items to the original sample.

Action Plan Implementation

Action plan implementation is one of the newest uses for the continuous auditing methodology, but it is gaining popularity. The action plan implementation verification process has become one of the main objectives of the continuous auditing methodology as described in Chapter 13. This approach, just like the scenario described for increased depth of a selected control, validates the strength of the targeted control by determining whether the control produces repeatable, reliable results. Just retesting the new control upon its initial implementation does not confirm that the control was properly designed and truly addresses the root cause. Usually control revalidation is performed too early to be sure that the enhanced control is working as designed. The continuous auditing methodology provides the most effective way to review action plan implementation that was required as a result of a previous audit exception. If a significant control gap was identified in a previous audit, business unit management is responsible for adequately addressing the risk. To ensure that business unit management properly addressed the risk, a continuous auditing program would be implemented to validate the effectiveness of the action plan.

Sarbanes-Oxley Testing

As with its use in action plan implementation, the continuous auditing methodology is gaining support in some internal audit departments to perform their Sarbanes-Oxley (SOX) testing. Since SOX testing requires at least an annual validation of the key controls, the continuous auditing program provides a more detailed analysis of the key controls. With the standard review process for SOX, key controls are sampled and tested on an historical basis to determine if they are performing satisfactorily. With the continuous auditing methodology, key controls are tested on a recurring basis to validate that they are adequately designed, in place, and operating as intended for the length of the continuous auditing program.

The recurring nature of the continuous auditing program provides a more effective validation of key control performance because it executes control testing over a period of time, which allows the control to be evaluated at different times of the year. The frequency aspect of the continuous auditing methodology provides real-time validation of control performance from the current month of testing instead of historical sampling, which selects transactions from different months but does not provide a profile of the business unit activity (such as staffing, volumes, etc.) at that time.

Control Self-Assessment Development

The continuous auditing methodology also is used as the driver for the consideration and possible implementation of control self-assessment. By way of background, control self-assessment is the process in which surveys are taken to solicit feedback from operational business teams as to the effectiveness of controls in place in their areas. Since the continuous auditing methodology tests the control effectiveness over a set period, sometimes the recurring results spark the interest of the business unit either to take over performing the continuous auditing testing on their own or to implement a control self-assessment process based on the key controls tested.

This area is not a primary use of the continuous auditing methodology, but the methodology has been used to assist in the development of the control self-assessment process due to its focused testing of key controls in operating business units.

 USERS

The continuous auditing methodology is a unique approach that is heavily used by internal audit departments around the world. However, due to the targeted approach, recurring testing, and expanded time frame, the continuous auditing methodology is being adapted to perform quality assessment testing, regulatory rule validation, and even control performance in business units outside of internal audit. Table 14.1 lists continuous auditing users and information users and describes how they use the recurring control testing technique to accomplish their own objectives.

Many different users have successfully developed and integrated the continuous auditing methodology into their business unit to provide effective

TABLE 14.1 Continuous Auditing Users

User	Description
Internal Audit	Primary use: • Expand risk-based audit universe coverage • Policy and procedure validation • Regulatory compliance • Key control depth testing • Management action plan implementation validation • Increase business knowledge • Proactively identify trends and issues • Establish and strength partnerships • Enhance audit committee reporting • Increase audit product offerings • Improve auditor development • Manage workload more effectively • Testing for externally relied-on work for external audit or examiners • Sarbanes-Oxley compliance testing • Process improvement project deliverable testing • Control self-assessment development
Compliance	Primary use: • Federal, state, and local law compliance • Internal policy and procedure validation
Enterprise Risk Management	Primary use: • Process control validation • Key control testing • Company-wide process testing • Internal policy and procedure validation
Process Owner	Primary use: • Key control testing • Sarbanes-Oxley compliance testing • Federal, state, and local law compliance • Internal policy and procedure validation • Control self-assessment development

(continued)

TABLE 14.1   (*Continued*)

Information User	Description
Senior Management	Primary use: • Evaluating risk of individual business units • Focusing resources to critical areas • Addressing outstanding risk exposure
External Partners	Primary use: • Relying on control testing performed

control validation. Table 14.1 illustrates a sample of continuous auditing users, but none has recognized the value and versatility of the continuous auditing methodology like the internal audit department. Each of the specific uses listed under the description column for internal audit have been described in the chapters discussing the methodology development, individual phase requirements, selling techniques, and uses.

SUMMARY

In this chapter, we identified and discussed examples of specific uses for the continuous auditing methodology. Conceptually, the uses of the continuous auditing methodology are endless and continue to evolve year after year as creative internal audit departments and business units identify the most effective use for themselves. The continuous auditing methodology has shown to be the preferred method for testing and verifying the implementation of action plans specifically developed as a result of an internal audit report. Business units have also adopted this method to validate the implementation of self-imposed action plans or ones requested from external examiners. As long as the methodology has been properly designed and links directly to the achievement of the business objectives, the customizable approach will provide effective and useful results.

The second part of the chapter presented a sample of the specific users of the continuous auditing methodology and the objectives that each group is accomplishing by using the approach. Each user focuses and perfects the continuous auditing program to attain different objectives. However, no matter what the objective is, the results of the methodology are based on recurring testing of critical controls.

CHAPTER FIFTEEN

Continuous Auditing Lessons Learned

 LESSONS LEARNED

In this chapter, we identify and discuss two specific concepts relating to the continuous auditing methodology: understanding that continuous auditing is a developing technique and that continuous audit is an effective concept but needs to be properly understood and developed. The most efficient way to discuss and describe these summary comments about the continuous auditing methodology is to organize it in a table. Table 15.1 contains the component details for the developing technique and Table 15.2 lists the component details for the effective concept. Both tables include brief explanations of each component.

In addition, we discuss a continuous auditing methodology team evaluation template that provides a tool to facilitate a meeting with internal audit team members responsible for the planning, execution, and reporting of the continuous auditing methodology throughout the entire frequency period. The specific section details are explained in this chapter; the actual template is included in the appendix.

DEVELOPING TECHNIQUE

The continuous auditing methodology is a unique approach, but it is not new. It has been around for a long time but until recently has never gotten support from internal audit departments as an approved auditing methodology that could produce valuable results. In the past five years or so, many internal audit departments have begun using the continuous auditing methodology or are drafting the appropriate methodology to support the introduction of continuous auditing into their departments to complement their current risk-based audit methodology. It is important to note several things that internal audit departments should be aware of as they move forward in the implementation process. Table 15.1 outlines the components to be considered as your continuous auditing methodology is being developed.

TABLE 15.1 Developing Technique

Component	Explanation
Understand the objectives	Table 14.1 in Chapter 14 explained that there are multiple users and even more objectives that each continuous auditing user utilizes the continuous auditing methodology to accomplish. Each user must be certain as to why they are using this customized methodology. The easiest way to validate your own objective is to be sure that it explains why this testing is being performed. As long as the objective is stated correctly, the continuous auditing methodology will produce data to evaluate the goal.
Identify the conditions	Chapter 11 detailed the specific conditions related to business unit management, internal audit, and technology. These conditions explain not only the questions you will face when introducing the continuous auditing methodology to your business partners but also the key success factors that must be clear to all internal audit team members to ensure program success. The chapter also introduced technology conditions to ensure that key systems get identified and the access needed to execute the continuous auditing program effectively is available. Remember that not all conditions have to be present at the start of the development stage of the methodology.

TABLE 15.1   (*Continued*)

Component	Explanation
Recognize the limitations	As discussed in Chapter 5, certain business processes (in particular, complex and judgmental ones) are not conducive to having a continuous auditing program due to their operational process requirements. You must be aware of the process requirements and decide whether a continuous auditing program would be beneficial, given the time and resources it takes to complete one. Also, be careful not to rush through the execution phase or assume that all testing periods do not need to be completed due to positive results early.
Understand the uses and users	As discussed in Chapter 14, there are many different uses and even more users for the continuous auditing methodology. As the concept is developed and refined, it will be incorporated into new strategies. Review the uses in the chapter as well as the users detailed in Table 14.1 to determine whom you can partner with to develop techniques and potential areas of coverage for your own department.
Follow the methodology	Table 3.2 in Chapter 3 identified and explained the specific continuous auditing methodology requirements along with details of a suggested format. At minimum, your methodology document should contain the five sections listed in the table and any templates that could be created to assist in the standardization of documentation.
Document approach and results	As discussed in Chapter 3 (the methodology formal documentation requirements) and Chapter 9 (the reporting requirements), it is important to create and maintain a formal continuous auditing methodology and a standard format for reporting. Table 9.4 identifies and explains the two types of reporting templates, including their advantages and disadvantages. Examine each one and determine the most effective template for your team.
Adjust to the process	As discussed in Chapters 5, 6, and 7, there are specific deliverables for each different phase of the continuous auditing methodology, and it is critically important to complete each phase as designed. Another important concept, when it comes to execution, is to ensure that the continuous auditing methodology is adjusted to meet the changing requirements of the business process. If a key control process is changed in the operational business process, the monthly continuous auditing program requirements must reflect that change to ensure that the most current process is being tested at all times.

EFFECTIVE CONCEPT

The discussion now shifts to how the methodology is an effective concept. How effective a concept it is depends on the dedication, planning, patience, and communication plan of the internal audit department during the development and implementation of the methodology. Table 15.2 lists and explains some of the critical components in recognizing the continuous auditing methodology as an effective concept.

TABLE 15.2 Effective Concept

Component	Explanation
Not implemented quickly or easily	The continuous auditing methodology is a straightforward testing approach that focuses on key controls in a business process and validates their effectiveness on a recurring basis. However, the methodology is not implemented quickly or easily because it requires that a formal methodology be documented and communicated to the audit team. Also, as discussed in Chapter 12, specific marketing components to the methodology rollout are required. Take the time to research and develop a comprehensive continuous auditing methodology and the marketing plan to support it.
Requires skill and planning throughout	As discussed in Chapters 5, 6, and 7, the specific steps and deliverables of the phase requirements are the keys to executing a successful continuous auditing program. To ensure that it is successful, the proper amount of planning must be completed, as discussed in Chapter 4, where the preparation for a continuous auditing program components were discussed. In addition, responsible auditors must have a certain level of skill because they are required to evaluate the business process and select the key controls for testing.
Develop achievable objectives	As discussed in Chapter 5, the foundation phase of the continuous auditing methodology requires identification and explanation of inclusions and specific exclusions of the objective. Developing an objective that is too large or complex to complete is one of the biggest mistakes internal audit can make when introducing a continuous auditing program. Every internal audit department wants

TABLE 15.2 *(Continued)*

Component	Explanation
	to create a huge objective for its first continuous auditing program to show how powerful the methodology can be; this is a mistake because objectives too large or complex cannot be completed effectively and in a timely manner, as required by the methodology. Especially for your pilot program, it is important to create an objective that is focused on the key control(s) and is achievable.
Communicated partner expectations	As stated throughout the book, communication should be the cornerstone for your internal audit department. The continuous auditing methodology relies on strong communication throughout the entire process, from inception to report. Remember to communicate effectively during the marketing, as discussed in Chapter 12, as well as throughout the phases of the methodology, as discussed in Chapters 5, 6, and 7. The report phase also needs strong communication, as detailed in Chapter 9. Keep communication a priority throughout the entire process, and ensure that the business unit partner has a clear understanding of the continuous auditing objective, what it has been designed to accomplish, what is specifically included and excluded in the scope, and how and when the testing is going to be performed from start to finish. Also, verify that business unit partners know what is expected of them. Explain that the success of the continuous auditing program is a partnership in which they must actively participate by providing requested documentation.
Obtain the tools and necessary training	The tools required to develop and implement a continuous auditing methodology include in-depth business knowledge, internal audit experience, and solid communication skills to facilitate the methodology development and execution requirements. Helpful training includes that which provides you with the fundamentals required to build and execute a continuous auditing methodology as well as experience and examples to illustrate the needs, successes, and challenges to be confronted as the methodology is built. Remember, the most effective tool is to always continue to develop your business knowledge. There is no tool more valuable than the continual development of operational business knowledge. This ongoing focus to

(continued)

TABLE 15.2 *(Continued)*

Component	Explanation
	learn about the business on every audit assignment will make you a very effective auditor.
Understand that this is a dynamic process	The unique characteristic of the continuous auditing methodology is that it is a dynamic audit technique that can be adapted to fit into any company as long as the specifics of the methodology have been explained and the testing is focused on the key control(s) supporting the control environment. Also, remember to keep the individual continuous auditing testing phase requirements dynamic (adjust to the process changes as required); before the testing begins, verify each time that there have been no changes to the control environment. If there were any changes, adjust the criteria testing requirements to match the revised business processes. This is the dynamic aspect of the methodology that is continually adjusted to evaluate the most up-to-date control environment.

 ## LESSONS LEARNED TEMPLATE

The Appendix includes a lessons learned template. It has been designed to provide internal audit teams with a tool to identify improvement opportunities and make suggestions to improve the existing continuous auditing methodology and approach. The tool is to be completed by all participants on an audit project; it is not to be used as an individual evaluation tool for performance. Feel free to customize the template as necessary to fit your needs.

 ## SUMMARY

In this chapter, we identified and discussed the continuous auditing methodology from the perspective of it being a developing technique and also an effective concept to validating control effectiveness. When discussing the developing technique, focus on understanding the objectives and consistently following the methodology. If you do not understand what the continuous auditing methodology is designed to accomplish, you are going to struggle to explain it to your audit department and to get your business unit partner to understand why you are doing it. Without that understanding on either side, you will struggle with recognizing any benefit from the continuous auditing methodology. The other critical component is to follow the methodology requirements consistently. At times the control environment may appear strong after only two months of testing; that does not mean that you should not complete the remainder of the test months. If you follow the methodology as it was designed, the continuous auditing program will provide valuable results. If you abbreviate any components or phase requirements, the methodology will not produce anything valuable to the business unit partner or the internal audit team. Always remember to execute the program as it was meant to be completed.

When discussing the effective concept, all of the components seem mission critical, whether it is understanding that the process of development and implementation takes time and effort or obtaining the proper training to complement your existing business and audit knowledge. It is important to realize that continuous auditing is a powerful, customizable audit approach, but it does require skill, planning, and dedication during every facet of its development and execution. Without recognizing those facts, you may be able to perform recurring testing on a monthly basis, but it will not meet your expectations because you did not dedicate the time and resources to planning, training, and implementing the continuous auditing methodology.

Remember to stay focused on your goal, understand your objectives, and keep communication as the cornerstone of your internal audit department.

Continuous Auditing Guidance

THIS APPENDIX INCLUDES FIVE documents: formal audit report template, action plan tracker, continuous auditing methodology template, lessons learned, and an example of a continuous auditing program. Each one will be briefly explained.

The formal audit report template is a color-based audit report format that can be used for reporting on your continuous auditing program activities and also for full-scope risk-based audits. It has been designed to provide readers with a clear message of the work performed, issues noted, overall opinion, and functional background of the area tested all on one page. Use of a color rating system avoids all the unnecessary discussions that surround every audit report ever drafted. This standard format simplifies the audit report process especially for continuous auditing programs.

The action item tracker is utilized to summarize and report business unit management action items on a recurring basis (to be determined by the individual user). Auditors spend a great deal of time finding issues, identifying root cause, and obtaining target action plans. This action item tracking sheet was developed to standardize the actions being tracked on a monthly basis. This format provides a complete executive summary that breaks down action items by risk and due date, then categorizes them by division for specific accountability. A second page tracks and reports on higher-rated risk action items that are outstanding after 90 days and lists the status for each action item. This action item tracker helps management focus on significant risk exposures and can be used for both internal reporting purposes and audit committee reporting.

The continuous auditing methodology document divides the methodology requirements into process overview, program outline, testing approach, and tracking and reporting results. This document is meant as a guide and provides a strong foundation for any company to use when beginning the process of formally documenting continuous auditing methodology.

The lessons learned document can be utilized at the completion of an audit to facilitate a discussion with all audit team members to ensure that the audit was executed efficiently and effectively. This document is in a question format that breaks the audit process down into four distinct categories: quality, cost, change, and audit team. While using the document to make your audit processes stronger and more efficient, remember that it is not meant to be used as an individual team member review of performance. The questionnaire is to be used to facilitate an open discussion on the methodology and how well the audit service was executed. The lessons learned tool can be used in association with any audit programs.

The continuous auditing program example provides the details of a continuous auditing program that was developed and implemented to validate the effectiveness and efficiency of specific aspects of the account reconciliation process. The documentation provides a basic outline of the information that, at a minimum, should be included when detailing the continuous auditing program.

EXECUTIVE SUMMARY

[Audit Name]
Audit Scope And Rating
[Date]

The results of our audit indicate that the control environment is *[Red/Yellow/Green]*. The rating definitions are included at the end of this report. The scope of the review was the time period *[include dates]*.

Audit Objectives	Objective Ratings		
	GREEN	YELLOW	RED
Objective #1			
Objective #2			X
Objective #3			X
Objective #4		X	
Objective #5		X	
		X	

RISK EXPOSURE

Risk Map

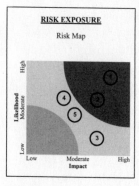

Significant Issues

Observations	Responsible Area	Implementation Timing
1. Condition Statement of the issue noted. Responsible Individual to complete the action.		Action Target Date
2. Condition	Action Owner	Date
3. Condition	Action Owner	Date
4. Condition	Action Owner	Date
5. Condition	Action Owner	Date

Background

Enterprise Process:
Subprocess:

General Background:

AUDIT OBSERVATIONS

Observation 1:
Risk Level: Yellow or Red
Condition:
Criteria:
Cause:
Effect:
Recommendation:
Action Item(s)
    1. Specific Action Detail
       Action Item Owner:
       Action Item Due Date:
    2. Specific Action Detail
       Action Item Owner:
       Action Item Due Date:
    3. Specific Action Detail
       Action Item Owner:
       Action Item Due Date:

Audit observation detail is repeated for the number of issues noted in the executive summary.

Audit Rating System:

Red—An overall unsatisfactory or unacceptable state of control. The red level of control denotes significant business risk or exposure to the company that requires immediate attention and remediation efforts. The overall control environment does not provide reasonable assurance regarding the safeguarding of assets, reliability of financial records, and compliance with company policies and/or government laws and regulations.

Yellow—A state in which the controls in place need improvement. If these controls are not improved, this could lead to an overall unsatisfactory or unacceptable state of control.

Green—An overall satisfactory or acceptable state of control, where risk is minimized and managed. The overall environment provides a high degree of assurance regarding the safeguarding of assets, reliability of financial records, and compliance with company policies and government laws and regulations. Control weaknesses noted, if any, are relatively minor.

INTERNAL AUDIT DEPARTMENT: STATUS OF ACTION ITEMS

Action Item Data

		Financial	Compliance	Operations	Human Resources	Information Technology	Legal	Facilities	TOTAL
I	**Action Items by Risk**								
	Higher	0	0	0	0	0	0	0	0
	Moderate	0	0	0	0	0	0	0	0
	Lower	0	0	0	0	0	0	0	0
	Total Action Items:	0	0	0	0	0	0	0	0
II	**Action Items by Status**								
	Due Date before 00/00/20XX **(past due)**	**0**	**0**	**0**	**0**	**0**	**0**	**0**	**0**
	Due Date on or after 00/00/20XX	0	0	0	0	0	0	0	0
	Total Action Items:	0	0	0	0	0	0	0	0

(continued)

(continued)

	Financial	Compliance	Operations	Human Resources	Information Technology	Legal	Facilities	TOTAL
III Action Items by Selected Risk								
Higher > 3 Months	0	0	0	0	0	0	0	0
Moderate > 6 Months	0	0	0	0	0	0	0	0
Total Action Items:	0	0	0	0	0	0	0	0
IV Action Item Summary								
Open as of 00/00/20XX	0	0	0	0	0	0	0	0
Add: New Action Items	0	0	0	0	0	0	0	0
Total	0	0	0	0	0	0	0	0
Less: Completed Action Items	0	0	0	0	0	0	0	0
In Progress as of 00/00/20XX	0	0	0	0	0	0	0	0

Higher-Risk Action Items: Greater Than 3 Months Old

Audit Name Observation and Action Item	Division	Report Date	Action Item Due Date	Update
2010 Payroll Audit Observation: System Access Action Item: System ID Security	Human Resources	08/27/10	09/30/10	A review of the HR payroll system is being performed to validate all user access to the confidential system. Management will be meeting to validate the completeness of the actions taken before closing the audit action item.

CONTINUOUS AUDITING METHODOLOGY TEMPLATE

Contents

I. Continuous Auditing Overview

Purpose

The purpose of this document is to detail the process by which Mainardi & Associates Internal Audit plans to implement and maintain a continuous auditing program.

Objectives and Goals

The implementation of the continuous auditing program will provide ongoing assurance that the control structure surrounding specific operational and financial environments and their corresponding key controls are suitably designed, established, and operating as intended. In addition, Mainardi & Associates Internal Audit will be able to expand coverage of the audit universe and proactively track the effectiveness and efficiency of implemented business action plans in a more timely manner.

Continuous auditing will also be used to validate compliance with internal policies and procedures, identify concerns, and highlight trends. In the future, continuous auditing could potentially help process owners implement a self-assessment method.

Understanding what continuous auditing can and cannot do is part of the key design of the program. While continuous auditing will allow Internal Audit to gain more audit coverage, it will not replace full-scope audits; instead, it will enhance them.

Implementation of a Successful Continuous Auditing Program

It is critical to ensure that both the internal audit department and business unit management recognize the purpose and requirements of the continuous auditing methodology. Without a clear, distinct understanding of the program's specific requirements and partnership, it will be difficult to implement the new methodology successfully. To facilitate the learning and education of both groups, the internal audit and business unit management conditions must be discussed and accepted in order for a successful continuous auditing program to be implemented.

First, internal audit must realize that there are distinct differences between a full-scope risk-based audit and a continuous audit. Additionally, even though the continuous auditing methodology has a more focused approach, that does not mean that there is less planning to be performed in order to execute the continuous auditing testing requirements successfully. Therefore, internal audit must perform adequate and effective planning to prepare and develop the three-phase requirements of the continuous auditing methodology. Continuous auditing is a specialized audit technique; it is not designed to cover every area in the audit universe nor is it implemented to replace full-scope audits. Consistency in planning, execution, and reporting are the keys to a successful continuous auditing program.

Business unit management must understand that a continuous audit is not just another audit; this technique focuses on specific high-risk areas and uses data selected from the most recently completed month to provide results in the most real-time fashion available—the most recently completed month. The critical component of business unit management understanding the continuous auditing process is the sole responsibility of the internal audit department. The internal audit department must provide a sufficient level of understanding and education regarding the continuous auditing methodology requirements. The successfully implemented continuous auditing methodology that takes less time, is specifically targeted to test critical controls, and provides validation that the selected process or control is working. Management must also be aware that results are reportable.

When applicable, formal action plans to address the identified control gaps are required.

II. Continuous Auditing Program Outline

Testing Overview

Target Area Selection

- The specific area to be tested will be selected from the current audit universe based on risk, audit frequency, and applicability of use (meets the continuous auditing program testing requirements).
- Target areas will include high-risk, high-transaction-volume areas.

Document the Testing Objectives

- The testing objectives will be created from the business objective and specifically state the purpose of the continuous auditing testing.
- The objective must be clear and adequately state what is going to be tested.
- The scope statement must detail the controls that are going to be included in the testing and all aspects of the business process that are *not* being tested as part of the continuous auditing program.

Frequency Determination

- The selected frequency must be detailed and documented and based directly on the frequency at which the business unit transactions produce a result.
- Consideration must be given to the number of transactions in the population as well as the dollar values (where applicable).
- Once the frequency has been determined, all associated testing must be completed as planned.

Documentation Requirements

- The testing plan will be documented and specifically detailed for each target area identified, thus maintaining consistency and efficiency.
- The documentation must be able to stand alone and completely re-present the reason the work was performed and the associated

documentation to support the testing conclusion. Ensure that there is sufficient documented evidence to support the continuous auditing testing conclusions.

Test Approach Communication

- Once the continuous auditing planning has been completed, in partnership with your business management client, it should be properly documented and communicated directly to the client.
- Internal audit must ensure that both the responsible auditor performing the work and the business unit client understand the expectations, requirements, and deliverables of the continuous auditing methodology.

Reporting Requirements

- Every completed continuous auditing program will result in a formal report that is issued, at a minimum, to the process owner plus one level. This ensures accountability.
- A standardized report template will be used to communicate the results of all continuous auditing programs executed.
- The distribution frequency, especially during a "6-9-12" continuous auditing program, will be at the discretion of the chief audit executive. At a minimum, the results should be fully distributed on a quarterly basis.

Performing the Tests

The recommended continuous auditing testing schedule (for business units that process multiple transactions on a daily basis) will be tested using the "6-9-12" audit frequency.

This frequency requires monthly testing be performed every month for the first six months of testing and then at quarter-end at month 9 and 12. The quarter-end test sample size is the same as the monthly testing previously completed; it should incorporate all three months of the quarter being tested. This frequency allows internal audit to identify potential trends and possibly use the results of the testing as a predictive tool to proactively address opportunities for improvement.

Mainardi & Associates Copyright 2010

III. Continuous Audit Testing Approach

All testing planning and execution will be documented in the same fashion and detail as any other full-scope audits by the responsible auditor. The documentation will contain the detailed planning steps and testing approaches as well as a conclusion based on the validated testing results. The documentation will be completed, reviewed, and approved according to the same guidelines as described in the current risk-based audit methodology.

To announce the beginning of the continuous auditing program to business unit management, internal audit will create and issue a notification memorandum notifying applicable personnel of the kickoff of the continuous auditing program. The correspondence will include, but not be limited to, the continuous auditing process requirements, document requests, time frames, and corresponding expectations.

The pilot program initially selected should have a specific, clear objective. Most successful continuous auditing pilot programs select a compliance-based control because of the specifically detailed acceptable performance parameters. Proper selection of the pilot program is critically important to the success of the continuous auditing program because of the testing frequency and interpretation of the corresponding data. Select a pilot program that has very specific parameters as to acceptable performance. This will limit the potential debate of exceptions noted.

Because of the recurring testing time frames of a continuous auditing program, it is important that business unit management recognize the importance of timely delivery of the requested business unit documentation for testing. The success of the continuous auditing program depends on the commitment of both business unit management and the responsible auditor to deliver and perform the work as requested and designed. If the requested documentation is not received in a timely manner from the business unit, it will be very difficult to complete the continuous auditing testing. The supporting continuous auditing work paper documentation will be in the same format and include the same critical fields that a full-scope test document would require. Those fields include, but are not limited to, date, source, scope, sampling technique, testing criteria, exceptions, conclusion, responsible auditor, and date.

IV. Tracking and Reporting Results

Continuous auditing results and corresponding exceptions noted will be tracked in the same process as any exceptions noted in a full-scope risk-based audit. The responsible auditor who executed the continuous auditing program will be responsible for populating and updating the issue-tracking database with any exceptions noted during the continuous auditing testing. All issues noted during the continuous auditing testing must have an action plan, and the action plans will be recorded, tracked, and followed up on until their implementation. Upon plan implementation, the responsible auditor must validate that the appropriate action was implemented properly as documented in the formal report. Once an independent internal audit validation has been performed, the open action item may be closed out of the tracking database.

INTERNAL AUDIT DEPARTMENT: LESSONS LEARNED (SUGGESTED QUESTIONS)

Objective: To provide audit teams a lesson learned tool to identify improvement opportunities and serve as a basis for making suggestions to improve the audit approach.

Quality of Audit

- Were all phases of the audit process and deliverables used? If not, why?
- Did you meet target dates?
- Were the right resources (skill sets) involved at the right time?
- Did team members receive appropriate training prior to the start of the audit?
- How well did your team do its homework?
- Was the supervisor/manager involved at the right times?
    - Reduced review comments
    - Cluster editing of report (staff and manager edit the report at one time, together)
    - Participation in scope and testing plan decisions
    - Available for questions when needed
- Did we effect positive change to the control structure?
- Do you feel that you provided your client with a value-added service?
- Would clients pay for the services rendered?
- Did you work in the client area?

Cost of Audit

- Did we perform continuous risk assessment?
- Were scoping decisions made at the appropriate time?
- Did we use effective testing methods?
- Did we effectively use information technology to increase productivity and reduce costs?
- Was the audit documentation completed in a timely fashion?

Culture Change

- Were team expectations discussed and agreed on prior to the start of the audit?
- Was there ongoing coaching and guidance throughout the audit?
- Were team evaluations completed in a timely manner?
- Was risk taking encouraged?
- Was communication up, down, and sideways?

Team Members

- Did you support your team members, when needed?
- Was the audit a challenge and opportunity?
- Did you increase your knowledge base?
- Did you have fun and learn?

CONTINUOUS AUDITING PROGRAM EXAMPLE: ACCOUNT RECONCILIATIONS

Account Reconciliation Process: Foundation Phase

- Objective
  - To determine that reconciliations are performed accurately, completely, and in a timely manner.
- Frequency
  - Monthly—for account reconciliations executed monthly.
  - Quarterly—for account reconciliations executed only at quarter-end.
- Testing Technique
  - Combination of manual and automated
    - Manual to independently validate the accuracy and completeness of the selected reconciliations.
    - Automated to validate that the completed reconciliations were submitted to the tracking database properly.
  - Inquiry and inspection
    - Inquiry into the tracking database and inspection to perform the completeness and accuracy review.

Account Reconciliation Process: Approach Phase

- Approach
  - Receive and review policies with process owner
    - Validate and verify the current account reconciliation procedures to ensure that the continuous auditing testing program accurately reflects the most recent operational procedures.
  - Judgmental sample of financial operations
    - Judgmentally select a sample of monthly and quarterly account reconciliations that have been completed.
    - Identify the account reconciliations that have the largest risk regarding number of journal entries and dollar amounts being processed through the selected accounts.
  - Request applicable reconciliations

- Submit a request for the selected account reconciliations to be tested, and actively follow up on the receipt of the sample selected to ensure sufficient time is available to complete the required testing.
- Validate compliance with policy and procedure
  - Execute the specific test steps as documented in the continuous auditing program.
  - Validate the account reconciliations were processed in accordance with existing policy standards.

Account Reconciliation Process: Execution Phase

- Execution Specifics
  - Discuss and validate the approach with the process owner
    - Prior to starting any testing, ensure the criteria being tested match current operational standards.
  - Request selected documentation
    - Determine the most effective method to select, and request the corresponding account reconciliations to be sampled.
    - Identify who will be responsible for physically selecting and delivering the sample to the responsible auditor. Some business units prefer to pull the documentation themselves while others will allow auditors to gather the samples.
  - Perform testing and record results
    - Execute the continuous auditing program requirements, and document the current level of compliance with policies and procedures.
  - Note noncompliance with procedures
    - Document potential exceptions that represent a difference from the processing standard criteria validated with the process owner prior to the start of testing.

Account Reconciliation Process: Execution Phase

- Execution
  - Validate findings with process owner
    - Review the test result specifics with the process owner to verify whether testing discrepancies represent true exceptions to the processing standard.

- Obtain action items and draft report
    - Once the exceptions have been validated, perform a root cause analysis with the business process owner and request action items to address the root cause.
    - Validate that the action plan submitted will truly address the root cause and not a symptom.
    - Draft the formal report and incorporate the action plans into the draft.
- Determine distribution
    - Once the report has been drafted and reviewed by the business process owner, discuss the final distribution list for the report issuance.
- Follow up and report on action items
    - Perform ongoing follow-up on outstanding action items until full implementation.

About the Author

AFTER 21 YEARS OF working in the internal audit profession in the financial services industry, Robert L. Mainardi started his own company, which develops and facilitates custom internal audit training, and evaluates, creates, and implements formal audit methodologies as well as consults on critical projects. Prior to starting his company, Mr. Mainardi was the Vice President of Internal Audit for the Penn Mutual Life Insurance Company and was responsible for the direction and oversight of the Internal Audit Department. He was responsible for Penn Mutual's internal audit activities as well as those of its subsidiaries. Prior to joining Penn Mutual, he was a senior audit manager for The Vanguard Group, where he was responsible for the Investment Programs & Services and Methods & Infrastructure teams.

As a professional speaker, Mr. Mainardi leads programs to help clients:

- Develop and maintain world class internal auditing functions
- Create, implement, and maintain continuous auditing programs
- Draft, finalize, and issue high-impact audit reports
- Establish and facilitate enterprise risk management programs
- Improve communication and client relationship development
- Develop and implement audit performance dashboards
- Identify, recruit, interview, and maintain quality audit staff

Mr. Mainardi is an active member of the Institute of Internal Auditors (IIA) and has been a Distinguished Faculty Member for almost 20 years. He is a member of the Vision University Staff and is a featured speaker at IIA and other professional association conferences and events each year as well as MIS Super Strategies and Audit World; the IIA annual International, General Audit

Management, Governance, Risk, and Compliance, All Star, Regional, and District Conferences. He received a BS degree from The Pennsylvania State University, where he majored in Accounting and Business Law. He also earned a master's degree in Finance from Temple University. Plus, he has merited the Six Sigma Green Belt certification from the American Society for Quality, which recognizes the recipient for unique expertise in problem-solving and statistical analysis. He also has earned the Qualification in Control Self-Assessment and is certified to perform internal audit Quality Assessment reviews.

Index